Paige

MY FATHER'S SON

A GAMING MEMOIR

MY FATHER'S SON

A GAMING MEMOIR

by Pete Cladianos Jr.

From oral history interviews with Pete Cladianos Jr.,
conducted by Dwayne Kling,
a narrative composed by R. T. King

University of Nevada Oral History Program

Publication of My *Father's Son* was made possible in part by
the Jack Douglass Memorial Fund for gaming history and
by gifts from Ken Adams, Sharkey Begovich, John
Douglass, William A. and Jan Douglass, the Charles N.
Mathewson Foundation, and the Peppermill Hotel Casino
in support of the UNOHP gaming history project.

University of Nevada Oral History Program
Mail Stop 324
Reno, Nevada 89557-0099
775/784-6932
ohp@unr.nevada.edu
http://www.unr.edu/artsci/oralhist/ohweb/oralhist.htm

All photographs courtesy of Pete Cladianos Jr.

Publication Staff
Book Design: Mary A. Larson
Senior Production Assistant: Linda Sommer
Production Assistants: Brooke McIntyre, Matt Slagle,
Allison Tracy, Elisabeth Williams, Kathryn Wright-Ross

ISBN #1-56475-380-8

To Kiki, my youngest daughter.

CONTENTS

Preface

THE UNIVERSITY OF NEVADA Oral History Program explores the remembered past of Nevada and the West. Through carefully crafted interviews with people who are primary sources, the program has amassed a useful collection of oral histories on a variety of subjects, including mining, ranching, Native Americans, federal management of public lands, the casino gaming industry, and many others. The collection currently totals about 4,000 tapes and 80,000 transcript pages.

Drawing from this substantial body of work, which is heavily used by students and publishing scholars, the program produces occasional books intended for the general reading public. *My Father's Son* is the fifth title in our series on casino gaming in Nevada. Through the memories of knowledgeable chroniclers who were directly involved in gaming over the years, this series illuminates the origins and development of various enterprises; the relationships between casinos and the communities of which they are (or were) a part; the evolution of gaming regulations and their enforcement; and other factors in the history of the industry in the state.

Casino gambling (or "gaming," as the industry prefers) was made legal in Nevada by the state legislature's passage in 1931 of AB 98, the Casino Gaming Act. Initially, the majority of Nevada casinos were small establishments containing a few gambling tables, perhaps some slot machines, and a bar. Most operators came from other states, where many had run rigged games in illegal gambling joints, but there were some early homegrown entrepreneurs. Among them was Greek immigrant and Reno grocer, Pete Cladianos Sr., who opened a "cigar store" (it offered gambling) and started a slot machine route shortly after AB 98 was passed.

Over the next thirty years, with the participation of his son, Pete Jr., and others in the Cladianos family, Pete Sr. built a diversified business empire that included bars, motels, hotels, rental properties, and even a mercantile business. Most of the Cladianos enterprises had at least one thing in common— slot machines. The slots were prominently placed where they would get the most traffic, and they generated a steady stream of revenue that could be used to expand Cladianos businesses and acquire additional properties.

By the mid-1960s, Pete Jr. had taken on responsibility for the day-to-day operations of the family enterprises. His father had long dreamed of opening a hotel-casino with unrestricted gaming, and, with the expansion and licensing of their Sands Motor Inn just west of Reno's downtown core, that was accomplished. Under Pete Jr.'s leadership, the Sands went on to become one of the larger and more successful operations in Reno and among the first gaming businesses in the nation to go public. In the mid-1990s, it also took a near-crippling plunge into the murky backwaters of Mississippi dockside gaming. As this is written, the Sands Regent Company has regained its equilibrium and appears to be successfully redefining itself in the face of intense (and growing) competition from gaming casinos on Indian reservations throughout the West.

The interviews upon which *My Father's Son* is based were done by Oral Historian Dwayne Kling. Mr. Kling brought forty years of gaming industry experience to the project, supported by considerable research into the history of the industry in northern Nevada. He is an adept interviewer, has a winning personality, and was successful in drawing significant memories out of Mr. Cladianos. The product of their collaboration, a 1,200 page verbatim transcript of thirty-three tapes, addresses a broad range of topics within the context of the life experiences of the chronicler.

Drawing from the transcript of the interviews, I have composed the book at hand to read as a memoir by Pete Cladianos Jr. These are not Pete's words precisely as spoken or even in the order in which they were spoken, but I have recreated his speech as faithfully as possible consistent with the aim of composing a readable volume from the elements of the interviews. In addition, Dwayne Kling's questions, which established the structure and elicited the detail of the work, have been subsumed into the narrative, and I have imposed a measure of chronological and topical order on the whole that was largely absent from in the transcript.

In general, oral origins notwithstanding, the text of *My Father's Son* reads like that of any other book. However, the reader will encounter two unconventional devices that are employed to represent important parts of the dynamic of spoken language: [laughter] indicates that the chronicler laughed in expression of amusement or irony; and ellipses are meant to represent halting speech . . . or a dramatic pause. As an aid to the reader, we also provide a glossary of gaming terms, which can be found at the back of the book.

Pete Cladianos Jr. read the finished manuscript in page proof form and affirmed in writing that it accurately interprets the content of the interviews upon which it is based. As with all its work, while the Oral History Program can vouch for the authenticity of *My Father's Son*, it makes no claim that the recollections upon which the book is based are entirely free of error. This is Pete Cladianos Jr.'s personal history. This is a remembered past.

R. T. KING
University of Nevada
October, 2002

Acknowledgements

PUBLICATION of My *Father's Son* was made possible by contributions from a number of Nevadans interested in advancing the work of the University Of Nevada Oral History Program (UNOHP). The UNOHP's gaming history series is supported by gifts to a special fund established for the purpose of collecting and publishing gaming-related oral histories. Principal contributors to that fund are: Ken Adams, Sharkey Begovich, William A. and Jan Douglass, the Charles N. Mathewson Foundation, and the Peppermill Hotel Casino. Additional support for this work was provided by the Jack Douglass Memorial Fund, established to honor the memory of the pioneering northern Nevada gaming figure who died January 6, 2002. We are grateful to all whose generous contributions helped make this project possible.

Introduction

I FIRST MET Pete Cladianos Jr. in 1984 when I joined the Sands to work on a prospective public stock offering. The company had a great track record of growth and profitability, but it needed public capital to expand and liquidity to settle sibling ownership disputes.

My previous experience in the gaming industry was with Harrah's and International Game Technology, two very different operations from the Sands. For me, signing on with Pete Cladianos was like diving into Lake Tahoe in February. The Sands was Pete's life, and he ran it the way he wanted to run it. That meant odd working hours and an open-ended job description: he would come to work between 11:00 a.m. and noon each day and leave at 2:00 or 3:00 a.m. the next morning, taking only a couple of hours each evening to play handball at the YMCA; he spent most of his time on the casino floor, visible to his employees; he made virtually every decision himself; and at busy times you could even spot him checking in guests at the hotel front desk or dealing cards to a big winner.

Pete Jr. is a second-generation patriarch of a pioneering Reno gaming family. He apprenticed under his father, Pete Sr., in the gaming, retail, and hotel-motel industries, developing his distinctive style and a tough-minded approach to business. He was also known to be flexible and creative in attracting customers to his properties. As CEO of the Sands, Pete took advantage of almost every business opportunity that he could dream up, from making the Sands the host hotel for the Reno Gay Rodeo to hosting each graduating class of marines from the Marine Warfare Center at Pickle Meadows.

Some in the Reno-Sparks business community may dislike Pete for his tough operating methods, but most have great respect for him. To Pete, business is business, and he expects people to honor their agreements, whether they have made a good deal or a bad one. He is now semi-retired, but when he was running his company, he gave no quarter and negotiated until he had all there was to get. He measured his personal success by the success of his company.

Pete's employees, particularly the lower level ones, liked him immensely for his common approach and his humble manner. He spoke to all and knew most of their names, and they felt their welfare was important to him. Equally important, he held no double standard, abiding by the same rules he imposed on his employees.

Pete was frugal in his personal life and in his business style. As an example, when the Empress tower opened with the company's first health club, Pete furnished it with a two-year old Sears exercise bike from his home. It did not dawn on him that something good enough for him would not be good enough for his guests, and he knew that bringing the bike from home would save the company the money it would cost to buy a new one. In the same vein, I recall when his sister saw a porter placing a hose into the trunk of his car. Sure he was stealing a company hose, she called security. They reported that the porter was bringing his own hose from home to water the hotel flowerbeds because Pete would not spend the money for a replacement hose. While most of us saw the humor in this incident, it was not lost on us that Pete was cost conscious and expected his employees to share his standards.

More than anyone I have known in business, Pete understood the "time value" of money. When I arrived at the Sands, I found that he was keeping two baskets behind his desk full of checks written but not sent to company vendors. He would hold checks until the vendor was about to stop doing business with him, then he would send out one or two and the process would start over again. I tried to get him to set a procedure for paying our vendors in a logical way, but he resisted for several years until the task of personally managing checks became too much. His ability to manage costs and control cash was the key to his great margins and success in the company. (Pete came to visit me one day after I had left the Sands for a stint at a computer start-up company, and he was quick to point out the basket of checks behind *my* desk.)

Pete Cladianos is someone that made a difference in Reno. He made things happen, most of the time with the help and advice of trusted friends like Art Wood, Chuck Zeh, David Wood, his sister Katherene, and others. He is his own man, true to what he believes regardless of the strength or political power of the opposition. He overcame the infamous "red line" that confined unrestricted gaming to the downtown core of Reno when he built a twenty-four room tower and connected the Sands Motor Inn to a gaming floor, thereby legally pushing unlimited gaming outside the red line. Pete has since been quick to weigh in on other matters that were unpopular with local business or political interests. In most cases he was proven right.

In my experience, Pete was (and is) the most basically honest individual I have ever known. He was true to himself regardless of the pressure of popular opinion. He may not have wanted to pay you on time, and he may have required you to be as tough a businessman as he was to get paid on time, but you always got paid. He had the rare ability to listen to all sides on a given business transaction and then make a decision and never look back. If the decision went wrong, he never looked to place blame on the person whose idea it was; he would just say, "That didn't work, so let's not do that again." He was always quick to take responsibility for decisions he made that did not work—a rare talent for a boss.

As an employer, Pete could be as uninformed and as unfair as any man, but he always let you know how he felt. There were never any hidden agendas or feelings. When Pete was done with you, you knew where you stood and what was expected. You didn't always get your way, but you always got your say.

Pete was fiercely loyal to those that he trusted and liked, and he enjoyed their loyalty in return. From the difficult times of employee lawsuits, through the opening of the Dynasty Tower without final approval, to licensing troubles in Mississippi, his staff and friends stood firmly behind him without hesitation.

That is not to say that he has treated all individuals with respect—he certainly has not. Much of Pete's reputation as a business tyrant is well earned. I have observed him yell at and berate employees, lawyers, vendors, family members, and others on many occasions, in most cases using profanity to drive his point home. Generally, this had little effect on the relationship. People knew that was just Pete being Pete, and when it was over, it was over. While I observed this many times, I never received that treatment myself.

Age and time have tempered Pete's toughness and the manner in which he treats people. Many of the business leaders of his time have tempered also, and I believe most that disliked him in the past consider him a respected peer today. I, for one, cherish the friendship and relationship I have had with Pete for these eighteen years, and I have enormous respect for what he has accomplished. I also appreciate how much I have learned by his example over the years.

Readers are sure to enjoy this memoir of a gaming industry legend who, with his father and family, began building a successful business long before corporate gaming forever changed the operational landscape. This is a story with its roots in an earlier, more colorful Reno, one in which families and individuals put a personal stamp on their enterprises. This is the uncensored truth from Pete Cladianos as he sees it. (And yes, he bought a garden hose.)

JON BENGTSON
Reno, Nevada

1

From the Old World

I AM GREEK. My family are from Zante (*Zákinthos*), an island in the Ionian Sea off the coast of Greece. The home of my father's parents was outside the little port city, Zante. (It had the same name as the island.) They lived up in the hills and were farmers, raising olives, walnuts, grapes, and currants. My mother's family lived in town. Her father had a little coffee-shop kind of place where he sold this, that, and the other thing—like an old Greek Seven-Eleven store.

I never got to meet any of my grandparents, because they all died during the Second World War. When the Germans occupied Greece, they systematically stripped the country of food for the German army, and both sets of my grandparents starved to death. During the war, my father's parents had moved down from their farm into the town of Zante and lived with my mother's parents. There, they and some of their children died.

In those days on Zante, the women had lots of children and did all the work. Both my father and my mother had stepmothers, because the women died off at an early age. (My mother had eight or nine brothers and sisters, only one of which was her full brother.) While the women worked and raised the children, the men spent much of their time in coffee shops. They used to drink black Turkish coffee there and sit and play cards and talk politics or whatever the topic of the day was.

My daughter Toni stands amidst the ruins of the old Cladianos farmhouse on Zante, c. 1971.

Up behind the Cladianos farmhouse, on a hillside, there was a big lime deposit, and my dad, his brother, and his sister would dig lime from this pit and put it in sacks and load it on donkeys and then walk the fourteen miles to the city to sell the lime. The lime was used to make cement. That was one of the ways they earned a few *drachmas* to live on. They also cut down trees, bundled up the limbs (they were probably sticks about as big around as your index finger), loaded them on donkeys, took them down to the little town, and sold them for firewood. They also sold produce locally, and olives. Olives, and the oil pressed from them, are very important in Greek life. They use olive oil for cooking; they use it as a hand lotion; they make soap out of it. My family and the people of Zante did all those things with the olives that they grew there.

My father didn't know the precise date of his birth, but he was about eighteen when he came to this country in 1912. By 1927 he considered himself to be a wealthy man, and he felt that at his age it was time for him to settle down and have a family. He decided to go to Greece to find a bride and bring her back to Reno. What he had in mind was pretty much an arranged marriage.

In those days, when a man wanted to get married, he usually talked to his father. He would identify the women that he had an interest in, and then his father would go talk to their fathers, and they would arrange a dowry. My mother was seventeen when she met my father. He and my grandfather had gone to arrange a marriage between my dad and one of her older sisters. After they left, Dad told his father that his interest had turned to my mother, not her older sister. So then they had to go back on another day and sit down and talk with my mother's father about arranging the dowry— it was going to be different now, because they were bargaining for his younger daughter. This is part of our family history.

Within a two-week period of the time that my father met my mother, they were married at a church in Zante. Of course, my mother could speak no English. She'd gone through high school, so she knew how to write and read in Greek, but she knew nothing about English. At first, life in Reno was very difficult for her, because she didn't know anyone. There were very few Greeks here, and most of them were men, but she was befriended by the wife of a Greek man (John Lougaris), a woman who actually was American, but who knew a little bit of Greek.

My father probably was less than an ideal husband at the time. He was a gambler in those days—he loved to play cards, and he made money playing cards. He also played the stock market and had some property, and much of the time he was gone from home, so my mother was forced to go through her first pregnancy without much support. In the first year that she was in Reno, she gave birth to a female child that died three days after she was born. It was a very difficult time for my poor mother, but my father and mother were bound and determined to have a family, so I came along in 1929.

When my dad had come to the United States, with help from

My father and mother shortly after their marriage.

his family, the plan was that he would join his older brother Dan in Kansas City. But Dad took ill on the passage across the Atlantic and had to be confined in the infirmary at Ellis Island. When Dad didn't show up at the appointed time in Kansas City, his brother left without him to take a railroad job in Sacramento. Dad wandered around Kansas City until he found some Greeks who helped him out.

My dad's first job was pushing a cart through the streets of Kansas City selling fruits and vegetables. He'd go to a wholesale produce market early in the morning and buy fruits and vegetables. Then he'd rent a cart and go out and sell them. If he paid a penny for a bunch of radishes, and sold it for two cents, then he had made a penny. That's what he did in Kansas City until, eventually, he made contact with his brother. He then went to California, where he went to work on the railroad where his brother was working.

My uncle was a big, strong, hardy guy that was used to hard work, but my dad was not like that. He was smaller, slimmer, and not so strong, so hard work was difficult for him. When Dad took up laboring on the railroad, he told his brother that if he had to work like this the rest of his life, he might as well forget it. [laughter] He talked his brother into quitting the railroad, and they went back to Sacramento and did various things, including operating a produce pushcart.

Eventually, down in Old Sacramento, about twelve or fourteen Greek men got together and opened a little bar and restaurant. Well, everyone knows what had to happen . . . . They began to fight and squabble with each other, and even-

Uncle Dan (left) and Dad, c. 1924.

tually my dad and my uncle sold out of that business. Two or three different times they got into deals like that in Sacramento. They had some really bad experiences, and later in life they would admonish the family that we should never, ever go into business with partners. I've seen my father and my uncle pass up deals that looked good at the time simply because there were partners involved.

(Jack Douglass mentions in his book [*Tap Dancing on Ice*, University of Nevada Oral History Program] that my dad was a loner kind of guy, and that's true. Because of the experiences that he'd had in Sacramento, all through his life he tried to stay out of partnerships. He did make that mistake a time or two, but he got out of them real quick, and none of the partnerships that he had ever worked out real good. He told me to stay out of partnerships, but, unfortunately, I didn't follow that advice at a critical time in my business career many years after his death.)

Eventually, my dad and his brother would set up a stand on a busy street corner (in those days they didn't have to talk to the city or anybody else about permits), and, instead of pushing a cart around in residential areas, they would sell their fruits and vegetables there, and maybe cigars and newspapers and that sort of thing. They learned that they could go outside of Sacramento and buy their produce directly from truck farmers and cut out the middle man. Rather than go to the wholesale produce people, they bought a cart and a horse, and they'd go right to the farmers and buy the stuff, and then they'd bring it in and sell it on the street corner.

Another thing they learned—and they learned it from copying other people—was to clean up their fruits and vegetables before putting them on display. Many of the old-timers had simply put out potatoes or radishes without cleaning the dirt off of them, but their produce would sell better if the vendor would clean it up, polish the apples and oranges, and so on. They did better than some of the other people, be-cause their produce looked better.

Then, for a time, my uncle and my dad split up. My dad went to San Francisco. There were other Greek people that he knew there, and he worked for a while on a commuter train that ran down the peninsula, selling newspapers and cigars and candy bars and that kind of thing. It worked the same way as the vegetables—he'd have to buy the merchan-dise, and then he'd get on the train, sell it at a little profit, and he'd keep what he made. He didn't know the language very well, didn't understand the customs, his clothes weren't the best, and people made fun of him.

One of the things Dad got from that experience was that he decided that if he was going to stay in this country, he had to learn to speak the language without an accent. He also determined that he had to dress like other people did, so they wouldn't look down on him. (Both my mother and my father learned to speak English without an accent. There were very few Greek people that ever accomplished that. Many times my dad said, "It was *important*." He worked on it, and he was a man that could concentrate, and concentration was what you needed to do that kind of thing.)

Eventually, my dad and my uncle were back in Sacra-mento doing the same old thing—they had a stand on a cor-ner in downtown Sacramento—and somebody told them that there was an opportunity to do what they were doing at Lake Tahoe. So they took the train from Sacramento to Truckee.

In those days, around 1915, there was a short line that ran from Truckee up to Tahoe City. The train went right to the pier at Tahoe City, and you got off the train, walked across the pier, got on the old *Tahoe* steamer, and the steamer would take you around to the five or six resort areas on the lake. There were Glenbrook and Camp Richardson and Chamber's Lodge and Tahoe Tavern and one or two others. My dad and uncle couldn't understand why anybody would say that you could have produce stands there, because Lake Tahoe at that time was just these resorts. It was difficult to get from one to the other, and everybody closed up in the winter and left. It was only a three-month season.

Before going back to Sacramento, Dad and Uncle Dan took the train down from Truckee to Reno. They walked around the town, and they noticed that the grocery stores were not merchandising their fruit and vegetables like *they* were doing in Sacramento—the grocers weren't cleaning their vegetables and polishing their fruit before putting them on display. Dad and his brother felt they could do some good here, so they worked up a plan to retail fruit and vegetables in Reno. The arrangement they worked out was that my uncle would stay in Sacramento to do the buying, because he knew the truck farmers that they had been buying from for their stand down there, and he could get the produce at the best price. Then, with his horse and wagon, he could take it to the train and load it on the train.

In those days there wasn't any refrigeration. They'd just dump ice on top of the produce, and then it would be shipped up to Reno on the train. They rented a little store on Commercial Row, across the street from the train depot, and my dad would unload the produce, carry it across the street, clean it up, and put it up for sale. He had no refrigeration, either, so he had to just stay there, and during hot summer days, he would stay as late as he could, so he could sell everything. Otherwise, a lot of the stuff would spoil during the night. And because he had the best *looking* produce in town, he eventually got the wealthier people and the more prominent people to shop with him.

My dad and his brother called their store the Economy Market. In the stories I've heard, there were only a few other grocery stores in Reno at that time. My dad stayed open seven days a week, and many of his sales were in the evening after other grocers had closed their stores. The other grocers decided that my dad was taking too much business away from them, and, since they had some influence with the city council, they got an ordinance passed that outlawed selling fruits and vegetables after six o'clock at night and on Sundays.

My dad had a lawyer who was a customer of his, a Mr. Ryan, and Mr. Ryan told my dad that for seventy-five dollars he would challenge the law, even if he had to go clear to the Supreme Court. Mr. Ryan felt that it was an unconstitutional law, but that my dad was going to have to let himself be arrested in order to start the case. My dad always said it took a great deal of courage for him to let the police arrest him and take him to jail, because he recalled the days in Greece when people sometimes would disappear and wouldn't be seen again . . . but he did it. When he was released, Mr. Ryan got an injunction, which allowed my dad to stay open until the case was heard. And when the case was heard, he won. The grocers chose not to appeal, and then the Economy Market could be open any time Dad wanted.

Dad and my uncle continued in the same business and kept that store until sometime in 1923. Many of the prominent citizens of Reno shopped at the store. One man that Dad got to know fairly well was George Wingfield, the banker. My uncle and my dad hoped to someday own a piece of real estate and put up a building of some kind, so they cultivated Mr. Wingfield's friendship. In the meantime, they opened up another produce store on South Virginia Street, just down from the river. It was a little bigger store, and in 1923 they sold both of their stores for approximately $38,000. At that time a church had bought a piece of property a little further out of the city and built a new church, so the congregation wanted to sell their property on the southwest corner of Second and Sierra Streets. My dad and my uncle bought the property, borrowed $55,000 from Wingfield's bank, and constructed a two-story building on that corner, which is half a block long and fifty feet deep—fifty feet on Sierra Street and 140 feet on Second Street. They called it the Cladianos Building.

The first floor of the Cladianos Building was store rentals, and the second floor was walk-up office space. They had about twenty-six offices on the second floor. The offices were mainly used by attorneys and doctors and dentists. Downstairs they had businesses like Harry's Business Machines and the Paffrath Photo Studio, owned by the McElwain family; also, an insurance agency, Slingerland and Hartford. We had all our pictures taken at Paffrath Studios—they only had one backdrop, so you could tell the pictures were taken there when you saw the backdrop. On the corner, eventually, they had a Hale's Drugstore, and my dad and Clarence Hale got to be good friends.

The Cladianos Building was a real dream come true for my dad and uncle. Those were prosperous times, 1923 through 1928, and the building was full, and everybody was paying rent. Things were going along great, and my dad would spend a good deal of his time playing cards and gambling. My uncle,

The Cladianos Building (center) as it looked in the 1980s.

even up to his last days, would say, "Oh, your father was an inveterate gambler, and I was afraid he was going to lose all our money, and I worried so much about it. I asked him to quit, and he never would, and I was just scared to death that all we had worked for was going to go down the toilet." [laughter]

My dad played cards around town in back-room bars and clubs. One of the places was in the Petricciani family's building on the corner of Center Street and Commercial Row. At that time there was a hotel upstairs, and on the ground floor there were some stores. The store right on the corner was what was called a cigar store. It had a soda fountain and sold all kinds of tobacco products, newspapers, candy, those kinds of things . . . and there was a little back room where they played cards. Of course, that was illegal at the time, but it was pretty common.

My dad's principal source of income was the rentals from the Cladianos Building, but he had lots of free time to play cards, and he was playing the stock market as well. The market was doing great, so he made quite a bit of money. By 1927 he probably had three or four hundred thousand dollars, something like that. He had it in his mind that he was soon going to be sort of semi-retired. He was going to get married; he was going to have a couple of kids. It was a fine life, and everything was wonderful. That's when he went back to Zante, married my mother, brought her back to Reno . . . and everything continued to go just wonderfully until the stock market crashed in 1929. [laughter]

I was born December 19, 1929. My sister Katherene is two years younger than me, and I had a brother named John, who was nine years younger. [John Cladianos died in October, 2000.] An older sister died three days after she was born, a year before I was born. They never did name her, because she was quite ill when she was born.

Dad, me, and Uncle Dan (left to right), 1930.

During the time that my dad had the produce business, he got *partially* involved in the mining business. When I say "mining business," I mean he made some investments in some mining claims. He had a claim or two in Tonopah and one in Goldfield and one or two in Silver Peak and so on. Those were the days before the SEC regulations, so there was a lot of speculation and a lot of stock being sold, and there were no guarantees. He lost a great deal in these mining ventures, mostly because there was a lot of chicanery and dishonesty. People would do things like salt the mines and then take some of that ore that they had salted the mine with and have it assayed. They'd get a good assay report, and then they would run around and tell everybody, "Look at this mine! It's going to produce four hundred dollars a ton," let's say, in gold or silver or both. Then they'd begin to sell stock in a mine with no worthwhile ore at all.

Dad was an investor only, and to his sorrow, every mine that he invested in went bad. In the early 1930s, he became associated with Charles Richards, who ran for Congress and lost by a very small majority. Then there was another man named Charles Myers. Eventually Dad and those two fellows bought a mine in Seven Mile Canyon, which is just below Virginia City. They poured a lot of money into that mine, but they had a lot of water problems there, so they had to do a lot of pumping, and they never made any money. Eventually, my father wound up with that mine, because the other fellows couldn't or didn't want to put any more money in it. Dad kept paying the taxes on the mine, didn't work it, didn't do anything except pay the taxes every year. I asked him one day why he did that, and he said, "I pay those taxes every year to remind to me never, ever go in the mining business again!" [laughter]

After Dad sold his produce business, the stock market really was what kept him going until the crash . . . and he was a good card player. He made money playing cards—not always, but in the long run he made money gambling. So he didn't feel like he had to have a business to go to every day.

These card games were all around town—places like the Wine House, Becker's, the Pastime Club, the Overland. They went on after gaming became legal, but they had been going prior to legalization. At the Riverside they had card games: poker and pan (*panguingue*). I never did learn how to play pan and never had any desire to play, but there were the addicts that played pan. My dad was a pan player and also a poker player and probably even played some dice here and there.

There was one stockbroker in town, J.A. Hogle, down on First Street, and they had a ticker tape. My dad'd go

"Dad made money playing cards . . . . He didn't feel like he had to have a business to go to every day."

there every morning and watch the ticker tape and buy and sell stocks. He was a speculative kind of guy, and he was look-ing for a quick buck. He'd go there and spend the mornings at Hogle's, and then afterward he'd have a leisurely lunch, and then he'd maybe play some cards in the afternoon, and then he'd come home. Before he was married, he stayed down-town pretty much all the time.

2

After the Crash: Dad Gets Into Slots

WITH THE ONSET of the Great Depression, my dad and uncle lost a lot of tenants, and they got to the point where they couldn't make the mortgage payment. So, they went to see Mr. Wingfield, and they told him that they were in trouble. Mr. Wingfield told them that if they'd pay whatever they could, then he'd go along with them. So they got by. Everybody was in the same shape that they were in, and the bank couldn't foreclose on *everybody*, so they just paid what they could, and the people that they had in there as tenants paid them what they could, and they just struggled along like that.

Then, in 1930, my dad had an opportunity to rent Petricciani's cigar store. And in 1931, when gaming became legal in Nevada, he bought four slot machines—he paid twelve or fifteen bucks apiece for them—and put them right inside the door of his cigar store. As a matter of fact, he put one of them halfway out on the sidewalk. The few dollars that he was making out of them made the difference between being fairly profitable or just running a break-even kind of an operation.

Some of my earliest memories are of Dad's cigar store. There was a little counter as you walked in, and a big barrel of Lyon's Root Beer sat on the counter, and Dad had ice cream . . . I remember going into his store, sitting on a stool and having root beer floats. He sold cigarettes, cigars, newspapers, various other items, but the slots and the card room in the back were what made him a few dollars.

Dad's cigar store space was actually a part of the Palace Hotel, and with legalized gaming going strong, when his five-year lease was up, the Petricciani family took the space over again to enlarge their Palace Club casino. Dad looked around town for another place to start a cigar store, but he was unable to find a spot that he thought was appropriate or a spot where he could afford the rent. So he decided to start a slot route business.

During the time that he had the cigar store, Dad was approached by slot operators who tried to talk him into allowing them to put their machines in his store. Their selling point was that they would service the machines, and that he didn't have to worry about them breaking down. That was a big issue, because my dad knew very little about those machines, and he had to teach himself how to fix them. But he felt that there wasn't any reason to share the money that those machines took in with anyone else. It was probably only ten or fifteen or twenty bucks a week, or maybe even less, but there wasn't a lot of money around, and so, rather than give half of it away, he used his own machines.

Then Dad began to think that he would try to put some machines out in other locations. He felt that he could do that, because he'd been in Reno since 1915, he'd been a gambler, and he'd been around all the bars and restaurants in the downtown businesses, and he'd met a lot of influential people in the community when he was selling fruits and vegetables. He had also established a reputation as a man of integrity and trust. Many people have said about him that he was a hard-nosed business man, but I've never heard anyone say that he was dishonest. Everyone said his word was his bond. If he shook your hand, it was like a contract, and that was important in business in those days, because written contracts were not the thing that people did—they just took your word for it, and if you broke your word, it got around. Then people didn't want to do business with you.

My dad began to call on other businesses in town while he was still running his cigar store, and he attempted to get some machines placed. He began to pick up a few locations. The first one was Hale's Drugstore on the corner of Second and Sierra Streets. That was fairly unique, because most of the places that had machines in the 1930s were bars. Most grocery stores didn't start getting machines until much later. Hale's was my dad's first location outside his cigar store, but by the time he lost his lease (around 1935 or thereabouts), he had a few other locations. One was the Roundup Bar, which was also in his building, a door or two to the west on Second Street from Hale's.

Before his lease ran out at the Palace Club, Dad began to use the basement of the Cladianos Building as sort of a shop. There he had a bench and a few tools, and he could work on his slot machines. It was kind of his headquarters. What little inventory he had, such as slot machine stands and extra machine parts, was stored there, and he kept his keys there.

Dad's slot machine keys were an interesting situation. All slot route operators did the same thing—they had a brass chain with many links, and, depending on how many locations they had, the chain might be eighteen, twenty-four, or thirty inches long. On each little link they'd have a brass tag that they'd stamp. Then they had the slot keys, square steel shafts that were probably about three inches long. On the end of each they had a letter or a number—for example, 214 Lake Street, or whatever you used for that location. When they went out to service the route, they had this long chain with tags on it and keys, so they knew which keys went to which machines. That was long before the days of master keys.

Now, I've heard two theories about master keys. Even back in those days I remember conversations between our service people and my father, and some said a master key was good, because it was handy and convenient; but if you lost it, or somebody took it from you, then they had access to all your machines. Those chains were cumbersome, but it was very difficult to lose one or for somebody to pick it up and run off with it, because it was heavy and it was hard to hide. I think that's the big reason why route operators kept these chains. As my dad's business got bigger, he had different chains for different parts of town, so that he'd have maybe one for the south side and one for the north side, and then he had one for Carson City and one for Yerington, and so on, so that you didn't have to pack the whole thing around.

Slot machines had a cash box in the bottom, which is different from the way things are nowadays, when the money drops through the machine into the stand and into a bucket. There was a cash box that was built right into the bottom of the machine. When the payoff tube filled, there was a diverter that came across the top of the tube, and then whenever the coins came in, they dropped through the chute right into the cash box. There was a lock on that cash box, and those keys were on a different chain, so that a serviceman didn't have a key to the cash box when he went out to service the machine, and that was an important point.

One of the things that my dad had to talk to people about when he wanted to place his machines in their business was the safety of their money, because half of the money in the coin box, with the exception of the taxes, was theirs. They had to feel that they could trust the operator and whoever worked for the operator and know that they weren't going to lose some of their money to theft.

I remember being with my dad when he explained how he handled it. He kept these two chains with his keys to the cash boxes locked in his safe. He had a big safe in his shop, and for many years he was the only one that would count money, or do the count at the location. That really became my dad's function in the business—to sell new locations, to act as a public relations guy, to drop in on these locations and talk to them, and to let them know that he was still personally interested in them.

When a location would run short of money, the first place they'd tap would be the slot route operator. It was easy for them to tell the slot operator, "Say, I need a hundred bucks for a couple of weeks. Just take it out of the drop." You took care of your locations like that when they were short of money and they needed it. It was a way to keep your locations loyal to you, and my dad handled all that kind of thing, as well.

One of the other things that route operators did was try to figure out the best places for equipment. In many places—like drugstores, for example—if you could get your equipment placed next to a cash register, it usually did better. If you couldn't get that spot—and it was difficult to get, because it was next to a counter, and the location owner wasn't always happy about giving up shelf space for that sort of thing—right inside the front door was usually a good location, because people going out of the store might have money in their hand or might even come in looking for a slot machine. In bars, the best location was usually where it was really handy for somebody to get off a barstool and walk two or three steps to the slot machine.

My dad spent most of his time calling on his locations, which meant that the more locations he had, the longer he worked. He'd do collections and his public relations work in the evenings, and he'd work on weekends. So it was an arduous job and long. He worked hard.

I started going around with my dad when I was ten years old or so. We counted all the money by hand, and I don't remember him ever owning a coin counter in his slot route business. We used to count twenty nickels in a stack, two stacks to the wrapper. Then you'd squeeze the wrapper and open it up, stick your index finger up there, drop the two stacks in, then bend one end, turn it around, bend, tap it on the table, and that was it. I enjoyed it.

My dad would always buy a round of drinks . . . all slot operators did this: when he'd come in a location that was a bar (they were almost all bars), he'd buy a drink for everybody there; and then when he'd leave, he'd buy a drink for everybody again. In little towns like Yerington or Carson or places like that, they knew his car, they knew when he was coming, they knew his location. They'd go right to the bar and wait for him, because they knew he was going to buy everyone a drink. Of course, I got a Coke or whatever I was drinking; and after I finished counting, whatever loose coins there were that didn't fill a wrapper, I'd get. I'd put them in my pocket, and that was my pay. I really looked forward to that, and my dad took me with him as often as he could.

When we counted, the owner'd be with us. In some cases it was his manager, somebody that he trusted, but it usually was the owner. Counting was a real personalized exercise— it was a time when my dad could talk to the owner, because, when you get experienced in counting money, you can just automatically count it, and you can carry on a conversation and never make a mistake.

Dimes were the most difficult coins to count, and I guess that's one of the reasons why dime machines eventually disappeared. By far the majority of the machines we had were nickel machines. We had some dimes; we had some quarters; but we had very few dollars. Dollar machines really weren't very popular, and I'm sure one of the reasons they weren't is that if a dollar machine ever hit a jackpot, it was like the Second Coming of Christ. They were as tight as you could get them—there wasn't any question about it. And people didn't have the money to play dollars anyway, so there were very few dollar machines.

In towns like Yerington or Carson City, we'd have at least two or three locations. Now, in Carson City, my dad probably had five or six. The Ship Bar down there had like a prow out front, kind of like the Ship and Bottle here in Reno, and that was one of his locations. A man named Ken Johnson, who later became a state senator, had a bar in Carson. There were two or three others.

Dad had machines in Fallon and Lovelock. He also had two or three in Fernley, on the way to Lovelock. Sometimes we'd do a swing—we'd do Fernley, Yerington, and Lovelock in one day, and that was a long day. It was hard work, but that was part of the business.

Dad operated machines on the California side of Lake Tahoe, but only in the summertime. Almost everything at Lake Tahoe in those days was open only in June, July, August, and maybe a few days in September. He had some machines in a bar owned by a man named Rose, two or three miles inside the California line. Then there was Young's Bijou—two brothers named Young had a market and a bar and a little resort, and they called it Young's Bijou. Near where Ski Run Boulevard is now, there was a little bar called Cecil's, and Dad had some machines in there.

On the Nevada side of Lake Tahoe, the tax for these machines, which was paid to the county, was about ten dollars a quarter. It was collected by the Washoe County sheriff, Ray Root, for many years. Root would show up, and he'd have his little list, and you'd pay him the ten bucks—sometimes in cash. My understanding was that the sheriff was paid a very small salary by the county, but by law he got a portion of the tax that he collected for gaming. To me, it was a very efficient system, because he was the man responsible for making sure every slot machine was paid for. He turned the money over to the county, if he was honest; and my recollection is that everyone considered Ray Root to be a very honest man. He took his percentage, and it was simple and easy and didn't cost the county anything. I don't know whether you could do that today, but that's the way things operated then.

Dad even had some machines at Camp Richardson, which was quite a ways into California. The way that worked was, the Placer County sheriff's headquarters was in Roseville or Auburn, and the sheriff had an undersheriff, a local resident who watched the Lake Tahoe shore for him so he wouldn't have to run back and forth through the Sierra.

When my dad had machines on the California side, the undersheriff just took it upon himself (maybe with the sheriff's knowledge and maybe without) to collect a tax on slot machines on the California side, where slots were illegal. It wasn't a tax; it was really just a fee that he kept. We paid this fellow ten dollars in cash for every machine . . . it was probably ten dollars for the summer, although it may have been ten dollars a month.

On more than one occasion we got a phone call from the undersheriff, and he would say, "Some people are coming up from headquarters," or words to that effect. "We have to put the machines away." So we'd hurriedly drive up to the lake and put the machines in the back room or put them on our pickup and bring them back to Reno and then wait till he called us back and said, "OK, now we can put them back."

On the north side of the lake at Buckhorn Lodge, right in King's Beach, a guy by the name of Johnny Rayburn had our machines. That was a good location. Buckhorn was good. We spent lots of time in there counting coin. Dad had machines in Tahoe Tavern. The Tahoe Tavern was a good location, because there was a hotel there, where a lot of people stayed. There were times when he had machines in Homewood at Obexer's. He also had some machines in Chambers.

After Labor Day, Dad gathered up all the machines and brought them down to Reno. By that time he had two or three men working for him, so he just did the collections.

He'd send the guys up to pick up the machines and bring them back. A man named Jeff was one of his men, and I spent some time with him.

When I began to work summers and weekends for my dad, when he was busy doing other things, I'd go out with a serviceman and help him load the machines. Once Jeff and I were driving to Lake Tahoe, and there was a young lady hitch-hiking right outside of Reno, so we stopped to pick her up. When we got to the state line at Verdi, Jeff stopped the truck and asked her to get out and walk across the state line. Then he drove across the state line, and she got back in the truck. I was completely mystified and didn't have any idea what was going on.

When we got up to Tahoe City, and she got out, I said to Jeff, "What was all that about?"

He said, "There's a law that if you take a woman across state lines for immoral purposes, then you're guilty of a federal offense."

I said, "Well, I didn't see anything immoral going on."

He said, "Well, you never know." [laughter] He was a cautious man. I used to have lots of fun with him.

Most of my dad's locations had three or four machines, but in the better ones, like Hale's, for instance, we got up to eight or more. Hale's Drugstore on the corner of Center and East Second Street in Reno became, if not *the* best, *one* of my dad's best locations. That was the second store that Clarence opened up. That store had eleven slot machines, and they did very, very well, and Clarence just kept eliminating drugs and adding slot machines. [laughter] He was making more money out of the slot machines than he was doing with his other things.

Clarence had a man named Phil, who was a long-time pharmacist. Phil would take money out of the cash register and play slot machines with it when no one else was around.

Not only did Phil play all the money he could take out of the register, but he played most of his paycheck, as well. Clarence knew what Phil was up to, and he told my father about it. "Well," they agreed, "we know that every nickel Phil gets goes in the slot machines, so we're going to get it back, anyway." They just let Phil keep right on playing. They'd estimate how much he played, and my dad would give Clarence a kickback to sort of take care of his losses, because they didn't want to lose Phil's business. Hale had several stores in Reno, and my dad had machines in all of his locations, except for the ones that were just pharmacies.

When my dad first went into business after he lost his lease on the Palace Cigar Store, he called himself Pete's Novelty Company. Many people in those days—and some even still—considered gaming to be a sin, so he didn't want anything in the name of his firm to associate him with gaming. In the late 1930s, when he moved from the Cladianos Building to the Lake Street location, he changed the name of his business to the W.P. Amusement Company, again not putting in the gaming name . . . but there was another reason for him to use the word "amusement." He formed a partnership at that time with a man named Walter Payne. Wally was a jukebox route operator. So my dad and Wally formed this partnership. My dad put slot machines into some of Wally's jukebox locations, and vice versa. It was a selling point—when my dad went into a location, he could say, "Well, look, I can furnish you a jukebox, too, and we can service it, and we can . . . ."

There was another man named Willard Wayne, who had pinball games, and they became associated with him too. They were all associated with this W.P. Amusement Company, but it didn't last too long. In 1939 or 1940, when the war in Europe broke out, both Willard and Wally joined the Canadian air force. My father bought them out when they went off to war, and so he then owned a slot route, a jukebox route, and a pinball game route.

Dad moved his business over to 128 East Second Street, which was directly across the street from Benetti and Douglass. [A prominent slot route operation located on the north side of East Second Street, between Lake and Center.] That was around the time Dad acquired the Jennings Agency (slot machines) distributorship and changed his business' name to the Rex Distributing Company. Again, he didn't use anything in the name that indicated that he was involved with gaming. At that time he also acquired the Rock-ola jukebox agency. So he was a distributor for Rock-ola and Jennings, and he put pinball games out on location, as well. He stayed at that address until he eventually sold his route in the latter part of the war years.

The Jennings slot machine was never a very popular machine. The machines simply didn't do as well as Mills. At that time, the Mills machine was *the* most popular machine, and most places—except for Harrah's and Harolds, that had Pace machines—used the Mills machines. Pappy Smith had a standing offer that he'd pay ten bucks for any Pace machine that you brought him, no matter what condition it was in. When my dad would acquire Pace machines, he'd just take them over and sell them to Pappy Smith.

My dad eventually gave up the agency, because people just didn't want to buy Jennings machines. When you had a location, and you had a Jennings next to a Mills, the Mills *almost* always made more money than the Jennings machine. Mr. Fitzgerald, for whatever reason, decided to fill his Nevada Club casino with Jennings machines, and I'm sure he did fine with them . . . just like Harolds and Harrah's did well with Pace machines.

My dad's locations had almost all Mills machines. He bought some machines from somebody in Virginia City—Bucket of Blood or something like that—and they were Caille machines. They were upright with a handle, and they had a wheel that spun around, and then a finger that came down and stopped the wheel. My dad bought ten of those and brought them to Reno to that 128 East Second Street location. They stood up five feet high, and they were about three feet wide. They had a metal front on them, but the sides and the back and the frame were oak, and somebody had painted the oak and the metal. Some of them were silver, and some were gold.

I worked very hard, along with an old man named Joe, in the back room of a shop with paint thinners and scrapers, getting all that paint off of the beautiful oak wood. Then my father had somebody come in and lacquer the oak, and he put those machines out on location. Possibly because they were a novelty, some of them did very well. They were mostly quarter machines. In those days, machines were machines. They were not like it is today, where every month, IGT has a brand new machine that nobody else has.

Back in those early days it was a fifty-fifty cut between the guy who owned the location and the owner of the slots. That was a pretty standard deal. The operator paid the license off the top, and the slot owner had to pay for all the parts and all the labor to fix the machines. Once you had the license paid, you just split fifty-fifty.

When I met Si Redd, the founder of IGT, one of the first things that he said to me was, "You know, letting a route operator come into a business and put his machines in there when the owner of the business has to pay all the taxes and take care of the business, has to keep the place clean, advertise, and so on . . . it's just like a license to steal!" [laughter] In those days, the gaming operators that ran casinos didn't want somebody in their place with their own machines—it was unheard of, as far as I know, until Si Redd and Bally's brought in the electromechanical machine.

The two Benettis were slot route operators. Louie Benetti was an older fellow, and his son, Louie Jr., came into the picture once the old man retired or died. There was a time when Louie Sr. was a partner with a man named Lovejoy, and he was also a partner with Jack Douglass for a time. At some point the Benetti operation was known as A-1 Supply. Bob Douglass, I believe, was a partner in it with Louie Jr.; then eventually, Al Figone ran A-1 Supply. This was after my dad had sold his bigger route but still had a small route.

Slot route operators furnished slot machines to many places, partly because there weren't any real big casinos like we have now. We had the Bank Club and Harrah's and Harolds, but most of the other places were pretty small. All the bars and little operations like I've described had slot operators that ran the slot machines in there. So slot routes were a big part of the gaming business in northern Nevada in the 1930s and 1940s.

The Fallon navy base [Fallon Naval Air Station] opened up early in the war. When my dad learned that it was possible to operate slots at the base, he called on them, talked to them, and found that they were receptive to the idea of him operating slot machines in what they called their ship's service building. It was a combination rec hall, soda fountain, and ship's store, the navy's term for a kind of convenience store for navy enlisted men. And the officers had an officers club, and slot machines could be operated in the officers club, as well.

So, Jeff (one of my dad's employees) and I drove out to Fallon one day in the summer with six or eight slot machines in a pick-up. We installed these machines in the ship's service, right across from the soda fountain bar, and we put four in the officers club by the bar. (They served liquor in the officers bar.) We coin-tested them, and everything was fine. We had a big crowd of sailors around us when we did this in the ship's service—the sailors were really excited about these slot machines. The officers club wasn't quite so crowded.

Well, we left and came back to Reno. The next morning there was a call from the Fallon navy base that every machine out there had stopped working. My dad told Jeff that we must have done something wrong: "Better run out there and fix them." So Jeff and I got in the truck and drove to Fallon. Well, when we got there and opened up the machines, we found that they had put so many coins in these machines that the cash box had filled up, the chute had run over, and the machinery was all jammed with coins. I'd never seen anything like that happen. We cleaned them out, but my dad had to send another man out with a key to the coin boxes, because we didn't have it with us.

We counted all the money, and we left, and we had the same call next morning—jammed up. So my dad got on the phone and talked to whoever the manager of the club was and said, "We better send some more slot machines down there." So we sent down another truckload of slot machines, and we eventually wound up with about fourteen slot machines in that ship's service, and we switched a lot of them over to quarters instead of nickels. There wasn't any more room, or we would have put even more machines in there. That's all we could put in.

That was the best location ever! The officers club did very well, too, but not nearly as well as the ship's service. There eventually came a time when the navy decided that they weren't going to allow machines in the service club anymore. (I believe they allowed them in the officers club, but they made us take them out of the ship's service club.) But until then, it was a wonderful location. We had to send a guy to Fallon to count those machines every two or three days.

My dad had some machines out at Stead for awhile, too. It was called Reno Army Air Base at the time. There was a

Greek fellow out there that ran the officers club. I think at the Reno Army Air Base our slots were only in the officers club. They didn't allow the enlisted men to play them.

My mother used to have parties from time to time at home for Greek men in the service that were stationed at the Army Air Base and the Fallon navy base. She would introduce them to other Greek people in town, and we'd have parties at our house, and I remember them as wonderful, joyous occasions, where there'd be a great deal of laughter and dancing and singing, and much of it Greek. We made a concoction that we called a French Seventy-Five, named for the famous artillery piece. We had a big, huge punch bowl, and we filled it with champagne and then poured brandy in it, and it really helped to make for a wonderful party.

3

Family Businesses

A SLOT ROUTE operator would sometimes actually acquire a location. Most locations were leased operations, where the location operator was leasing the premises from the owner of the building—most of them were three-year or five-year leases. So when a location went broke or closed up or whatever, the slot route operator—I saw my dad do this, and I'm sure other operators did the same thing—would acquire the lease to that property, and he would open it and run it. My dad did that with the 116 Club, which was the forerunner of the Stein on Center Street. He did it with the L&L Bar in Yerington. He did it with Lovelock Mercantile Company in Lovelock. He did it with the Ship Bar in Carson City for a short time—maybe one or two others.

The idea was to operate a place till you could lease it to somebody, with the proviso that whoever you leased it to would agree to keep your machines in there. The real aim was to be in the route business, but in order to help your route business, you'd take over these places. Sometimes the man who you loaned the money to would give you his lease as security, so when he couldn't pay, you'd wind up with the lease. Dad got the El Rancho Bar out on South Virginia Street that way in the early 1940s or late 1930s.

The buildings that became the El Rancho Bar were known as Farley's Dude Ranch when Dad acquired the place—about twenty-five to thirty motel units that had been converted from stables.

Originally, the buildings were stables for George Wingfield's racetrack. Wingfield had a practice track just east of where these buildings sat, on Gentry Way. When Wingfield sold all his horses or moved them, Farley converted the stables into single-story motel rooms. Then Farley lost the property to the bank, and my dad bought the property from the bank. He had been operating machines in the bar, and he bought the whole property. He became the landlord of the El Rancho Bar.

Swede Oleson and a guy named Jack were leasing the bar when my dad became the landlord. He became the lessor, as well as the slot machine operator in that bar, and he began to run the place as a motel, rather than as a dude ranch like Farley had been operating it. Dude ranches were very popular in those days. It was a well-known fact that you could get a divorce in Reno in six weeks. Most people that came for divorces didn't have much money, but a lot of wealthy women came, and many of them stayed in dude ranches, which were really nothing more than a few units and some horses and a cowboy or two to keep the ladies satisfied, in terms of entertainment and so on.

There were a couple of locations that my dad wound up with that became quite significant in his life and mine. One of them was the 116 Club on South Center Street. Dad leased it to a man named Dalrymple, who everyone called Dal. As you walked through the bar, you came to the restaurant, and the restaurant was leased to Willi Brueckner and Marcel Peters. They'd been around Reno for quite some time in other restaurant operations. They ran a wonderful dinner house. I went there with my mother and father on occasion, and the food was absolutely wonderful. The first time I ever tasted avocado was there . . . .

Whatever happened, my dad eventually bought Dalrymple out, and then he ran it himself. He continued to lease the food operation to Willi and Marcel, and he operated a roulette wheel, a crap table, two twenty-one games, and about ten or twelve slot machines. It was during the war, and there was lots of business from Stead Air Force Base, which at that time was known as the Reno Army Air Base. Plus, local people would come in there because of the restaurant.

On busy weekends there, I learned how to rack chips behind a roulette wheel. I was maybe thirteen or fourteen. There was no question that we were breaking the law—it was just that anybody over eighteen that wasn't crippled was away at the war . . . and the sheriff, Ray Root, was the guy that was responsible for taking care of any law breakers, and he wouldn't bother us. My dad did it to try to teach me a little bit about the operation. He wanted me around, because he was spending less and less time in Reno because of all the other businesses that he was running.

Towards the latter part of the war, around 1944, Dad got involved in the Lovelock Mercantile business. Lovelock Mercantile was a huge general store in Lovelock. Half of the main street on one side was the building that the Lovelock Mercantile owned. They sold everything from brassieres to tractors. They had a grocery store; they had a soda fountain; they had a clothing store; they had a furniture store, a hardware store, and so on, but they didn't do very well. Most of the people in Lovelock, when they wanted to make big purchases, would drive to Reno. Plus, there was bad management and what have you.

In the corner store of the Mercantile, on the corner of Main Street and Highway 40—the main transcontinental route at that time—was a soda fountain and a little coffee shop kind of operation. Because parking was real handy and easy, a lot of tourists stopped there in the summertime to get a soda or what have you. So it was a pretty good slot location in the summer, and I remember my dad would increase the number of slots there in the summer and cut them back in the winter.

Dad loaned those Lovelock Mercantile folks money, and they never could pay him back, and eventually he acquired a majority of the stock in the company that owned the building. He had control of the company, and he operated the corner store, and eventually, somehow, he acquired the whole company. Now he had this huge operation in Lovelock. He tried to run it with managers, but he just kept losing money. The slot machines would make money, but the rest of the store would lose more than he would make.

Dad had his slot route, he had the 116 Club, he had the Mercantile, and he had the El Rancho on South Virginia. He was doing very well, but he was working too hard. He also had loaned money to some of his slot locations . . . and in not all cases were the locations able to pay him back. In some instances it was a situation where he'd give a guy a hundred bucks, and the guy'd pay him back; and then the next time, he wanted two hundred, and he'd pay that back; but at some point, he *couldn't* pay you back. So something had to give, and he sold part of his slot route to a man named Williamson. Williamson came from California, the Vallejo area. He had "acquired" a great deal of cash, and he needed a way to legitimize this cash. He bought Dad's business so that he could treat his cash as slot income, pay taxes on it, and thereby launder it. He made payments to my dad once a week in cash, and my father would march over and put that cash right in the bank, because he wasn't hiding it.

In the deal between my dad and Williamson, there was no caveat that my dad had to get completely out of the business, so he continued in a small way in the route business. In all the places that he owned, he operated his own machines, and Clarence Hale stayed with him, because they were still friends. When he sold the route to Williamson, he said, "Look, certain of these locations are mine. They're going to stay with me. I'm not selling them; I'm just selling you these others." The Roundup Bar, for instance, went with him. He cherry picked them, so to speak, and kept the good ones.

I helped Dad more and more with those places, and I got to where I could, for instance, meet with Lena Jacobs, who was running the Roundup Bar, and sit down and count the coins with her. I could go in with Clarence Hale and his son, Jim, who was my age (we went to school together), and Jimmy and I would count the money.

I was able to help my dad in that regard while he was heavily involved in the Lovelock Mercantile, trying to extricate himself from it. He began to spend three to four nights a week down there. He'd move down there on a Monday morning and stay there until Thursday. After he sold most of his route, he was able to devote more time to the Lovelock Mercantile store. He also sold the 116 Club, but he did have the El Rancho, which was doing a tremendous amount of business. Around 1944 or 1945, Jack and Swede left the El Rancho. Dad took over the bar and put in a crap table and a couple of blackjack tables. He ran those and eight or ten slot machines.

Dad gave up on the Lovelock mercantile after a couple years and began to close it up department by department. The first department he closed was the meat department. Then he closed the grocery store, and so on. One summer he sent me down there to work, so I could get some experience. I would work there for three days a week, and then I'd come back to Reno and work at the motel and in the slot route business.

The company that had owned the mercantile store also owned an alfalfa ranch, and my dad sent me out to the ranch to work on it at the end of one August, during the harvesting time for alfalfa. I worked there two days, and that was an experience I'll never forget. I had to run behind the baling

machine, or walk really fast, and pick up bales—which probably weighed eighty to a hundred pounds—and throw them
on a truck bed. (This was called "bucking bales.") I did this
from sunup to sundown, and it was hot, and the alfalfa stuck
in my hair and in my ears and everywhere else on my body.
At the end of a day I'd feel whipped. I did that for two days,
and I said to myself, "I've got to figure out a way that I don't
wind up having to work like this, because I can't stand it. I
can't handle it." Many is the time through the years that I
thought about that, especially when I was going to college,
and said, "If I don't beat these books and get my degree, I
may wind up behind a baling machine again, and I don't
want to do that."

The El Rancho was a good gaming and bar operation,
because of the divorcée trade and local trade, and the motel
was a help to the business of the bar. Then World War II
broke out, and things got even better. The motel-hotel business was a great business to be in during the war. Since the
government had ruled that there would be no new civilian
construction, there were no new hotels or motels being built
anywhere in the country. Yet, industry was operating day and
night, seven days a week, producing goods for the war. The
country had become very prosperous, with a great deal of
travel going on—some business related, and a great number
of service people—but with the same number of accommodations.

Accommodations were extremely scarce. The government, in order to stop people from profiteering, had established an office of rent control. Everybody that operated a
motel or hotel had to show the government what rates they
were charging in the years 1937 and 1938, which were Depression years. The government only let you charge a certain percentage over that amount. In my father's case, he
was allowed to charge $3.50 a night per room; but the way

the regulations read, it was per occurrence, so that if you rented a room to somebody for two hours or eight hours or ten hours, you could rent the room again to somebody else in the same twenty-four hour period for $3.50. It wasn't "hot sheet" business—there were just so *many* people traveling and looking for rooms. I recall being out there and seeing three or four cars parked in front of the motel with people sleeping in the cars, waiting for a room to come available. People were traveling across the country, going from town to town, needing a place to sleep and needing to shower and so on. So instead of $3.50 a day for a room, motel owners were getting seven to ten bucks a day for a room.

I worked with the housekeeping crew, the two or three people that my father had out there, and we'd run in and change the sheets and sweep out the floor and wipe up the shower a little bit, and then usually the new tenant would be standing right by the door, wanting to rent it. One of the people I worked with said, "In this business the motto is, 'There's two good sides to every sheet.'" I never forgot that. We usually put new sheets on the bed, but every now and then, we'd run out of sheets, so we'd just flip them over. [laughter]

Ten dollars a day in those days for a motel room was a lot of money. You didn't spend a lot of time fixing them or cleaning them or anything, so the labor factor wasn't very high. People were being paid seventy-five cents or a dollar an hour to clean rooms. For amenities, we didn't have to worry about anything except soap and a couple of towels.

The bar operation at the El Rancho was making a great deal of money. A lot of folks would spend time in the bar waiting for their room to become vacant, and people that were interested in a little extramarital affair and needed a place to go to do that, would spend time in the bar, waiting for a room to open up. We were also the first motel that you'd hit on the way down from Virginia City, where there were three or four whorehouses, and those girls, when they were off during their time of the month when they couldn't work, would come down and spend time at the Rancho Bar. That was good for business, because men would come in there because of the women.

The operation was very successful, and my father was working very hard with long hours. He found somebody to lease the El Rancho Bar to, with a proviso that he operate the slot machines in the bar. He was not a live-game guy at that time—when he ran the bar, he had a man named George Brazil in there who ran the gaming for him. Dad understood and knew the games, but he didn't want to get involved in them, even though the live table games were the big money makers. My father *always* felt that slot machines were the place to be, and that's what he concentrated on. He liked them because they were not labor intensive; there was probably less chance to be cheated; and for various other reasons.

Dad leased the bar to a man named Kenny Kendall, who was married to Ella Mae Morris, the singer. Kenny's brother, Babe, tended bar for Kenny, and the place slowly changed over from the popular local spot that it was and became a hangout for slot cheats, gaming cheats, crossroaders, and that kind of element. The El Rancho took on a bad name. My dad still owned the place, and he suffered some fallout from that. He tried to make it clear to everyone that he had nothing to do with the operation, other than running the slot machines in there, and when Kenny's lease was up, he refused to lease to him again.

There was even a murder at the place. Somebody got shot and killed in the men's room, and whoever killed him, tore the window out of the men's room and jumped out the window and got away. When the police came to investigate the killing, they found three guys in the bar: Carl Wheeler, who was a crossroader; a man named Goody, who always carried a pistol with him, and when he'd get drunk he'd lay it up on the bar; and Joe Reed, who was tending bar in the place. There were also three or four others in the bar, and no one admitted that they'd heard a shot or any noise whatsoever!

With Kendall gone, my dad leased the place to Guy Meyers and George Stone, and they ran a clean operation. They turned it back into the popular place it had been before. They hired a guy named Jackson, who was a piano player who had played at the Townhouse downtown. Jackson was a great guy. He was going blind, but he could drink shots of whiskey for eight hours a night and still be able to play the piano and not fall off the stool. He was a popular entertainer.

The years of Kenny Kendall's being a lessee at the El Rancho Bar were interesting years for me. I got to know that there was another life besides the normal, run-of-the-mill kind of life that most people live.

4

Small Town Hell Raiser

MY FATHER was the dominant person in the family. Absolutely—wasn't any question about that! We thought that that was the way it was supposed to be. (I think my mother did too for a long time, but after twenty-five years of marriage, she decided that it shouldn't be that way, and things changed a great deal.) During my youth it was unheard of for any of us to dispute anything my father would say. He had a very commanding presence. Even though he wasn't a big man—he was only five foot eight—when he came in a room, everyone recognized that he was dominant. It wasn't until I was in my late teens that I ever even thought about disputing anything that he said to me.

We had dinner every night together as a family, but when I was young, family affairs were rarely discussed in front of the children. My mother and father would decide between themselves if we were going to go on a vacation, or if one of the children was going to have surgery, or go to a summer camp, or what have you. We could make our requests, but we were not included in the deliberations on these matters. If we were going to buy a new home or a new car, those kinds of things were never a part of the children's life, because of the old Greek tradition that children were to be seen and not heard. And if there was a dispute between my mother and father, we were always kept away from that kind of thing. The conversations at the dinner table were pretty much about how we were doing in school, what we were going to do over the weekend, how we dressed, whether we were behaving or not, what punishment might be meted out if we weren't behaving, and that kind of thing.

My dad felt that I should begin to work and earn some money at an early age. I was around twelve years old or so, maybe a little younger, when I got my first job selling Sunday newspapers. My mother would take me down to a little news and magazine agency on Third Street, and we'd buy our papers there. The owner, Mr. Saul, had the town sectioned out into areas, and he gave me the area where I lived.

My folks had moved in 1938 to 125 Circle Drive, on the corner of Monroe and Circle Drive in the Southwest part of town, so I had the area from Mount Rose Street to California and as far west as Plumas. I would knock on all those doors and ask people if they would like a newspaper delivered on Sunday; and if they did, then I'd make a note of the address, and on Sunday mornings I'd bring them a newspaper, and they'd pay me. It would take me all morning. I'd start out pretty close to daybreak to get my papers. I had a little cart that Mr. Saul furnished, and I'd put the papers in it—the *San Francisco Examiner* and a local paper. I'd buy them from Saul for, say, twenty cents a paper, and I'd sell them for twenty-five, so I'd make the nickel. If I had any papers left over, I ate the loss. Saul didn't want them, because they were history, so the idea was to keep hustling and to keep selling until you got rid of all your papers, because you weren't going to get your money back for any of them.

My mother was a very gentle woman, and one of the things that she tried to instill in me and her other children was that we should not ever participate in any violence of any kind. We should be courteous; we should be polite. She tried to train us in that manner to the best of her ability, and she was vigilant in that area. If we would show bad manners or wouldn't use a napkin or talk with our mouth full, she corrected us. I think she instilled honesty in us, because she was a very honest person; and whatever courage we had came from her as well as my father. And, of course, she went to great pains to make sure that we did attend church when we could and observe the religious holidays and know about the Greek religion.

Within our family, the division was that our mother raised the children, and my father ran the business without any input from her. She was happy enough to do it that way, and, anyway, she had her hands full with three kids.

We always had everything we wanted, but we weren't in a situation where we were spoiled or where we had much more than we needed. Everything was adequate, and it was good quality. We Greeks love to eat, and we had the *best* food. My dad knew about the produce business, and my uncle, who used to come and stay with us, made sure we had the freshest produce and the best meats, because eventually he got in the meat business, as well. We ate very well, and we lived in a very fine home.

When I was born, we lived at 622 1/2 Ryland Street, which was a little house in an alley about a block west of Wells Avenue. Shortly after I was born, we moved to a house at 737 West Fifth Street. It was a brick home that had two bathrooms and three bedrooms, and it was a pretty decent home for those days. That was probably in 1931, and we lived there until 1938. In 1938 my father bought a fine home at 125 Circle Drive for $17,000. It was brand new with hardwood floors and tile bathrooms, built on two lots.

We had everything that we wanted, but, when it was time for me to get a car, I got a Chevrolet. We had nice clothes, we had food, but everything was always given to us in a way that we understood that we should be grateful for it. We shouldn't ask for anything more than what we really needed, and we should begin to think about trying to work for it.

One of the things that my dad made it a point to tell me was, "Look, you are the oldest *male* child. When I die, you're going to take over." He started talking to me about that when I was really young, in my early teens, maybe even earlier than that. It was pretty much handed down to me that my brother and sister were my responsibility, and that I needed to be cognizant that, because I was the oldest one, I had these special responsibilities.

I was told that in everything I did, I should keep my brother and sister in mind. And all the things that we ever did in business together, even though I was the president of the company, we shared alike—one third, one third, one third. I got that from my father. He said to me, "You don't want to have arguments about money. The way to prevent that is by treating everybody alike. And you, because you're the oldest person, have to take the bull by the horns, and even though you do more work and have more responsibility, you need to share everything with your brother and sister *evenly*." I did that for most of my life. We did have some extenuating circumstances when my brother became ill, but the family came first, absolutely! Religion and family were, and are, the most important things in my life.

From the earliest time I can remember, my dad talked about college for all of us, and if any of us ever said, "Well, I don't know why I should go to college," we were instantly silenced. It's only because of my father that I did graduate from college.

My father was quite a role model. He had the greatest willpower of any man I've ever known. Around 1940 or so, he just decided he was going to quit gambling, so he did. And about two years later he decided to quit smoking. He smoked one more cigarette, and that was the end. I wish that I could be like that. It took me *eight years*, for Christ's sake, to stop smoking cigarettes! [laughter]

I started grammar school (there was no kindergarten) at the Mary S. Doten school. At first, Mother sent me to school in a pair of short, black, velvet pants. All she knew about school in Greece was that children should be dressed nice to go to school. Most of the kids in Reno came to school in overalls or some such informal attire, but my mother felt it was important that we learn to dress properly. So here I was, a really shy child at that time, coming to school in short, black, velvet pants! [laughter]

I would wait until the bell rang, because I could hear it from the front lawn of my house, and when I heard the bell ring, then I'd run to the school. That way I could keep from being harassed by my classmates. I had a great deal of trouble over these clothes, and I wound up in some fights, forced to defend myself. I'd come home on occasion with a bloody nose or scraped hands or elbows or black eyes.

My folks were wondering why I was having all this trouble, and I would try to explain to my mother that it just wasn't going to *work*—that I couldn't *go* to school in black velvet pants. Sometimes she would relent, but other times she still felt that it was her duty to make sure that I looked nice.

At the end of first grade, I was held back a year. The school said it was because I couldn't yet speak English well enough to keep up, and they were right. But I think there was also another reason. I was always thinking about how I was going to escape when the school bell rang and class was over—how I was going to escape these bullies and get home without getting my head knocked off. I was worried more about that than I was about trying to learn anything.

There may have been other factors. My brother was born in 1938, and he had pneumonia, and they thought that he was going to die. My mother was also quite ill, because he was thirty days late in coming. (The doctor gave my dad his choice about whether to save the mother or the child, and he said, "Well, I have to save my wife, because I have these other two children to take care of.") My brother lived, but he was very ill.

We were living in this small home; I was having trouble at school . . . and my father could afford it, so he sent me away to military school when I was eight years old. The school was in San Rafael in Marin County, California. When I went in September, I didn't come home until Thanksgiving, and then for Christmas vacation I came home. Then I came home for Easter, and I was in San Rafael until the first part of June. I was lonely and sad. It was a long time to be all by myself without my family . . . without my mother, especially. And my dad, of course—I had love for him, as well.

I only went a year that first time, but I went back later. I came home after a year, and during the time I was gone my family had moved from West Fifth Street to Circle Drive, so

when I returned, I began school at Mt. Rose. Then I went to Billinghurst for junior high school, and then on to Reno High.

I had some of the most wonderful times of my life as a student at Reno High. It was a carefree time. We used to cut school once in awhile. There was only one truant officer in town. His name was Neil Scott, and I got to know him intimately. [laughter]

"I was lonely and sad. It was a long time to be all by myself without my family . . . ."

Just before you got to Lawton's on West Fourth Street, there was a cave. We just called it *the* cave, and everybody knew what we were talking about. We had beer busts out there, and we'd go out there and sit around and smoke when we were playing hooky. It was quite a popular place with the high school group. Also, there was sort of a sand pit out at the end of Seventh Street at that time, and we'd go there and see whose car was fastest from a dead stop to a spot two or three hundred yards up a paved strip, and we'd try to see how much rubber we could lay. That was another one of our recreations. [laughter]

Lawton's was run by Mark Yori. The Yoris were an old-time family here. They owned Yori Land and Livestock, and they made a great deal of money in the ranching business. At Lawton's they had a casino, a restaurant, a meeting hall (sort of a banquet hall), and a huge swimming pool. There were natural hot springs out there. They had two or three diving boards, and they had a high board. One of my first experiences in swimming was diving off of that high board—first jumping off and then learning how to dive off that board. That was quite an accomplishment for me, because I wasn't really a good swimmer. Also, Lawton's was a place for high school graduation parties and that sort of thing.

The proms were held principally in the gymnasium of Reno High or Huskies Haven, which was a building on the corner of South Center Street, right where the Washoe County Library is now. It was an old two-story building that must have been supported by city recreation money. They'd have dances there, and it was a place that we could go after school. Huskies Haven was open after school up till probably seven or eight o'clock. Usually, Friday night and Saturday night, they'd have dances. Kids would bring their records there and play them, and on big occasions, like a graduation dance or something like that, they'd have live music. But most of the time it was just an old Victrola. I didn't have a whole lot to do with Huskies Haven.

I had peculiar ideas about dating and about girls in those days. I'm not quite sure how that all came about. I think I had a certain shyness—more so than other boys—when it came to talking to young girls that I attended school with, and I had very few dates. Instead, I fell in with some older boys who frequented little bars around town where women hung out. These women were at least twenty-one years old, and many were casino workers. I had a better rapport with them.

I was friendly with many of the girls that I went to school with, but they were just like buddies, really. I didn't consider them to be objects of a romantic association. The females that I was thinking about in those terms were ladies that I met in these little bars around town.

There was a place called the Bluebird Club on Commercial Row, between Virginia Street and Sierra Street, and it was a place that didn't really care how old you were. I was tall for my age, and I didn't have a great deal of difficulty being served there. There was a shortage of men, so it made it easy for those of us that were of high school age to go in and strike up a conversation with the ladies. A great many of these women were looking for some male companionship, and once I learned the ropes, so to speak, I pretty much kept away from high school girls, other than the friends that I'd made.

From time to time the guys I hung out with would go up to the Virginia City houses of prostitution. A group of us would drive up there, maybe four or five of us, but none of us ever had very much money. At that time, it cost three dollars to have sex with a lady in the house. As we wouldn't have enough money for all of us to go in, we'd draw straws, and if we had six bucks, then the two guys with the longest straws got to go in. The rest of us would wait out in the car and think of all the things that were going on inside. [laughter]

"*I was tall for my age.*"

There was prostitution in Reno, but the cribs in the red light district were pretty well policed by their own personnel (not the police department), and they wouldn't let us in. Virginia City, because it was so out of the way, didn't seem to care too much. If you had three dollars in your hand, you could get through the door real easy.

At Reno High, I attended a speech class taught by Roger Joseph, who helped me get over my shyness. He would assign us certain subjects, and then we would write out a three-minute speech and deliver it before the class. It was a very difficult thing for me to do. I was extremely nervous about speaking to the class, and I would be apprehensive and have a very difficult time delivering a speech. Roger Joseph was a wonderful teacher, and he could see that I was nervous about all this, so, at his suggestion, I'd come in after class, and he would help me in my delivery. He also helped me to get over my shyness.

There were two or three other people at Reno High that were very important in my life, because of the examples they set and because of their dedication to teaching young people.

One was Bud Beasley, an extremely devoted man. Anybody that went to Reno High School in the last fifty years or so knows Bud Beasley. He's influenced many lives. One of the things that Bud did for me, as well as for other boys like myself, was instill in me the idea that even though much of the time in sports you might sit on the bench, you were still important. You didn't have to be a star. You could still play, you could still be an athlete, you could do your part.

I didn't play much in organized sports during my high school and junior high years. I was an uncoordinated boy, who had a great deal of medical problems, including broken arms and legs and ankles and that kind of thing. I participated in athletics only because Bud encouraged me. He made me understand that I didn't need to be a star, but that it was important that I learn team work. He also led me to understand that individual sports, like wrestling and tennis, were important and something that I should learn. Teamwork is one thing, but you need to depend on yourself in certain instances, and Bud would force us to wrestle and box during physical education classes.

Our principal was Roger Corbett, a gentleman who ran a strict ship; but when you were a disciplinary problem, you were first confronted by Vice Principal Gallagher, who was in charge of discipline. Gallagher would mete out the punishment, which generally consisted of being barred from certain social events if you had too many absences or played hooky or were late to school or scuffled in the hallways or disrupted the classroom. If Gallagher couldn't calm you down, then you had to face Roger Corbett, and Roger Corbett would stare holes right through you. He was a very fair-minded man, but we all pretty much accepted that his word was law, and he kept us from straying too far. After he retired from the school system, he went to work for the district attorney's office as an investigator.

Herb Foster was the football and basketball coach at Reno High. He was a gruff, outspoken militarist, and he brooked no nonsense. The little bit that I played on the football team taught me that Herb Foster didn't put up with any foolishness. If you wanted to play, if you wanted to practice, if you were serious about it, Herb would allow you to do so. If you fooled around, and you weren't interested in it, Herb would cut you.

I made some lifetime friends in school. One was Roy Torvinen, who became a district court judge here. He was also a member of the legislature, and he was city attorney in Reno and probably one of the most honest men that I ever met in my life. I spent many years trying to get him to be not so honest—he took honesty to a length that was probably too much. Every time I wound up in Roy's court, he'd see that I was removed to another court, because he didn't want anybody to say that because of our friendship he would do anything untoward. That worked to my disadvantage.

On several occasions, especially in the case of my mother's estate, I was thrown into the court of a judge who was inferior. Some judges simply were not the type that Roy was. They didn't view things like he did, and they didn't have the honesty that Roy had. So, because of our friendship, I sometimes wound up before judges that were less than the judicial type of person I could have had. When Roy ran his election campaigns, I helped him with money and with work, and I used to say to him, "Roy, your opponent is attacking your character. You need to do the same thing to him." He absolutely refused to do anything along those lines. He always said his record would be the thing he'd stand on, and he would never stoop to attacking anyone's integrity. He never lost an election that I can recall, so he probably did the right thing in not paying attention to what *I* told him.

Harry Rovetti was the most aggressive of my friends. While still in high school, he started two or three businesses, and for a short time I worked with him in one—draining septic tanks at Lake Tahoe. Harry was the glue that kept our group together: Roy, Bob Moore, Frank Sala, myself, and Harry. He was the guy that would get us together. We learned to scuba dive together. We water skied for many years together—he got us interested in that. (We bought a boat together after we got out of college, and we all learned to ski together.) We'd go on trips together to Mexico, to Hawaii, and Harry would organize all this stuff—he was a guy that just couldn't sit still.

Unfortunately, Harry died about twenty years ago from cancer, and we have drifted apart more than I would want to, but without Harry there was no glue. We are still in touch, but I know that if Harry was here, we'd be in touch a lot more. These are the folks that I went on to college with, that were instrumental in making me understand, along with my father, that college was important.

The other group of people that I became friends with was somewhat more adventuresome. I had a great deal of freedom. The old Greek tradition is that the oldest son takes over for the father and inherits everything. Then it's up to him to see that his brothers and sisters are taken care of. In my case, that wasn't true. My father always treated the three of us equally. We inherited equally from him, and he paid us equally . . . but he did give me a great deal more freedom than my brother and sister; especially my sister, and she is only two years younger than me.

I had a job that allowed me to get out of the house almost every night—I was a janitor at the Cladianos Building, and I cleaned the offices on the second floor nightly. That allowed me to be out, because I couldn't start until after they all closed. And the fact that I was out put me in touch with other boys that were out a lot. Among that group was a Greek boy whose name was Angelo Anastasakis. His father owned a little restaurant down on Commercial Row (I believe it was called the Popular Cafe), and my dad had a couple of slot machines in his restaurant. He was a man who worked all the time, and Angelo also had a lot of freedom.

Angelo had an older brother named John who was away in the army, so Angelo had inherited John's car. He was only fourteen years old or so, but he had transportation, and that was the reason we could do a lot of things that other kids couldn't do. It was hard to get around if you didn't have your own automobile.

In our group of boys, there was one named John Burns, who came here from back East. His mother worked at the Riverside Hotel as a waitress, and her husband worked in the gaming industry. They both worked swing shift, so John had a great deal of freedom too. That was one reason we banded

Lounging with John Burns (right) next to the V&T Railroad tracks near South Virginia St. and Gentry Way, 1946.

together. We remained friends until he passed away a few years ago. Unfortunately, John was one of so many in my generation who succumbed to alcohol and cigarettes. He just wouldn't stop either one, and they killed him.

We had in our group a guy named John Meckes, whose folks owned a little convenience store off of North Virginia Street, up near the university. They were open in the evenings, and John had a lot of free time, so he was also out there with us.

I never have been a joiner, and although there were clubs in high school, I didn't belong to any except an informal, unauthorized fraternity known as Gamma Eta Kappa. We were called "Geeks" after the initials. There was another fraternity with more boys in it, but the fellows that I was acquainted with were members of the Geeks. Since these were not really school-sponsored fraternities, we were not able to hold events at the school, but we would hold them other places . . . pretty much what we're really talking about here is beer busts! [laughter] That was the extent of our social events.

In my second year of high school, my father became aware that I was drinking in bars, dating older women, visiting Virginia City brothels, and occasionally committing petty thefts . . . and other things. He became quite disturbed. The last straw was when the police called him to come downtown and get me out of the drunk tank. So, in my second year of high school, I was sent back to the San Rafael Military Academy. It was an altogether different experience than I had had the first time.

San Rafael Military Academy was composed of, essentially, two kinds of students. There was the student from a very wealthy family that wanted its child to go to a private school. Then, there were other students that attended because they were disciplinary problems or had been asked to leave public schools.

At San Rafael Military Academy, life was regimented, discipline was severe, and physical training and athletics were mandatory. It was a wonderful experience. My year there taught me that I was responsible for my failures, whatever they might be, and I had to pay the price. Through my father's wisdom in sending me there, I was able to learn that lesson. I also made one or two life-time friends at that place, and I learned a different culture.

At the end of my year at San Rafael, my father wanted me to stay another year. I promised him that I'd learned my lesson, and that I could be trusted to come back to school, and that I wouldn't engage in the activities that had caused me problems before. So he gave me that chance; he allowed me to come back. Unfortunately, I didn't keep my promises. I still had some difficulties, but once he allowed me to come back, it was too late for him to do anything about it, and I graduated and went on to college.

Company C, San Rafael Military Academy, 1944. I am third from the left in the back row.

When the United States entered World War II, there were a couple of Japanese kids in my school, and they moved them and their families down to Inyokern to the internment camp. It was really foolish, but I guess the government didn't know what the hell was going to happen. I guess it couldn't be helped. The father of one of the kids, Mr. Fuji, had a nursery on Wells Avenue, Nevada Nursery. We had a kid named Buster Chikami, and they moved his family, also.

There weren't very many Japanese in Reno then. And we had only one black student in Reno High, Ken Hyliger. (He wasn't a Negro that was descended from slaves that they brought over here—he was an immigrant that came from England, and I got to know him pretty well.) We did have a few Chinese families, and we had some American Indians. But most of the kids at Reno High were Caucasian, so we simply didn't have the kinds of problems that existed in the East and other places.

When I was growing up, we had a few Indians in Reno, and there was prejudice by the white folks against them. I felt that the Indians were kind of inferior. We had two or three that attended school with us. There was Phelan Sampson, his brother Floyd, maybe one or two others. We treated them like they were one of us, but downtown we would see Indian men that had had too much to drink, staggering along a street or sitting in a doorway—not a great number of them, but once in awhile.

Ken Hyliger and I have remained friends. (1997 photo)

The feeling was that Indians simply couldn't handle alcohol, and I guess that's why the government didn't allow them to drink. We took advantage of that, and that's another way that we raised a few dollars when we needed it to go to Virginia City or what have you. We would go to a liquor store and buy Indians a quart of beer or a bottle of whiskey. They'd give us the money, and we'd charge them fifty cents or a dollar to buy the alcohol for them. We did have some prejudice against Indians. Blacks, no. And I think the reason is, there simply weren't that many blacks here.

I didn't experience any prejudice against Greeks, but my dad told me many stories about it. When he first came to this country, not only was there prejudice against Greeks, but there was prejudice against Polish people and people from Czechoslovakia and Turks and so on and so forth; but when I grew up in old Reno, we didn't really have that kind of problem.

Back then, before the casinos took over, there were a lot of businesses downtown. There was a place that we used to go called Wilson's Drugs. It was on the corner of First and Virginia Street, and it had a soda fountain. We'd go to there after school, and the big rage in those days was a chocolate Coke. They'd give you a glass of Coke and put a dollop of chocolate in it, and then you'd stir it up.

Sears and Woolworth had stores in downtown Reno. Herz Jewelry was on Virginia Street, and the I. Magnin women's clothing store was there. Sunderlin Shoes was there. Many stores were along Virginia Street, most of them on the west side of the street. The east side of Virginia Street, between Commercial Row and Second Street was pretty much restaurants and casinos. The Monarch Cafe was between First and Second, and there was a Victory Cafe on the corner of the alley, where the Primadonna was built later. And then, across the alley, there was Southworth's Cigar Store.

"Pop" Southworth, as he was known, was a councilman and one of the civic leaders of the town for many years. He was very friendly with the gaming interests, and he essentially represented them on the city council. One of the reasons he took care of them is that he had the cigarette concession in most of the gaming establishments. It sort of went hand in hand—they gave him all the cigarette concessions; he made sure that they were well represented on the council.

In the middle of the block between Center and Virginia, on the north side of First street, there was a brokerage house called J.A. Hogle. My dad spent a lot of time in there, playing the stock market. They had a ticker-tape machine, and they would flash the tape up on a screen on the wall and enlarge it. Folks would go in there and read the tape, look for their stock, see the trades going across, and watch the price of the stock fluctuate. My dad would spend two or three hours in there every morning, and, of course, there were press releases and that sort of thing that came in there, too. You got all the latest financial news in J.A. Hogle's, and it was the only brokerage house in town for many, many years.

On the northwest corner of Second and Center Street was Hale's Drugstore. That was one of my dad's best slot route locations. He had six or eight slot machines in there. Hale was doing pretty well with them, so he threw out some drugs and added more slot machines. There was a club on Center Street called the Inferno. We used to go there to look for girls. The Ship and Bottle on Center Street was one of my dad's slot locations, so I didn't hang out in there, but when I was working for my dad, I'd go in there with his service men to fix the machines or count the money.

There weren't many real restaurants in the town center. Most of those places were just bars, but there were some exceptions. In the 116 Club, my dad leased out the restaurant to Willi Brueckner and Marcel Peters. The food was wonderful there, and they had a great reputation. The Club Fortune had a restaurant, and they had a pretty good reputation. The Trocadero in the El Cortez Hotel was quite a famous night club locally, and they served food. (The casinos didn't serve any food in those days.) A lot of these places were really just gin mills. They were just bars. I mean, you just went in there for one thing . . . . Well, two things: ladies and alcohol. [laughter]

When I wasn't in school, I used to meet my dad for lunch in the Golden coffee shop or the Overland coffee shop. When the Mapes opened, we'd eat in the Coach Room a lot. At the 116 Club, they didn't serve lunch, but we used to eat dinner as a family in the 116 Club. In those days in Reno, it was unusual for families to go out to eat—it was usually a special occasion.

When I was going to school, we didn't have a cafeteria, so, once we had wheels, we'd go to the drive-ins. Lee's Drive-In was on North Sierra Street, between Fourth and Third Streets on the west side of the street. Then, around the corner, there was a drive-in for a time called the Boys' Drive-In. The rougher element in town hung out there, so I was there—not because I was a rough guy, but because I liked to hang out with the few guys that rode motorcycles and so on.

There was a great number of servicemen in Reno during the war years, because troop trains used to pull into town and stop and let the servicemen off for an hour or two. You'd see a lot of service guys, mostly army people, walking up and down the streets and in the casinos. Everybody liked service people, because we knew that they were putting their lives on the line for us and for the country, and we were *all* patriotic folks. It wasn't like the later wars when there were some dissenters.

As teenagers, if the war lasted long enough, we would have to go to war ourselves, and we used that as a method to get things that we wanted. Sometimes we'd go into a bar to buy a drink, and the bartender would ask for our I.D., and we would say, "Look, we're not twenty-one years old, but in a year or two, we're going to be drafted, and we're going to go to war and fight. You mean to tell me that you're not going to give us a beer?" And it worked pretty good. We also used that when we talked to older ladies, ladies that were over twenty-one. We'd say, "You know, maybe I'm only eighteen, but don't forget, I'm going to be out there laying my life down for you." It was a pretty good line.

During the war, they rationed gas. We had coffee rationing. We had sugar rationing. We had butter rationed, and also meat. (You needed red points to get meat, and you could only get so much meat.) To help put food on the table, my brother and sister and I, with my mother's help, had a Victory Garden: carrots, tomatoes, potatoes, green beans. Because there was a shortage of food, the government urged everyone to grow their own vegetables, so that commercially farmed food could go to the armed forces. Greek people like to eat a lot of greens, so we grew different greens, and we'd also pick dandelion greens. My mother would boil the greens and put olive oil and lemon juice on them.

Later on in the war, my folks expended a great deal of effort and money for Greek War Relief. The Greek War Relief was organized by AHEPA, the American Hellenic Educational Progressive Association. It was organized in the early 1920s to help Greek people in this country network with each other, learn the English language, understand the customs of this country, and so on. For Greek War Relief, money was donated to them, as well as clothes, shoes, hats, that sort of thing. It was for the people in Greece that were being starved by the German occupation army, because the Germans took away everything. We were closely involved with it. We felt we were helping them in the only way that we could.

I began to follow the progress of World War II shortly after Pearl Harbor. My mother could see that I had quite an interest, and she bought me two or three big scrapbooks. I would cut articles and pictures out of the paper and paste them into the scrapbooks. The Pacific theater was pretty much all in one book, but the European theater was two or three different books. When the Italians invaded Greece, I started a book, because we were very interested in the war between the Italians and the Greeks. We were quite proud of the Greek nation and the Greek army, because the Italians suffered defeat after defeat after defeat. Then Hitler decided that he had better get into the war, and he turned the German army loose on the Greek army, and then they didn't have a chance.

5

Hellenic Reno

IN BIGGER CITIES, the Greek church was usually the focal point for the Greek community. Most of the time, there would be a Greek school associated with the church, so that Greek-Americans could learn to speak, read, and write Greek. Since there wasn't a Greek church in Reno, we didn't have that opportunity when I was a kid. Although my mother taught my sister to write some Greek, I never learned; but I did learn to speak it, because the first language in our home was Greek.

My sister and my mother and I learned English out of the same book for a few years when my sister and I were going to grammar school. I had to repeat the first grade, because the teacher felt I didn't understand what she was saying. It was probably true—I didn't know enough English to understand what was going on. When I was held back, my mother decided that we were going to have to speak more English in our home, and that she was going to have to learn to speak it. My dad had long ago decided that *he* had to learn the language as well as he could; and so, for all of these reasons, we all tried to speak English more than Greek. So we lost a lot of our ability to speak Greek, and I never did learn to write the language.

Greek Easter is a week-long event with church services every day, and since there was no church in Reno, there were several times when I was young that we went to Sacramento and spent a whole week there going to church. At other times we'd only go down for the last two or three days, for the weekend, because there's a big service Friday night and a big service Saturday night. Then, Easter Sunday, there's a short service in the morning followed by a big celebration where the Greek tradition is to barbecue a lamb. Of course, you've been fasting all this time, up until the day of Easter; then you get to eat barbecued lamb and all the things that you had given up. Greek Easter was a very important time for us—a religious time and a holiday time—and we did keep that tradition.

The other tradition that we kept up was celebrating name days. I don't think they do this anymore, but when my parents lived in Greece, they didn't celebrate birthdays. They only celebrated their name days. For example, my name is Pete, so I would celebrate St. Peter's Day, which is August 15. We began to celebrate both our name days and our birthdays in this country, because the American custom was to celebrate birthdays. We had friends who celebrated their birthdays, so my mother felt that it was important that we be able to celebrate our birthdays as well as our name days.

There may have been thirty to forty Greek families in the Reno area when I was young. A few were from the island of *Zákinthos*—Zante—that my folks were from. One man who was here when my father got here was a man named John Lougaris. He had fought in the First World War in the U.S. army, and he'd been gassed, so he was collecting disability. He was partially disabled, but you wouldn't know it. Lougaris was a friend of my dad's, a tenant in the building downtown that my dad and my uncle had built in 1923. He lived to be ninety-seven or ninety-eight years old, and the Veteran's Administration Hospital here in Reno has a wing named after him.

Lougaris became a lawyer without going to law school. He studied under a judge up in Virginia City, and he used to buy fresh vegetables and fruit from my father's store and take them up to Virginia City to the judge. My dad and my uncle always said that they were responsible for John becoming a lawyer, because it was the only way the judge could get fresh fruit and vegetables up in Virginia City!

There was also a Pappas family in Sparks that became *very* important in my life. James and Catherine Pappas had three sons and a daughter. Jim worked on the railroad, and Catherine was a housewife. One of their boys, Gus, died as a teenager, drowned in Washoe Lake. He was out there with his brothers trying out a boat that they had put together. The other two brothers attended college, went in the army, came back after the war, and started a little business called Nick and Paul's Service. It was a gas station and repair shop located at 40 B Street, and it was the last business on the east end of Sparks at that time. They stayed there over forty years. Nick married a lady named Vaslie Argeres, and they had four children. One was named Althea, and she's now my wife. Little did I know, many years ago, that someday I'd marry one of the Pappas kids. I remember when my wife was born— she is twenty years younger than I am.

Another Greek family in Reno was the Angelides family. Angie Angelides was a wonderful person. She started the only Greek school that we ever had here in Reno. For many years, she, with some help from some other Greek ladies, taught the younger children how to read and write Greek. It was after I had graduated from college and gone in the army, and so I never got to attend that school, but my wife did, and it was one of the ways that some of the young folks learned to read and write Greek. If it hadn't been for Angie, that never would have happened. Her husband was a supporter of the Greek church and Greek organizations in Reno.

Danny and Perry Varzos were also staunch members of the community. Danny Varzos was an entertainer in his youth. He was a piano player, but he also learned the food business.

He became a restaurant manager, and he worked for my father for awhile in the early 1950s.

There was a family in Sparks called the Lemberes family. The lady's name was Stella—she came over here from Greece. Her husband died when her children were very young, probably in the 1930s. Her brother, Nick, lived with them and worked for the railroad. He stayed single all of his life, and he helped her raise her four children—three boys and a girl. The girl's name was Dula, and she became a very close friend of my mother's. For years and years, until she became crippled and in a wheelchair, she always went to the cemetery on my mother's birthday and left flowers for my mother.

My folks were very close with the Lemberes family. The youngest Lemberes boy, Alex, went to West Point with my dad's help. My dad knew a senator and a congressman, and when Alex applied, they helped him get an appointment. Alex retired from the army with the rank of full colonel, and he now lives here in Reno.

Another man who was very important in the Greek community at that time was a man named Angelo Pappas—same name as my in-laws, but not related. (Pappas is a name that is as common among Greek-Americans as Smith is in English. It's really a shortened form of a lot of Greek names.) Angelo was a detective on the Reno police force for thirty-five, forty years, maybe. If any of the Greek folks got into any difficulty with the Reno P.D., Angelo would come to their aid and help them out, especially those Greeks that didn't speak English well. Angelo was married to a lady named Rose, who is not Greek, but she also became a strong supporter of the Greek community and church.

In the early 1930s, when the country was in a depression, there were some Greek families in Reno that were having a very difficult time. They were quite poor, and they were really having some trouble feeding their families. During this time people like Bill Pappas, Angelo Pappas, my father, John

Lougaris, and other folks that I've probably left out, went to great lengths to see that these families were fed and clothed. They actually gave money out of their own pockets in a collective effort to make sure that Greek folks in this community wouldn't suffer. That, of course, pulled the community together and made for a pretty solid group.

My parents were friendly with some Greek people that lived in Portola. There were two brothers up there, Tom and Gus Nichols. (In Greek, Tom's first name was Athanasi.) Tom, who became my godfather, operated a bar and a restaurant in Portola, and his brother operated a laundry and had a little trucking company. We would many times go to Portola and spend a day, maybe go on a picnic at Beckwourth, or they would come down and spend a day with us.

Tom had six children. The oldest girl was a girl that I had a crush on. Her nickname was Kiki, and I always have thought that was a unique name. I christened my youngest daughter with the name Kiki before she was born. (Her real name is Leslie, but I always call her Kiki, and all of our family calls her Kiki.)

Another man that was important to the Greek community was Chris Kakouris. Chris worked at the Washoe General Hospital in the surgery department. He was an orderly, and when Greeks wound up in Washoe Hospital, he'd do little favors for them. He'd make sure that they got the kind of food they wanted—within limits, of course—and he'd do everything he could so that they'd be comfortable in the hospital. (I was a patient at the hospital on several occasions. When I was young, I had a problem with breaking my legs and my arms, and I'd wind up in the hospital. When I'd start playing team sports, I'd wind up with a broken leg, and that was the end of my season!)

Peter Demosthenes and family were old-time Reno residents that had come from Greece, probably in the early 1920s. Mr. Demosthenes started an ice-cream creamery that he called the Velvet Ice Cream Company. The building still stands just past the police station on Second Street, very close to Wells, and there's a sign around on the east side where you can still make out the word "creamery." Mr. Demosthenes produced what we thought was the best ice cream in the world. He became quite wealthy. He dabbled in real estate, and he was a great supporter of the Greek community, as well.

There was another man who was important in my younger life, who is dead now. His name in English would be Rose, but in Greek it's a long name with many syllables (*Triantafyllo*), so let's just call him John Rose. John Rose was in the army with Mr. Lougaris during the First World War, and he was also gassed. He was a close friend of John Lougaris and my father, and many times I would go down to meet my dad in the Cladianos building, and John Rose would be there. Everyone smoked cigars at the time, and I remember the smell of the cigars and the big brass spittoons in those offices and how they would chew their cigars and spit out pieces in the brass spittoons. Later in my life, as a teenager, I became a janitor, and I used to clean those offices up on that second floor, and the whole place smelled like cigars.

These men were all very nice to me. They used to buy me candy and sit and talk to me and tell me about Greece and about their experiences in the war, and how difficult it was for them when they came to this country, how difficult it was for them to learn the language, and how important religion was in our lives. Unfortunately, John Rose died fairly young. He had been wounded more severely than Lougaris— he was unable to work at all, had a limp, and he walked with a cane.

Most Greek men belonged to the AHEPA, the American Hellenic Educational Progressive Association, and at their meetings they would raise money or use their dues to bring a Greek priest to Reno at least once a month. Because we had no church, the services were held in the same hall that the AHEPA met in, a place called the Pythian Building on North Virginia Street. The meeting hall was on the second floor, and we would have our church services there almost monthly. Sometimes they'd be held on a Saturday, because the priest would usually come from Sacramento, and it would be the same priest that would do the services in Sacramento on Sunday. There were even times when my father or other Greek men would drive to Sacramento and pick up the priest and bring him here and then take him back.

Sometime in the late 1930s or early 1940s, the women's auxiliary to the AHEPA was formed. The national group eventually started a chapter here in Reno, and the name of that group is the Daughters of Penelope. My mother and Vaslie Pappas, my future mother-in-law, were charter members of that group—they both served as president and held many other offices, as did my father and Nick Pappas, my future father-in-law in AHEPA.

The ladies' auxiliary was very supportive of the church, and one of their main functions was to try to get a Greek Church in

Dad is wearing his AHEPA fez, and he has put one on me.

Reno. Eventually, both of these groups were successful, but not until 1964 or 1965 was a Greek Church built in Reno.

My mother and father had to teach themselves English. It was a big step for them to take office in an organization and have to deal with the city council and other government groups, but they didn't lack the courage to do that. They stepped up to the plate and did the things that needed to be done, and I think their example was a great inspiration to myself and my sister and brother. We knew that if we just followed their example, we could be successful.

The AHEPA and the Daughters of Penelope started a fund so they could have the regional and national conventions for both of those groups in Reno. They hosted those conventions and made money with them. My father was a chairman of one of those conventions. I remember him putting in very long hours, but it was all to raise money to eventually get a Greek church. They also did a great deal of work during the Second World War, raising money for Greek War Relief.

The AHEPA bought a lot on Lakeside Drive that was zoned for churches, probably around 1960. It was an acre lot, and they paid $10,000 for that acre. They continued to raise money, and, around 1964 or so, some of the more substantial members of the community, including my father and my future in-laws, the Pappases, signed a mortgage at the Security National Bank and borrowed enough money to build a church. The church was opened in 1965.

Unfortunately for my family and myself, my mother's funeral services were the first ever held in that church. She was fifty-four years old, had a heart attack, and passed away. Because my father and mother had been so helpful in raising and giving money for the church, they named the church St. Anthony's Greek Orthodox Church in honor of my mother, whose name was Antonia and whose saint was St. Anthony.

Later on, there was an addition to the church that my father donated $38,000 to help build, and they named that wing after him—the Pete Cladianos, Sr. Social Hall. It's a large hall that's big enough for a basketball court. It has a kitchen in it, and a lot of Greek affairs and Greek holidays are celebrated there.

One of the most important days for Greeks, outside of Easter and Christmas, is Greek Independence Day, celebrated on March 25 every year. The Turks ruled Greece for some 400 years, but 300 years ago or so, the Greeks finally were able to rid themselves of the Turks on March 25, and that's the day that we still celebrate. Those celebrations were held, before we had the church, in the Pythian Hall, and many of the young folks, like myself and my sister and my brother, would take part.

Many pageants were religious. Some were based on the war with the Turks. When I was probably between nine and twelve, my mother sent away for an authentic *Evzone* costume, a uniform that the Greek soldiers wore—a big white skirt with many ruffles in it, a velvet jacket, a velvet fez with a long tassel on it, and pointed shoes with a tassel at the turned-up point of the shoe. I dressed in that costume and appeared in several little skits and plays until I outgrew it, and then I passed it on to my brother. My sister had her own costume, as many of the other young girls had, and they would participate, as well.

My dad encouraged me to join the AHEPA. I was proud to join, and as soon as I joined, I got elected or appointed to the job of secretary-treasurer of the local chapter. It was my job to make sure dues were paid. Once in awhile there'd be a member that would be a little slow in paying dues, and I would have to go after him—it afforded me the opportunity to have conversations with older Greek men and to hear about the struggles they had coming to this country and living in this country—and a lot of success stories, as well.

My mother was noted for her cooking. One of the things that I have not been able to find since she passed away is somebody who cooks as good as she does, although my mother-in-law, Mrs. Nick Pappas, is right up there! My mother would cook for special events at home and then bring her dishes to the church for special events like Greek Independence Day, Greek Easter, and Christmas. One of *my* favorite dishes was a dish called *pastitsio*.

The Cladianos family, c. 1950. Left to right: John, Katharene, me, Mom, and Dad.

There were other things that my mother used to cook that were very tasty, and one of those items would be a dish the Greeks called *horta*. *Horta* means "grass" or "greens." Greens come in different varieties, and one of the varieties is a dandelion green. I recall going down to the Lemberes farm in Sparks and going out in the pasture with my sister. We had a little hand trowel and would dig up dandelion greens and put them in a sack or a pan. In the pasture there were cows and sheep and so on walking around, and many times these dandelion greens had manure on them, but my mother would wash them thoroughly. My father and my uncle just loved these greens. It took me a long time to get used to them, but once I did, I really liked them. Some of them are quite bitter, but when they're boiled and drained well, and you put lemon juice and olive oil on them, they're good. Many times the poor Greek people would eat them as their main course—or the only course that they had—with some bread. Bread is a big staple in the Greek diet, and we put olive oil on bread.

6

Crossroaders and Slot Thieves

WHEN I WAS YOUNG, I hung out with a rough crowd. Some were crossroaders, some were thieves, some were . . . . I look back on my life, and I reflect that at any time, I could have been caught in some criminal activity, and my whole life would have changed. My dad wouldn't have been able to get me out of some of these things. Of course, he didn't know what I was up to. It was a life that was exciting—there were so many varied things that we were involved with. We drew the line, however, at strong-arm robbery.

It was a good time. We never stopped and said, "You know, I don't think we ought to be doing this, because we might get caught." We just lived under some kind of a lucky sign.

Jim Owen went to military school with me. His father had died when he was young, and Jim lived with his mother and his Uncle Mack. Mack was involved in the gaming industry in Havana, Cuba, and he would go down there in the winter time and work in that industry and send Jim away to military school. Jimmy and I have been close friends ever since meeting at San Rafael. He even worked for me for awhile at the Sands as head of my engineering department.

After a hitch in the navy, Jimmy returned to Reno and started dealing in clubs. When he got fired from one for reporting some dishonesty among his crew, he became disillusioned. It seemed to him that honesty might not be the best policy, after all. He turned to his uncle, and his uncle taught him how to make a good living as a crossroader.

Jimmy started out in the crossroading business as a man who would do what's called cold-decking. He would slip a deck into a twenty-one game that was sorted out so that the first twelve hands out of the deck would be winners for the players and losers for the dealer. It's interesting how this worked:

Crossroaders need to work in crews, because it takes several people to do this kind of thing, and it works much better when you have the dealer in on the play. The dealer's job is simply one of placing her deck out at the appropriate time in front of the man who's going to slip the cold deck into the game. These folks spend many hours out there courting dealers into helping them in this kind of a venture, and the logic they use is, the dealer doesn't have to do a thing. Usually, it's a woman dealer, and she doesn't have to handle any marked cards. All she has to do is place her deck out there at the end of her shuffle for a cut when the man with the cold deck walks up to the table.

The first thing these folks do is fill a table with their crew. They sit there and play the minimum until the appropriate time, and many times one of the crew will engage the pit boss in a conversation as far away from that table as he possibly can—a man has a dispute about something, and he wants the pit boss to settle the dispute, and once the pit boss's attention is away from this game, then the man with the cold deck can put it in the game.

In Jimmy's crew, he was almost always the man with the cold deck. They would take a blue deck and a red deck, and they'd arrange winning hands. Sometimes in the first hand out, there would be four deuces and four nines and then a couple of blackjacks, so that in six spots on the table, there'd be six winners—four double downs and two blackjacks. And next hand, there'd be threes and eights, so they could double down; and the tens would come along after that, so they'd win the double-down hand, and the dealer would break or have a low point total.

The crew would come up to the game, and when they got close to the game, they'd see what color deck the dealer was using, and the man with the cold decks would get the appropriate deck out of his pocket. He'd hold it in his right hand, with a jacket or a sweater over his arm, covering up his hand, so people couldn't see that he had a deck in his hand.

When a crossroader crew walked up to a game, hopefully there'd be an open spot where they could make a bet. If there wasn't an open spot, they'd simply make a bet between two spots.

They'd time it so that the dealer was shuffling the deck when they walked up. At the end of the shuffle, the only thing required from the dealer was that the dealer would place the deck in front of the man that was going to cold deck the game. The cold-decker, instead of cutting the deck with his left hand, would pick the deck up off the table and put it in his pocket; and with his right hand, he would place the cold deck down. The dealer then would pick the deck up and begin to deal.

During the time the cold-decker was doing this, the players in his group that were on the game before he put the deck in would get up and leave. Two new players would come in, and each would play three hands apiece at $500 a hand, or whatever the limit was, and they're the ones that would win the money. Their goal was to win twelve hands. They'd win double downs on eight of them, and they'd do it as quickly as they could before anybody noticed. Many times they were interrupted, but sometimes they got off a play like that, and then they'd get up and leave.

This was back in the days before Harolds Club (and others) began to keep a record of the serial number on the ace of spades on every deck as it went on the game. Harolds began doing this after they realized that their games were being cold decked.

Crossroaders would do this only in the bigger clubs. You couldn't do it in a small place that only had two or three games, because you'd be noticed too quickly . . . and many of those games could have been crooked games, as well, so it was much more difficult. The large clubs were the targets. From time to time, Jimmy's group would drive to Las Vegas and spend a few days down there and do this same kind of thing in the bigger clubs in Las Vegas.

Then clubs began to take a lot of measures that made it much more difficult. Harolds Club installed bells at every table. If there was a bet over $100, the dealer would ring the bell to get the pit boss's attention. So, no matter what the pit boss was doing, if a bell or a light went off, the pit boss would pay close attention to that game. Dealers also began to holler out the bets. If there was $100 or some figure more than that, the dealer would holler to get the pit boss's attention if he'd been distracted. But the crossroaders did have a heyday there for awhile. They did very well with it, Jim said, and when it got too risky, he turned to cheating slots.

There was a great deal of money to be made in cheating slot machines, so Jim decided to learn that. Some of Uncle Mack's friends taught Jim how to cheat slot machines. In those days it was done with a gaff through the escalator, down in the machine. The idea was to stop the fan on the clock on the old mechanical machines, and also to line up the reels. Sometimes they had to use two gaffs or two wires, one to stop the clock, and one to line up the reels, and they would ratchet (manipulate) the handle on the machine so that you could move the reels around and get the bars lined up. Once you got the bars lined up, you'd let the clock begin the run again; and then you'd hit the handle real hard and the jackpot would set.

The man that was doing this would walk away from the machine quickly, and his associate, who would be very close by, would walk up to the machine. (Those people are called collectors.) The collector would holler that he had a jackpot, and he'd stand there and collect it.

Collectors were just people they would pay to do the one job; ordinarily, collectors were not part of the gang. They were innocent people that didn't know anything about cheating a slot machine, because the less they knew the better. The gangs would recruit these people, and they'd simply say to them, "You don't need to do a thing. You just walk up when you get the signal, holler 'Jackpot!', stand there, collect the money, and then we'll give you a hundred bucks," or a piece of the pot. They'd have a prearranged place to meet, and that's when they'd split the money. It was important that these collectors be different people, because there weren't very many big clubs in town. You couldn't use the same person all the time, because pretty soon the clubs would get wise to what was going on.

Jim told me that the Golden Hotel was a favorite place for them to practice when he was learning, because the Golden paid the least amount of attention to their slot machines. He would go in the Golden and practice on their slot machines for hours on end, for many days in a row, so that he could be proficient in setting up jackpots. But he never once collected a jackpot from the Golden during the time that he was doing this, because he didn't want to bring any heat on himself. He just used it as sort of a laboratory.

Cheating slots is very difficult, and you need extreme concentration. Jim has said time and again that there were many people that tried it and couldn't do it. He told me that you couldn't go in and do this if you were going to be concerned about whether you were going to be caught. When you did this, you had at least two associates. The best set-up would be when you had a machine with machines on either side, so you could have one of your confederates playing the machine on one side, and one on the other. They'd watch behind your back and to your right and to your left, and they'd warn you if someone was coming. They would cover for you. That was the most ideal setup.

If you were one of three guys, then you could focus on what you were doing. Your whole mind could be set on getting those gaffs or wires in that machine, getting them set up for the pot, and then walking away. As soon as you were able to set the machine to pay, you passed your tools off to one of your associates, and they would quickly leave the casino. You would be clean. The person that actually did the work wouldn't have anything on him.

Jim's group didn't carry any I.D. They had no car keys in their pocket. Their procedure was, if anyone questioned them, to say, "I don't know what you're talking about. I don't know anything about cheating slot machines. All I did was play that machine and walk away." They had nothing on them if they were asked to empty their pockets. There was no proof of where they lived. They simply said that they were from some other city, and they didn't have anything on them, and they came up here on the bus. On many occasions Jim, and people like him, were questioned, but because of the fact that he took these precautions, he was only caught once.

There was a four-reeler there in Sparks that was *so* easy to do. [laughter] Some machines were harder, and some were easier, and they tested the machines by testing the handles. Handles on the machines had to be somewhat loose, and if a handle was a tight handle, and they couldn't walk the reels with the handle, they'd leave the machine alone. So they'd walk around the clubs, and they'd test these handles.

There was a four-reeler at the Nugget in Sparks that had a twelve-hundred-dollar jackpot that they took off at least ten times in about three months. The Nugget was getting a little bit disturbed, and they were sure that there was something going on, so they notified the Sparks Police Department. The next time that Jim did that machine, as he walked away from it—he had already passed his tools to his confederates—a couple of folks that worked for the Nugget grabbed him. They called the Sparks P.D., which took him over to the police department. They questioned him for an hour or two, but he denied everything. He had nothing on him. They asked him how he got to Sparks, and his story was that he'd walked from Reno. They asked him where he lived, and he gave them his uncle's phone number, because he knew that his uncle would know exactly what was going on. So they called his uncle, and they asked his uncle about Jim and if he had a car and if he lived there. His uncle said no, he had no car, and yes, he did a lot of walking for exercise. So they really didn't have anything on Jim, and they let him go, but they had a record of him. They took his picture.

Jim told me that during his career, he knew that Harrah's had his picture and the Nugget had his picture. I'm not sure in those days that the clubs cooperated too much with each other when they found these crossroaders. In later years, they did cooperate, because they found it was to their advantage to cooperate when they found a thief, or somebody that might be a thief, and then they'd share that knowledge with other clubs to try to eliminate that sort of activity.

From time to time Jim's crew would go to Las Vegas and do some crossroading there. One of the things that they did down there is they would, with the aid of confederates on the inside, get a set of mis-spotted dice in a game. The ones that they liked the best were dice that only had threes, fours, and fives on them. They would get the dice in the game and make some big bets and then get them out of the game and walk away. They were quite successful in doing this until one particular night in the Silver Slipper.

They found the Silver Slipper to be a wonderful place for cheating of all kinds, and they made two or three plays over a period of a few days. One night they were attempting to put a cold deck in a game. They got the deck in, but the pit boss noticed that they had $500 bets out there, and he came across the pit and told the dealer to stop dealing the cards. They knew they had been found out.

Jim, who had walked away from the game after getting the deck in, heard the commotion and came running back and scooped the chips off the table—that was their bankroll. He stuffed all the twenty-five-dollar chips that he could in his pockets and ran out the door and across the Strip. Of course, people were chasing him, but he eluded them. Eventually, he got to the Desert Inn Golf Course. It was fenced off, so he climbed the fence, chips dropping out of his pockets. Once over the fence, he began to run across the golf course, and it was so dark that he didn't see a water hazard and ran right into it. [laughter] He had his alligator shoes on and his Kupenheimer suit, and he ruined them and lost a bunch of quarter [$25] chips in the water. On the other side of the golf course, he had to climb another fence, and then he called a confederate to come get him.

Jim finally got back to the hotel where the group was staying. He had avoided being apprehended, but he'd lost quite a few chips. Then they had a problem trying to cash in. The Silver Slipper had altered its method of operation. When Jim's group sent a guy into the club with one of the chips to test them out, the minute he put it down to cash it, the cashier summoned somebody. The guy they had sent ran out, but it was clear that it would be very difficult to cash these quarter chips in, so they gave them to some guy in Las Vegas that was straight.

They had lost their bankroll. They had to put together a new one. Usually the way you did that was you borrowed it from somebody and had to pay a usurer's interest rate. In Jim's case, he was able to get another bankroll from his uncle, because his uncle understood the situation.

At some point when Jim was a slot thief, he believes his group managed to win the first $25,000 keno ticket that was paid in northern Nevada. They convinced a writer at Harvey's that he should help them win this big ticket. He practiced concealing eight numbered balls up his shirt sleeve until, without being detected, he could get them into the tube in place of balls from the basket. The first eight balls in the tube would be these eight balls, and the eight, of course, corresponded with the number that they would play on the keno ticket. That's how they won the $25,000. Harvey's never knew the difference, and nobody else ever found out.

Some crossroaders were beaten up when they were caught. Larry Moss had that trouble, and I think that was one of the reasons Larry began to carry a gun. In Jim's crew that never happened. Jim stopped this kind of activity around the early 1960s and tried to sever his relationships with these folks, because he decided that that life didn't have a future.

During the time that Jim was involved in these activities, he made it a point to distance himself from me, and I didn't know about him. I went in the army in 1953, and Jim came back here from his navy hitch at about the same time. When I came back, Jim was quite distant, and he rebuffed me on several occasions, and I didn't understand why. I thought maybe our friendship had come to an end, but he did that because my father was in the gaming business and I was involved in the gaming business, and it wouldn't be good for anyone to know that we were friends—for either him or me. So all of the things that I'm relating, I learned after the time that Jim decided to quit crossroading.

Jim's reason for quitting this was that no one seemed to be getting ahead. First of all, you had to have a bankroll to do this thing: if you were going to cold-deck a game, you needed several thousand dollars to make the bets, and you needed to sit there and play till you were ready to put the cold deck in. So you tried to be very careful to keep your bankroll together. Once you took off a game—you made a score—then you cut up the money, and Jim noticed that most everybody that was involved in the thing took their share and immediately spent it in riotous living and drinking and gambling on their own. A lot of these people played horses, and they played keno. They had other activities that caused them to go through that money really fast, and then they'd want to get a piece of the bankroll to play themselves. Jim was the guy that was in charge of the bankroll, and he had to fight off a lot of attempts to take the bankroll.

What motivated these people to keep doing what they did was that, when they did make a score, they'd go through their money so fast that they'd have to make another score real quick, because they were out of money. After a few years of that, it didn't take a very smart man to figure out that this didn't have much future. Jim was one of the very few who decided early on to get out, but he didn't have any other way to make a living. He cast around for some kind of job that would offer him some security, and he wound up working for Ray's Heating and Sheet Metal, an old-time Reno firm owned by the Scolari family. He saved whatever money he could, bought a piece of property in Carson City on Hot Springs Road, and went partners with a man named Clore in starting a business called the Desert Sheet Metal Company.

Jim got married, and he and his wife wanted to have children. Then it turned out that he and his wife were not able to have children, so they adopted two. From time to time after he quit, Jim was beseeched by people in the crossroading business to come back, but he wouldn't. He didn't want to be in a situation where he could go to jail and have a small child at home. He said it was fortunate that he had these children, because he might have been lured back into the business. There was so much easy money . . . but he never crossroaded again.

7

Court Martialed!

WHEN I ENTERED the University of Nevada in 1948, it was almost ordained that I would follow in my father's footsteps after graduation. Then, in my last year or two of college, my father began to talk about me doing something on my own. He and my mother both encouraged me to think about a profession. They would say, "You don't want to be known as somebody who succeeded just because his father had a business and he took over that business. You want to do something that you can say, 'I did this on my own. I accomplished this.'"

I didn't know what I was going to do. The degree itself was the only thing my friends and I were thinking about when we started college. What we would get it in really didn't matter. As we progressed and got towards the end, we began to think, "Well, what am I going to do when I get out?" That caused me to do somewhat better after an awful rocky start. My intention became to go to law school with my friends; but, although I got accepted to two schools, it didn't come about.

My first year in college was just playtime. I wasn't serious about anything; I didn't study; I didn't care whether I made good grades or not. I was having a wonderful time. I had moved out of the house when I became eighteen years old, lived out at the El Rancho on South Virginia Street. During my first year of college I was still helping my dad with his slot route and helping at the motel, and

I had a great deal of freedom, but I did not use that freedom productively. Consequently, I flunked both semesters of my first year at the University of Nevada.

My father was livid. He was adamant—I *would* get a college education. Trying to figure out what do, I thought about Jim Piculas, a friend whom I'd gone to military school with. Jim was attending the City College of San Francisco. At that time it was a two-year college. He told me I could go to San Francisco, not mention that I had already been to college for a year and had flunked both semesters, and register at that school. So I told my father I had a situation that would work out for me, and I moved to San Francisco, enrolled at City College of San Francisco, and lived with Jim.

I spent three semesters at City College, and my grades were good. My father was pleased, and I was pleased with myself. The professors were interesting people, whereas that had not been true at the University of Nevada.

Another reason I did well in City College was that I had become involved with Leona Bruce, a woman who was ten years older than me. Leona had once worked for my father, but when I met her, she was a twenty-one dealer working out at Carson Hot Springs. We were romantically involved during the time that I was going to college in San Francisco. Our relationship helped me stay focused on my schoolwork, partially because I didn't have to spend a lot of time searching for a girlfriend, as I did when I was at the University of Nevada, and as many young college boys do. I had this steady woman, and she was a good influence on me.

Leona had not had the opportunity to get a college education, but she knew the value of one. She encouraged me to continue my education and get a degree. Coming from someone I was romantically involved with, that was a powerful message. She also encouraged me to go straight and be honest in all I did. Even though she was a crossroader herself, and would deal seconds and cheat her customers, she could see there was no future in that kind of life.

As I look back on my life, for a long time I was torn between two divergent value systems. One was represented by my mother and father (and, for a short time, Leona), pushing me as hard as they could toward getting an education, being an upright citizen, and making a success out of my life. On the other side were

". . . I had become involved with Leona Bruce."

the friends and boyhood pals to whom education didn't mean a thing. They looked for the easy way out, and there was a lot of dishonesty. It was a life that seemed to have a lot of good times and no hard work . . . and you didn't have to go to school. I seesawed back and forth with this for several years until I was finally able to put it to rest and decide that, as my friend Jim says, "You can do a lot better on the square than you can any other way."

After three semesters at San Francisco City College, I returned to Reno and again enrolled in the University of Nevada. I had the grades to get back in, and Leona was there—I could see more of her if I came back. I was so in love with Leona that I wanted us to be married, but she knew that it wouldn't work, and she resisted. My dad was also opposed. Fearing that I would not let go of the idea, Leona left town to end our relationship. I later learned that she had gone on the square and married a guy over in California.

My second go 'round at the University of Nevada was kind of a mixed bag, but my history grades were great, because I liked history and had some professors I liked. One in particular was Wilbur Shepperson, who was one of the best professors I ever had. I got to know him well. He was a wonderful teacher and a wonderful person. I also joined the History Club, and that helped me with Professor Hutchinson. (The rumor was that he gave better grades to students that belonged to the History Club—he was the Club's faculty adviser.) I also took some courses from Professor Russell R. Elliott, another dedicated professor.

I got my degree in history in June of 1953. My friends—Bob Moore, Roy Torvinen, Frank Sala—applied to go to law school, and my father encouraged me to do the same thing. I applied and was accepted at Georgetown University Law School and at George Washington Law School—the two law schools that my friends had applied to.

I was a college student, and I had a right to look like one.

While I was in college, the U.S. went to war with Korea. Frank Sala and I joined the naval reserve to get a deferment so that we would not be drafted. (If you were in a reserve unit, you'd be allowed to finish college as long as you kept your grades up.) The naval reserve had a chapter in Reno, and once or twice a year we'd have to report to active duty in San Diego. On three different occasions I had to go to San Diego for two to four weeks, and on each occasion we went through sort of a shortened boot camp. Frank and I had some experiences in San Diego at the navy boot camp that were really disagreeable to us and eventually led to my leaving the reserve.

I'd never been a violent person, never precipitated any fights, but I had gotten into two fights in San Diego and hit somebody before I even realized what I had done. So I suspected that I wasn't going to do well in the military. Nonetheless, I applied for the Reserve Officers Corps. Then they changed the rules and told me that if I accepted a commission, I would have to go in for four years. I wouldn't do that, and I resigned from the naval reserve. About three weeks later, I received my draft notice.

I'd been accepted to law school before I got my draft notice, but that didn't matter to the draft board. My college graduation ceremonies took place on the eighth of June, 1953, and I was to report to the Oakland army induction office on the ninth. It was a bittersweet graduation. I felt wonderful, and my folks were proud and happy that I had graduated, but we had this pall over the whole ceremony. I was proud that I'd finally managed it after all the times I had decided to give it up, but I was on my way to Oakland.

After basic training, I became a clerk-typist and eventually wound up as an instructor for clerk-typists. Then an opportunity came along for me to be assigned to the Presidio at San Francisco. I liked what I was doing, but I decided to go. Sometime around the first of 1954, I was assigned to personnel under the adjutant general's corps. I worked in the mail room of the personnel section and lived in a barracks and pulled K. P. and guard duty and so on. I wasn't satisfied. I wanted an easier life.

I knew that a married man could live off post, so I went one day to the first sergeant, and said, "Hey, Sarge, the last time I went on pass I got married. I'd like to live off post."

He said, "Here, sign this," and he stuck something in front of me, and I signed it. Then he gave me—and I didn't realize what it was at the time—a request for separate rations. He said, "Sign this, pack your stuff, and get out of here."

A couple of other fellows and I rented an apartment off post on Arguello Street. One of the big reasons we wanted it was so we wouldn't have to pull K.P. or guard duty anymore. Things were great for awhile, but eventually I got caught.

I had received separate rations under a ruse, so they charged me with embezzlement. But I was getting just thirty dollars a month! [laughter] I had collected this thirty dollars a month for eight or nine months, and for that I was charged with embezzlement, which was a general court martial offense, and I was tried and convicted. The worst thing about the whole affair was that I had to tell my folks about it. When they came down for the trial, my mother was in tears . . . and it was all because I couldn't get over the belief that I should have everything I wanted whenever I wanted it, and that "good" wasn't good enough. I had to have the best of everything.

My dad hired a lawyer for me, a retired army officer that had been in the JAG corps. But it was a cut-and-dried affair, and there wasn't any question about it. I was sentenced to a year in prison and a bad conduct discharge. That was really a blow to my folks, because after I'd graduated from college and had been selected for law school, it looked like I was going to be a success. Then this came along. I was sent to the stockade at the Presidio.

After a month or six weeks, my kind of case was automatically reviewed by the commanding general of the Sixth Army, and I happened to have a friend, Alex Lemberes, who was an aide to the commanding general. (He was the Greek whom my father had helped get an appointment to West Point.) Lemberes was a captain, and he interceded with the commanding general and told him that I didn't intend to steal any money from the army—that my intent was to just live off post, and that's what caused me to do what I did; that I came from a good family; and so on and so forth. The commanding general reduced my sentence to six months, and my bad-conduct discharge would be remanded if I served the rest of my time in the army without incident.

Before my court-martial I had met a beautiful WAC named Pat Cox, and we had become romantically involved. She remained loyal to me throughout my time in the stockade, and when I got out, we lived together off post. I think we were in love . . . . After six weeks or so, I succumbed and married her in February, 1955, even though my parents were adamant that I shouldn't.

I married Pat without my mom and dad being present, and it was a difficult decision. But lo and behold, after we'd been married for a month or so, they came to visit us along with my sister Katherene. She had been divorced, sympathized with our situation, and prevailed upon them to give in and allow me to marry Pat. They came up there to give me their blessing, and I had to tell them that I was already married!

I was married to Pat for sixteen or seventeen years, and those were good years. It was a good marriage. We had two children: a boy, Pete III, and a girl, Antonia. Our marriage eventually ended because Pat's whole philosophy of life changed. She got involved with the women's liberation movement, and her outlook on life and her whole demeanor changed. She was not the same person that I had married. She had been a kind, gentle, loving, wonderful human being that had feelings, and a great wife and mother.

After getting married, I applied for early discharge. The time that I had spent in the stockade did not count towards my service time, so I had to do that time over again, and I did. But the army had an early discharge program—if you applied to a school that the army recognized, they'd discharge you early to enter this school. So, even though I already had my degree, I applied for summer school at the University of Nevada in 1955, and the army released me early.

8

El Rancho II

I HAD IT IN MY MIND to go on to law school . . . but in 1954 my father had built and opened an eighty-unit motel on East Fourth Street that he called the El Rancho Number Two. He was still running the business in Lovelock; he had the motel on South Virginia; he had the Cladianos Building downtown; and he had the El Rancho Number Two. The sum and substance of the whole thing is that he got exhausted, went to a doctor in Reno, and was told that he had a bad heart. Well, it turned out that the doctor didn't know what he was talking about, but there's no question that my father was exhausted. (As it turned out, he had a strong heart. When he finally died at eighty-nine years old, his doctor at the time said that his heart was the toughest part about him.)

My dad still wanted me to go to law school, and so did my mother. But I felt that maybe I had been the cause of my dad's supposed bad heart. Because of my court-martial and all the other problems that I'd made for my parents, I felt I owed it to Dad to take the load off him at a time when we all thought he was quite ill. I did not go to law school. I stayed in Reno, and I think I did a fairly decent job of looking after Dad's business.

When I took over the management of the family businesses, Dad and mother went to Greece for several months, and he recovered his energy. After that, he and my mother would go to Hawaii every winter for a month or two, and that helped him, also. It wasn't that I could step in and run these businesses as well as he could, but with his guidance, and with him there to mentor me when I ran into a problem that I didn't know how to handle, I was OK. Everything worked out for the best. For many years I thought that it was a shame that I had not attended law school, but I found that my friends who had gone to law school all wound up in business.

Dad started thinking about doing a hotel-casino project, but he was also thinking about acquiring motels in other parts of the West. In those days a lot of our motel customers were people that would be doing a big loop around the West. Most were from the Midwest or the East, and they'd load their family in the car for a trip that would be two or three weeks long. They'd come out old Highway 40, which was the road that went through Reno at that time, and stay overnight in Reno. Usually, they'd go from here to San Francisco, then to Yosemite. From Yosemite they'd go to the Grand Canyon . . . .

My dad's thinking was that if he could have a motel in each of the spots tourists were visiting, he could refer them from one to the other, and it would be good business. Holiday Inns did that kind of thing, and he was thinking along those lines. But we never did get involved in that kind of business. We kept gravitating back to gaming, because the gaming business seemed to be getting better and better all the time. We knew the business, Reno was doing better all the time, and it appeared that our best bet would be to get something established in the way of a hotel-casino in the Reno area. My dad used to say, "Don't play the other man's game, if you can help it. If you know your game, play your game."

Outside of the brief ownership of a drive-in theater in Richmond, California, and, of course, Lovelock Mercantile, Dad concentrated on the Reno area. He eventually traded the Lovelock Mercantile property for an apartment house in

Reno. It was a seventeen-unit apartment house on Court Street called the Crest Apartments. The apartment business was similar to the motel business, except you were renting units by the month. With my dad's guidance, I became the manager—we had an on-site manager that lived there, but I supervised her. The trade for the apartment house was a good way for us to get out of Lovelock. Lovelock was really a drag. We weren't making any money; in fact, it was costing us money. We had spent twenty years running that place just to pay off the mortgage—which we did.

My dad wanted us to learn the construction business, because he knew that there was a great deal of profit in construction. He didn't want us to be *in* the construction business, but he wanted us to understand it so we would be able to do projects of our own without having to depend on contractors. We began to do little upgrading and remodeling projects out on South Virginia Street, because it was an old building. In those days, you could do that. We'd just hire a carpenter or a brick mason or whatever we needed, and my dad would direct them as to what he wanted to do, and he would have me there, whenever possible, so that I could learn.

I got some more knowledge in the construction field building my first house out at the end of Canyon Drive. My dad had contacts with people that sold furniture, carpeting, drapes, and that kind of thing, because he'd just gone through all that with the El Rancho on East Fourth Street and the addition to the El Rancho on South Virginia Street. My sister Katherene was involved in decorating and purchasing furniture and fixtures for the El Rancho on East Fourth Street, and she picked up that kind of knowledge and did a splendid job on that sort of thing for us on all the other projects we got into afterwards.

All this time I was working in the apartment house, running the two motels and the slot route, and acquiring property. The next building project that we got into was on a

"The whole operation had different addresses for its different components." The El Rancho Motel on East Fourth Street, 1960.

piece of property on the corner of East Fourth Street and Wells Avenue adjacent to our El Rancho Two. My father wanted to build a restaurant, a cocktail lounge, and a lobby area for our motel.

My dad didn't know anything about the food business, and he didn't want to operate the restaurant himself. Fortunately, on a trip to Los Angeles, we met the principal owners of the Denny's chain and got them interested in opening a restaurant in Reno on our property. We would construct the building so it looked like a Denny's, but our lobby would be on one side and a cocktail lounge would be accessible from our lobby and from Denny's. Denny's would be our tenant on a twenty-year lease. When we began to construct that building in 1959, we allowed some room for slot machines. Our aim was to put in some table games also, but it turned out that we didn't have the room.

Eventually, we wound up with about twenty slot machines. We had fifteen in the lobby area, allowed by ordinance. Then, because technically the whole operation had different addresses for its different components—the lobby area in the motel was 777 East Fourth Street, and the Denny's was 795 East Fourth Street—we were allowed slot machines in the restaurant. We had two to four in there, and then the balance were in the bar, because the bar entrance was on Wells Avenue, and it had the address of 425 North Wells.

We opened the restaurant in the spring of 1960. We knew before it ever opened that it was going to be successful, because once we put a sign up and began to build, we had innumerable people stop and say, "Well, when are you going to get open?" Even though East Fourth was a major thoroughfare back then, there were no restaurants anywhere near. The closest were in downtown Reno. We opened that restaurant at noon on a Thursday. (Denny's would always open a new restaurant in the middle of the week on a day that wasn't quite so busy.) We had had a sign out there, and Denny's had done some advertising that they were going to open on this particular day at noon. A line began to form out in the street at about ten thirty in the morning. When they opened the doors, the restaurant immediately filled up. We had many people waiting to get in, and our slot machines began to hum pretty good. We had started out with just eight or ten slot machines in the lobby, because we didn't really know how it was going to work out, but it was a huge success!

In the mid-1950s, we had a situation that broke out in the motel business that related to price signs. In those days all the major gaming attractions were in downtown Reno, and motels and hotels that were close to the gaming did the best. Places that were further out didn't do so well. Those places that were way out on the periphery began to hang out little price signs to attract guests. They'd put out a ten-dollar sign, so that people would stop to get a ten-dollar room. At first we weren't concerned about it, but as it went along, more and more motels would put these signs out, and eventually we got in a situation where sixty to seventy percent of the motels had a sign out. It was unsightly, and it also began to turn into a bait-and-switch hustle. When you had a bunch of ten-to-twelve-dollar signs, somebody would put out a nine-dollar sign; and then somebody would put out an eight-dollar sign. Pretty soon, you had signs out at five and six dollars, and people were coming into motels and saying, "I want a five-dollar room."

And the clerk would say, "We don't have any. We just ran out, but we do have an eight-dollar room," or words to that effect. It was giving Reno a bad name. Las Vegas was having the same difficulty at that time.

Reno had a local motel association that we belonged to, and I began to attend those meetings and got elected vice president. The major topic at the meetings was these signs and what we were going to do about them. We were contacted by the Las Vegas Motel Association, and they told us that they had the same trouble, and they had an idea of what could be done.

Their idea was that the state legislature should be lobbied to allow the lodging industry to create a commission to control lodging facilities in the state of Nevada, and this commission would have the power to forbid price advertising on billboards or on any other signs outside of the premises. (It would allow properties to post a sign inside their office.) We had the support of the gaming industry on this issue. They wanted to attract higher-income people as gaming customers, and all these cheap price signs did was attract people with lesser incomes.

Rodney Reynolds owned the Silver State Lodge, a motel-type facility on West Fourth Street, just west of Keystone Avenue. The old buildings are still there. Rodney was a state assemblyman, and he advised us how to best approach the legislature. Before we did that, however, we met jointly with the Las Vegas group, and we formed a state motel association. A man named Henry Bridgeman became the president, and I became the regional vice president for northwestern Nevada. We got the state motel association behind the idea of this commission, and we sold it to the gaming industry, and then we began to lobby the legislature. In the late 1950s we lobbied two different legislatures, and we came within two votes of getting this lodging-commission act passed, but we failed. I spent a great deal of time in that effort, and I learned much deal about the workings of state government and the workings of the legislature.

I eventually became the president of the state motel association. After failing to get a commission established, we were successful in getting an ordinance passed in Reno, Sparks, and Washoe County to eliminate price signs.

Not only did we have that problem here, but it spread to other parts of the country. When these ordinances began to get passed everywhere, chains looked for a way around it by putting the rate in their name. Motel 6 and Super 8 said, "Well, we'll just make our name 'Motel 6,' and then you can't do anything about it," which is true. You couldn't. [laughter]

In the 1950s, as I recall, Fitzgerald was the first man to put a restaurant in a casino in Reno. He had such great success that Harolds and Harrah's and others followed suit, because they could see that restaurants kept people in their casinos, and when you could do that, it made you more successful. When Denny's opened in our East Fourth Street property, my father suggested that this was an opportunity for us to learn the food business.

Denny's was a lot like fast-food places, only a little bit more elaborate. They had guidelines for everything, and one of Denny's secrets was portion control. The food cost was, in Denny's guide, somewhere between 25 and 30 percent. If you could hold it under 30 percent, you were doing a good job. Denny's also had their jobs broken down, and they had a labor cost attached to every item. So we learned that a hamburger had a certain amount of labor cost as well as a food cost. If you could come up with a labor cost and a food cost combined that was under 50 percent, then you had 50 percent left over to go towards rent, utilities, and the other expenses that you have when you run a restaurant. Denny's at the time, if I recall correctly, had a gross profit somewhere in the 20 percent range, so they were very a profitable operation.

Another thing we learned is that food business becomes more profitable when you have high volume. Your food stays fresh, because if you're moving a lot of food, it doesn't spoil.

And with the high volume, your waitresses and bus boys and so on make more tips, so you tend to get better employees—they look for jobs where they can make more tips, because the food business historically has been a very low-paying job, and those people exist on their tips. So we learned the basics of the food business, and I'm really just talking about a coffee shop operation. We certainly didn't feel qualified to run a gourmet dinner house, but we did feel that we knew a little bit about running a food operation.

In the 1950s, Harolds Club had one of the first packages in Reno. It was called the Reno Super Tour. Pappy Smith, with Roy Powers's help, started this package that was sold only in Canada, principally in Vancouver. Pappy realized that Canadians were an especially good market. Canadians are pretty conservative, generally speaking, but they love to play slot machines. The Reno Super Tour was essentially a package that Canadians could buy only during the off season. For twenty-five dollars, a couple would get a room for two nights and breakfast both mornings. Pappy began to sell his package October through April or May, and it was very successful in bringing people down here during the off times. Maybe Reno's weather isn't so good in the winter, but it certainly is a lot better than British Columbia's!

Pappy originally had his package customers staying at the Pony Express Lodge on Prater Way, which was owned by Harolds Club, but the package was so successful that he ran out of rooms. Then he contracted with other motels in town to furnish rooms for his package. We were one of the motels that was contacted. Most of that business was done at our East Fourth Street motel, because Pappy wanted his people to stay near Harolds Club. He had a bus that traveled from Harolds Club to the Pony Express Motel, and it went right by our door, so it was easy to pick our people up and take them to Harolds Club. It was off-season business, and it was weekday business, and it worked out great for us, even though the package room rate was very low. That was our first experience with Canadian customers in big groups

We learned that there were also bus tours that came from Canada. Beginning in October, as the season in Reno was beginning to slack off, they'd come in on Sunday and leave on Thursday morning, here for four nights. At first, the Canadian bus groups were staying at motels further out of town, because they were the only ones that would take bus business. Most of these tours were a mom-and-pop type of operation. There might be a lady who was married to a bus driver, and she'd sell a group; or maybe it was done through a garden club or a trailer court or an apartment house or a co-op or something like that. Harolds Club sent people up to Vancouver, and they'd go to apartment buildings and trailer courts and so on, and give these people matches and literature and ashtrays, and show movies of Harolds Club, and give them coupons. It was a wonderful promotion on Harolds Club's part. Other casinos may have gotten involved, but Harolds Club was the leader, the founder of this kind of business.

We began to book these buses into our motel on East Fourth Street. It became a big part of our business there in the wintertime, because we were one of the closest motels to downtown that would take these buses. We took them for the room revenue, and our own few slot machines would get some play . . . nothing big, just grind action, but those machines were sitting there, and if our motel rooms weren't full, we didn't have any players. We'd always get some players from the Denny's and maybe a few from the bar, but when that motel was filled up, we noticed a difference in those slot drops.

We learned that the public relations aspect of the business was important. Customers like to feel at home. They like to be talked to. They like to feel important. They like to be recognized. So, because we worked right there and checked people into their rooms, we had a lot of repeat business. Humans love recognition. We learned how important that was, and it became a keystone of our business.

In many of the clubs downtown, dealers could not talk to the customers, because the bosses felt that it would take their minds off of their dealing. They also didn't want them to open up a situation where there might be collusion between the dealers and the customers. My father felt that was a poor way to run a business, no matter what business it was, and he preached to us to recognize the customer and make him feel at home. We carried that philosophy into our first casino operation, and it was something that really helped. Many of our customers made comments that our club was friendly, and they felt comfortable there, and they liked it much better than bigger clubs downtown that had more gaming and other things to offer than we did.

Back then, Bill Raggio was district attorney of Washoe County. I was acquainted with him and with many of the lawyers that worked in the city attorney's office and the district attorney's offices, and I would have lunch with them and stayed in close contact with them. Some were high school buddies of mine who had gone on to law school.

Raggio had a problem with a man named Joe Conforte. Conforte was operating houses of prostitution in mobile homes, and when he wanted to evade the law, he would move them so that it was difficult for the officials to pin him down. Prostitution was legal in the small counties around Reno, but he would violate other ordinances, and there was a move afoot to rid the area of these mobile homes that were houses of prostitution.

There is a place down around Fernley, near Wadsworth, where the county line between Washoe County and Lyon County is the middle of the Truckee River. The river had shifted course several times, so there was kind of a never-never land in there—neither Washoe County nor Lyon County was sure whose land it was. (Actually, Storey County was involved in that, as well, because the Storey County line was in that area.) Joe would move his trailers back and forth down there, and no one ever really knew what county the trailers were in.

My friend, Bob Moore, was the D.A. of Storey County, and Raggio was the D.A. of Washoe County, and Tom Ross was the D.A. of Ormsby County. The D.A.'s would form posses, and they'd have deputies from each county go with tow trucks to wherever Joe had those trailers, empty the trailers of people, arrest the girls, and tow and impound the trailers. They needed a lot of personnel to do this, and they didn't have that many; so, because I knew all these people, they deputized me on a few occasions, and I went along on raids.

Conforte began taking the wheels off his mobile homes and removing them from the site. The first time we showed up at a site where he didn't have wheels on the trailer, we were really stumped. We couldn't tow it away. So we started taking spare wheels and tow-trucks with us, and we would put the wheels on and tow the trailers to an impound lot.

Eventually, Joe opened a house somewhere down in the Wadsworth area, and Raggio, as D.A. in Washoe County, got a court order to burn it down. I went along on that mission with Raggio. We went down there with a group of deputies, emptied the house out, arrested the girls, and Raggio set fire to the place. Raggio and Conforte fought with each other like that for many years. It's all a matter of history, and that was my small part in it.

9

Launching the Sands

MANAGING the two motels and the Cladianos building was a full-time job, but I liked what I was doing. Business was good. Times were good in Reno in the late 1950s and early 1960s, and we were growing. My dad had an active mind, and he was always thinking about new projects, and he began to acquire property up on North Virginia Street, between Sixth and Seventh Street. He found a piece of land there that somebody had for sale, that he thought was a good bargain, and he bought it. It was where the Circus Circus garage is now. His idea was to build a hotel-casino.

For many years, Dad had looked for property in downtown Reno within the red line, but the existing casinos had sort of checker-boarded that area—Harolds Club and Harrah's and others had bought key pieces of property within the red line in order to stop anyone from coming in and building a place that might be a major competitor to them, so he was stymied. Dad couldn't get within that red line, so he decided to acquire property outside it. He wanted to build a big place, a place like the Sands is now.

Dad had the vision to see that he shouldn't get boxed in with a small piece of land and not be able to grow, so he began to acquire property up on North Virginia with the idea that someday he'd build a hotel-casino there. The downtown area is chopped up pretty bad in small lots—fifty-foot lots, even some thirty-foot lots in there. So it was a long, drawn-out process. You had to acquire land pretty much lot by lot by lot. He concentrated on that block, because he was able to buy three lots in the middle of it in one purchase. There were buildings on these lots. One was a cleaners and one was a liquor store owned by a Swedish fellow—Viggo Peterson was his name, and the store was called Viggo's. Viggo would sell you whiskey, no matter how old you were, as long as you had the money. [laughter] But he was a good old guy.

After he bought the property, Dad kept those stores. It became my responsibility to keep them rented. We had an apartment house, the Coronet Apartments. We had the dry-cleaners. We had the liquor store. Then, over on Sierra Street, he acquired other property, and Carlisle's Printing was renting a store from us there.

Dad bought these properties with the cash flow from the motels and the Cladianos Building. His long-term idea was to get into the hotel-casino business. He knew he was capable of doing it, because he knew the hotel business and he knew the gaming business. (The only thing he didn't know and didn't care about was the food business, but we could lease out the food business, and when we built the Sands, he leased it to Denny's. And it worked! It worked great. That was Dad's idea, and it worked at the Sands for a long time.)

As it turned out, we never had a casino there. We sold the property on North Virginia to Circus Circus when the Silver Legacy was being built. What happened was, as Dad was acquiring that property, he was at the same time acquiring property in other areas, and the motels and everything we had were doing very well. He'd acquire these properties with a down payment and assume a mortgage or borrow money on them, and so the interest payments were deductible from our income, and that made it easier to acquire them. He acquired several properties around our El Rancho Two motel on East Fourth Street—across the street and behind it. He acquired properties behind the El Rancho Number One on South Virginia Street, as well.

Dad ran onto three couples that had a piece of land where the Sands sits now. The land had 150 feet of frontage on Arlington Street and 220 feet of depth running along Austin Lane, an alley that ran through the middle of the block, from east to west. At any rate, my father purchased this piece of land, and because the North Virginia properties that he was acquiring were not in one big parcel, he said, "We will build a motel on this piece. We can borrow the money for it, it's a project we can do, and it's closer to downtown." The key in the motel business in those days was to be within walking distance to downtown, and this property was closer to the city center than the North Virginia property.

The property north of Austin Lane was owned by an old-time Reno family named Austin. On it there was a little motel called Will's Motel, consisting of eleven little cottage-like units. It was as deep as our property, and it had 200 feet of frontage on Arlington, so it would be a great piece of property for us . . . but the Austin family didn't want to sell it. Period. They didn't care. They were well off, and it didn't matter.

There were two brothers named Christianson, who lived in Los Angeles, where they owned a well-to-do house painting and decorating business. They liked to gamble, but they didn't like Las Vegas. They liked Reno. They were frugal, and they used to take the bus to Reno for a weekend to gamble. They felt that the motel rates were too high, so they began to acquire property to build their own motel. Each had a son, and they were going to have their kids run the motel. So they began to acquire property in this block that we were in, but they started in the middle of the block facing Third Street. Several homes along there were on fifty-foot lots, and the Christiansons started to buy these lots and hang on to them. They bought right up to the back of our motel, and they didn't want to sell, so we were landlocked.

Finally, the Austins got in a situation where they were amenable to selling their property, and that was a break for us. We couldn't afford to buy the whole piece, but Union Oil wanted the corner, so we made a deal with Union Oil—they bought the whole thing, and then they sold us the piece where we built the original casino that we opened up in 1970. Later, we added twenty-four rooms and the building that had the Denny's and the little casino in it.

We had opened the Sands Motel in 1965. My dad's idea was to build more units and get a little casino started, so the next step in his program, when he was able to acquire the Austin property, was to put up a building that had a restaurant in it—and he leased that to Denny's—with an area that could be the beginning of a little casino, and the motel office would be in that, also. We called it the Sands Motor Inn.

The first phase of the Sands Motor Inn was the eighty-unit motel that we built on the original piece of property that we purchased in 1963. We had a contractor from Las Vegas, a man named Ben Davey, and I worked with him on an eight-to-ten-hour-a-day basis, five days a week. My brother and sister took over the management of the motels, and I spent the entire construction period, nine months or so, working daily with the superintendent of the construction company, so we were able to bring the project in at quite a substantial savings. My sister helped us save a lot, too—she picked out all the furniture, fixtures, wall coverings, and interior finishes, so we had no need to pay a decorator.

My father had contacts with people that he had done business with in the Lovelock Mercantile Company, most of them being in the Bay area. From them he had bought carpeting, drapes, furniture, mattresses, and so on, because he

Building the Sands Motor Inn, 1965. I spent the entire construction period working daily with the superintendent of the construction company.

used to sell most of that stuff in Lovelock when he had the store down there. These contacts were very helpful in us being able to purchase the furniture and fixtures at the best price possible. We had a very good quality of furnishings.

To build the Sands Motor Inn we got a loan from Union Federal Savings. We were able to get that loan because we had a strong balance sheet and because there wasn't any gaming attached to our project. On paper, it was strictly a motel project, otherwise, they wouldn't have loaned us the money. Our projections were based on what we had done in our other operations, and we felt that the operation at the Sands would do much better, because we were much closer to town.

We had learned in the years that we had been in the motel business that people liked a room that was large. Most hotel and motel rooms in those days were built on a twelve-foot module, so the rooms were twelve feet wide. We built the Sands on a fourteen-foot module. That two feet doesn't sound like a lot, but it makes a great deal of difference in a hotel room. We had previously built some rooms fourteen feet wide and some twelve feet wide, and we learned that the fourteen-foot rooms would bring us more revenue, because people would pay more money for that room. We were one of the few places in town that had a fourteen-foot-wide room, and people would come to us for that reason. It was more expensive to build, but it worked out in the long run, and after we built that first section of the Sands Motor Inn, we never built a room any smaller than that. As a matter of fact, we also went from a twenty-five-foot-long room to a thirty-foot-long room, and that's still one of our key features. If not *the* biggest, at least we're right up there in the size of our rooms, and that has been a factor in our success.

We opened the Sands in February of 1965. I then resumed my position as manager of the other motels, as well as the Sands. Nineteen sixty-five was a wonderful year for us, because the Sands was an instant success. Unfortunately, in September of that year, my mother had a heart attack and passed away. She was only fifty-four years old.

Mother had diabetes; she had high blood pressure; she was overweight. Today, it would be simple for cardiologists to recognize that she was a prime suspect for a heart attack, but they didn't know that. Her sudden death was an extreme blow to us. For several days, I was unable to do anything at all. My father was devastated, as were the rest of us. Fortunately, we had loyal friends and employees who took care of our business for us until we could pull ourselves together and go on. After my mother's funeral, the priest said, "My son, life is for the living. You need to go on, even though this happened." Eventually, that got through to me, and I decided to get started again and get back to the things that we were doing.

In 1970 we opened another building with an additional twenty-four units, because we needed 100 units to get an unlimited gaming license. (We had eighty units on this side of the alley.) We built a five-story building on the north side of the alley, and it had twenty-four units in it, so that gave us

The first addition on the Sands going up.

a 104 units, so we got over the hundred-unit mark. That was the red line stipulation. You had to have 100 units to get an unlimited license. Otherwise, you were stuck with only operating fifteen slot machines.

We applied for a gaming license during construction of the building on the north side of Austin Lane, and the city council turned us down. They said that we didn't have 100 contiguous units. Their interpretation of the law was that they needed to be "contiguous." We didn't read that in the law, and our attorney didn't read that in the law. I don't think that really was the law, but the casinos in downtown Reno—principally Harrah's, Harolds, the Primadonna, and the Mapes—had their minds set on keeping gaming within that red line district. The casinos backed their councilmen, and they made it their business to ensure that the council voted the way the casinos wanted them to.

When our application came in for an unlimited gaming license north of the railroad tracks and outside of the red line district, the big casinos didn't want it. As we can see today, the center of gaming eventually shifted north of the railroad tracks, so they were right to be concerned—once gaming got out of that downtown area, it was probably going to move, because gaming is a business that *has* to expand.

If you don't expand, you die. If you look around Reno, you see that. That's one of the things that happened to the Mapes. They weren't able to expand the Mapes, so eventually it died. Riverside, the same thing. If you haven't got the land to expand, you're going to die. If you look at all the other operations around here that are doing well, they were all able to expand. Look at the Atlantis and the Peppermill. In our case, if we hadn't been able to acquire this land and expand, we'd be closed by now.

Anyway, when we first applied for an unlimited license, they turned us down. So I conceived the idea of tying the two buildings together, making them "contiguous." As regards my method, it came to me when I drove by a school that was being built and saw that the roofs of the buildings were sheet-metal forms about twenty-four feet long by four feet wide. They were hollow, square tubes, and they'd lay those tubes on top of the buildings and then put roofing on top of them, so the airspace acted like insulation.

I bought four of those hollow tubes, and we hung them across the alley and tied the two buildings together with them. We painted them the same color as the buildings, and then we reapplied for a gaming license on the basis that we had a "contiguous" building. My dad and I both had to lobby all the council people over a several-month period to get them to understand and agree with us that this was a project that was legal under their ordinance. We even brought them over to the Sands during one of their sessions, and they walked around and looked at our property. We explained that what we wanted to do was going to better the town, because eventually our program was to acquire more property and make something that the town could be proud of.

Our "contiguous" buildings, tied together with hollow, sheet-metal forms. This came to be known as "Pete's Passover."

Marshall Guisti and George Carr were two of the councilmen. Another fellow on the council was Charlie Cowen. He was a nice guy, but Fitzgerald fed him free lunch every day at the Nevada Club, and he voted against us, as I recall. At any rate, we finally got approved, even though there were a lot of questions about the purpose of this thing we had hung across the alley—you couldn't walk through it or over it or under it or anything else. We finally got our license, and we opened with forty slot machines in the spring of 1970. On my wall I still have the *original* first registration card. The first room that we rented was on February 21, 1970.

When we built the Sands, the big casinos had downtown Reno pretty well tied up through their clever practice of acquiring small parcels in checkerboard fashion. Harrah's did this to a great extent. Harolds, of course, bought all of Commercial Row and little pieces all up and down the street. If they couldn't buy it, they'd lease it. Cal-Neva did this in that block they were in. They eventually wound up owning the whole block where they are now, and they bought it up piece by piece by piece.

The big boys made it very difficult for anyone to open a new casino downtown. Most new casinos were small. The only big one that got started down there was the Sahara (later the Flamingo Hilton). They bought the property from Ernie Primm, who had been putting it together for many years while he was in business in the original Primadonna on Virginia Street. He moved over to Sierra Street and began to buy up that property, and then he went through his big hassle with the city council to get that included in the gaming district. Then the Sahara came along and bought it from him. All the other operations that started out down there were small operations.

My dad simply couldn't put enough property together down there to get an operation started. That's what prompted him to start putting together property in other places that he thought would work. We even looked at property in Las Vegas. We looked at some stuff on the Strip; we looked at some stuff downtown; but we didn't ever get a foothold in Las Vegas.

10

Big Bertha and the Electro- Mechanicals

EACH TIME MY DAD would do a project, he'd set up a corporation. He had one for the El Rancho on South Virginia Street and another for El Rancho Number Two on East Fourth Street. The Lovelock Mercantile Company was a corporation, and he had a partnership with his brother for the Cladianos Building downtown. So he had three corporations and a partnership by the early 1950s. Later, as he set up a new corporation, he'd loan his three children the money to buy stock in the company, and then the company would get funded, and we would draw salaries from the company and pay him back the loans.

We set up a new corporation when we built the Sands Motor Inn—it was called Sands Motor Inn, Inc. We even set up corporations to be operating corporations. We had a corporation that would own a property, and then we'd have an operating corporation. We had the El Rancho operating company.

All these corporations consisted only of members of my family—essentially, they were my brother and my sister and I. My dad even began to give us stock in the existing corporations that he had, the two El Ranchos and the Lovelock Mercantile Company, through an annual lifetime exclusion gift program that the IRS permitted. Every year he'd give each of us stock in those companies, so we eventually became the sole stockholders in them, as well as in the new ones that he set up. When my mother died in 1965, she owned half of the stock in these companies, because when he set up these original companies, it was community property. We inherited the balance of the stock—what he hadn't already given us—from my mother when she died, and that's how we became owners.

From very early on, Dad made us officers in those corporations. I was usually the president, and my sister was the vice president, because she was only a couple years younger than me, and our brother was usually secretary-treasurer. My father didn't hold offices in these companies, but he directed us, and under his guidance we ran these companies. Dad wanted us to get the experience of being officers in corporations and understanding the responsibility that was involved in running a business.

When our first expansion of the Sands opened in June 1970, it contained twenty-four rooms giving us a total of 104, a Denny's restaurant, the lobby area, and a bar and cocktail lounge. We also put in forty slot machines.

We bought the machines from Bally Distributing Company, at that time being run by Si Redd. We also put in a Bertha machine, which was a percentage machine. (A percentage machine is a slot machine where the profits of the win are split by the owner of the machine and the owner of the casino.) It was owned by Bally, and we had a dice machine that Bill Pennington, the Circus Circus co-founder, owned. He had a little route with those dice machines. The rest of the machines we owned, and they were all Bally electromechanical machines. They cost about $3,500 each, and it didn't matter what denomination they were.

When Bally came out with that electromechanical, it pretty much knocked everybody else out of the market. Harolds and Harrah's were still running Paces, and Fitzgerald was running the old mechanical Jennings, but everybody else went to Bally's, because they were a far superior machine in terms of the drop.

I guess Harolds and Harrah's customers were satisfied with their Pace mechanical machines, because they held off for a long time before they bought any new ones. There were customers that didn't play anywhere except at Harolds and Harrah's, because of the Pace machines—they were used to them. Plus, it was a big expense for a casino to switch over to Bally's, and I'm sure that Harolds and Harrah's thought long about that. They hung on to their Pace machines for a long time, but they had to give in eventually, because there wasn't any question that the new electromechanical machines and the machines that came along after them did four or five times what the old mechanical machines would do. Bally's had control of the electromechanical slot machine market then. If you wanted a good machine that would make you money, you didn't have anywhere else to go.

Si Redd ran the Bally office for northern Nevada, headquartered in Reno, and I believe he had an interest in the company, as well. Si was great for spending money on research and development, and he wheedled as much money as he could out of Bally's. He had his people in Reno working on developing a video poker machine. Si had the vision to see that video poker was going to be huge; Bally couldn't see that. As far as that goes, there weren't a lot of us around that *could* see that. And we didn't visualize that anybody would play a video machine after having had reel machines all these years.

Si felt that video poker was going to work great, but Bally's wouldn't produce it. So he eventually left Bally's. They bought him out of their stock that he owned, and he resigned as their agency manager here. Si took with him the concept of the video poker machine. Si also bought the rights to the Bertha somewhere along the line, but somebody else had come up with that Bertha idea. If Si saw a competitor that had something better than he did, he'd buy him, if he possibly could, and if he couldn't buy him out, he'd run him out of business. He'd sue him. He'd tie him up in court. Si was a pretty ruthless guy, but he was very shrewd, and he had a lot of vision.

When Si left Bally's, he formed a company called SIRCOMA. SIRCOMA soon came out with a video poker machine. It looked like a regular slot machine, only it had a video screen. You put them on stands, just like regular slot machines. It took a little while for the customer to get used to them. The *real* growth in video poker came when someone, and I think it was Si, decided to install them as bar-top machines. Then, they did very well, indeed! Initially, they met some resistance from bartenders, who got up in arms because they thought that their tips would all go in the video poker machines. That turned out to be really shortsighted. The video poker machine came to be the bartender's best friend, because it gave him the opportunity to talk to the player. The customer bought change from the bartender, and the bartender touted him on the machines, and bartenders made more money than ever, once the video poker machines got placed in the bars.

Si wouldn't sell a poker machine. He was smart enough to keep them and operate them as a route operator. So if you wanted poker machines, you had to do a percentage deal with Si Redd. Si would lease anyone any kind of machine, and he would help people who were getting into business and were short on up-front money. You could bring operators in, and Si would bring the equipment in. You didn't have to buy it, but when you got enough money together, then you could buy the machines.

For a long time Si wouldn't sell video poker, because he had too good a thing there, but eventually he began to sell the machines. The first time we found out that he was selling a video poker, the price was twelve thousand bucks! It was an unheard of price, but Si didn't care whether he sold them or not, and he put the price up so high that not very many people bought them. He was just as happy that you didn't. He did the same thing with the Big Bertha machine. The first price on a Bertha was $40,000. Well, Bertha was a machine that was probably *the* most profitable single machine around, but you couldn't run a bank of Berthas. You couldn't have thirty, forty, fifty Berthas, but you could have fifty video pokers. That was the difference between Berthas and video pokers.

You could have, depending on the size of your club, one, two, three, four Berthas, and they'd do great; but if you had fifteen, they wouldn't do that good, because they were an impulse machine. If you put them in a high-traffic area, people would see this big machine, and they'd put a dollar or two or three in it, just simply because it was an oddity. Big Bertha was probably somewhere between seven and eight feet tall, and it was probably four to five feet wide. It was a *huge* replica of a slot machine. It had huge reels and a big reel glass and a huge handle on the side, just like a regular slot machine, and so it was a curiosity.

Customers would stand around and watch a Big Bertha being played. The best place to have them was right inside the front door, or wherever there was a heavily traveled lane. You'd put it there, and if somebody was playing the machine, you'd stop a whole lot of people, and they'd stand around and watch. Then, of course, some of those spectators would come up and play the machine.

Si made sure that the Bertha had a lot of loud bells on it. If it had a payout, everybody would look around to see what happened. These were dollar machines and had a big payout tray at the bottom, and the silver dollars would fall in there from up high, so they made a lot of noise.

You had to have room for Big Bertha—you had to have the ceiling height. They took a lot of space, but they made a lot of money. My recollection is eighty dollars a day was a pretty decent drop for a slot machine back then, but Bertha would probably do $300 a day.

Si and Bally's fought it out in the courts over video poker, and eventually Bally began to produce a video poker machine. However, they decided to tilt the screen. IGT (SIRCOMA had become IGT) machines were flat on the bar—you looked through a glass surface at the monitor and watched your cards come up on it. Bally's tilted theirs. Up to that time, all video poker players were used to IGT machines, and this was a different animal. Eventually Bally figured that they had better make their machine look as much like IGT's as they could, so they made a flat one that went into the bar just like the IGT machine. When it was harder to differentiate between the machines, then Bally's started to do better.

11

Grinding It Out

WE PRETTY MUCH SETTLED on the Cal-Neva's operation as a model for the kind of club we wanted to run. We didn't want to be a high-end operation. We felt that there were far more people out there that would like a "grind action" kind of casino, so we'd have a much bigger audience to draw from.

It was apparent that the better customers for us would be tourists, as opposed to locals, because we knew the hotel business and were going to have a hotel connected with our gaming operation. If we had a bed base, or a room base, that was big enough, we'd have a built-in clientele. Anyway, we couldn't find a place to build in downtown Reno, and the locals were concentrated downtown. The down side to concentrating on tourists, of course, is that when tourism is down, you don't have good business. (The local customer is good year round, except maybe for the month of December, when everybody is Christmas shopping.)

We were able to maintain a high occupancy rate, around 92 to 95 percent, most of the time that we ran lodging businesses, because we also courted business travelers. They were good for us in the off season, because they only stayed with us Monday through Thursday, and then they were gone. That left our weekends open for weekend gamblers from the region and package business.

We put in our first table games in the 1972-1973 time frame. We also kept adding more and more slot machines, and we expanded the building we were in. The building had parking in the front, off of Arlington Avenue, and we added on to the building and pushed it out all the way to the street to give us more floor space. With the floor space that we added, we installed more slot machines.

We were doing so well with the slot machines that my brother suggested that we put in a live table game, a twenty-one table. My dad said, "Sure, but what do you guys know about operating a blackjack table?" My dad was sort of semi-retired by that time, since my mother had passed away, but we used him for his experience and his knowledge in the business whenever we needed him, and this was an occasion that we needed him. We told him that we'd grown up in this business, and we knew a little bit about it. We certainly weren't experts, but we were just going to run a low-limit game, and it would be good experience for us. Dad said, "Fine. Why don't you guys go ahead and get your feet wet."

It took two or three months to get a license for the game. We kept thinking that we were going to hire a dealer, but we never did get around to it. Two or three days before we were to open the game, my brother and I and Jerry LaCroix began to practice dealing. We'd been downtown and watched dealers, and we practiced a little bit, then opened up the game one day . . . and we still hadn't hired any dealers.

We just kind of took turns dealing. Well, it didn't take very long before we could see that that wasn't going to work, so we hired one day shift dealer and one swing shift dealer. We were only open two shifts, but we'd stay open at night as long as we had business, and then we'd open again at ten o'clock in the morning. We would break the girl, so we got our experience dealing and watching the game in that manner.

Ed Weiss, a fellow I went to high school with, had been in the business almost from the time he got out of high school. He started as a dealer, and he worked as a pit boss at the Cal-Neva Club for many years. He came over several times and gave us some tips. He watched our dealers and was very helpful to us. My brother and Jerry also knew people in the business, and they also got help from their friends.

It was only a few months before we put in another table. Then it filled up too, and we put in a third one. Of course, we had to hire more dealers. Between LaCroix and I, we split the swings, and my brother worked mostly all days. I worked the swing because I had a lot of other things to do during the daytime—I was responsible for three motels, an apartment house, and some other properties that we had been acquiring up on North Virginia Street, mostly rental properties.

My brother and Jerry and another fellow named Tom Piculas and my sister and her husband, Mark Latham, would do the drops and service the machines and act as change people. We didn't hire a change person for the longest time, probably a year or so after we opened. We did all of that ourselves, and we did it from the point of view that we wanted to learn the business, and we wanted to meet the customer. We wanted to be there. Those were hard and long days, but it was exciting. We were making money.

We had formed a little partnership called CC&J, which stood for Cladianos, Cladianos, and Johnson (my sister's name from her first marriage.) As CC&J, we leased the casino from the Sands Motor Inn, Incorporated, which was a corporation that my dad had set up. For tax reasons we formed this partnership and leased the casino and paid rent to the Sands, and then the partnership ran the casino.

Our motel had 103 units at the time, but also we began doing a lot of local business in our casino. We were getting people from St. Mary's Hospital. We were also getting a lot of black-and-whites (dealers and people that worked in other casinos), because they would park on the streets near the Sands and stop in after their shift.

We had a Denny's Coffee Shop at the Sands, just as we did down on East Fourth Street. We built a portion of the first expansion building specifically for Denny's. They put the fixtures in, and we leased them that part of the building. Our Denny's helped the entire operation, because they were doing very well. There were several motels up and down West Fourth Street and across on Arlington and on West Street, but there weren't any other restaurants nearby. Before we put in our Denny's, you had to go down to one of the casinos to eat. Denny's had a good reputation, so a lot of people would come in and eat.

Between 1970 and 1978, our growth was pretty rapid until the building wouldn't accommodate more. We topped out around 1976 at 185 slot machines and eleven table games. I think we had nine blackjack tables, a crap, a wheel, and a keno game. Carrol Rippy was our first keno manager. We

didn't know anything about keno, at all. We did know that it was a game where you had to have somebody who understood the game run it—it wasn't like getting a deck of cards and dealing twenty-one.

Our first pit manager was John Oliver. John had been in the business many years, working at Harrah's Club, Harolds Club, and some other

Carrol Rippy was our first keno manager. clubs before he wound up at the Palace. We hired him when we got up to five black-jack games. If we were going to take the next step, we needed to get professional help. We were doing well with the five games that we had, but customers were leaving us because we didn't have a crap table or a wheel.

When George Karadanis opened the Sundowner across the street from us around 1975, their operation was slanted towards pit play. They opened up a whole pit—crap tables and a couple of wheels and blackjack games and so on. So it was easy for our customers to walk out of the Sands and over to the Sundowner to play craps or the wheel, if they wanted to. We'd lose customers because of that, but it was sort of a wash, because when Karadanis opened up his 400 rooms, that put another 800 potential customers a day just across the street from us.

Karadanis's slot operation was not as good as ours, because he didn't buy Bally's. He bought a competitor's machine because he got them a lot cheaper. They made him a good deal, and his knowledge of the slot machine business wasn't deep enough for him to understand that Bally was a far superior machine in terms of the drop that you could get out of one. So slot players would leave the Sundowner and come over to our operation because we had Bally machines and it was an easy walk.

We saw a tremendous increase in our slot business when the Sundowner opened, but we also saw a deterioration in our live game business. The Sundowner was doing a better job of attracting that kind of business, partially because of a policy put in by their casino manager, Chuck Clifford. Chuck allowed his dealers to keep their own tips, whereas our dealers pooled their tips and then split them up on a shift. When Chuck allowed the dealers to keep their tips, he got some good dealers from around town that had a following, and many players followed their dealer friends to the Sundowner and played with them. We spent a lot of time at the

Sundowner to see what their operation was like, and we saw dealers were very outgoing and friendly to the players, and they had a great pit operation. We were going in that direction too, but we learned from the Sundowner that we had to go stronger and further—we had to have a real friendly place where employees, especially the dealers, would talk to the customers.

We never went for letting dealers keep their own tokes. There's a down side and an up side to that idea. The down side is that if a dealer keeps her own tokes, she can kind of go into business for herself, and that type of dealer is not necessarily the best thing you can have in your casino. What we tried to do was develop a loyal team of employees, with the idea that if we all made money, they'd make money. We were right there working with them all the time, and we'd go out and have drinks with them after work; but we also tried to retain some distance between us. On some occasions we went too far, but we did have a great rapport with our employees, especially our dealers, and I think it contributed a great deal to our success.

Competition from the Sundowner showed us that we needed to have a full casino; and if we were going to have a full casino, we had to have professional people. We didn't know a lot about craps or the wheel, and the crap table was a place where we could get hurt. We were raising our limits all the time, because we'd lose customers if our limits weren't high enough, but we didn't want to get too high, because then we'd be subject to a possible heavy loss. So we got up to around five hundred dollars as a maximum limit. That was a pretty good limit for us, and we attracted players that wanted to play at that rate. Karadanis was pulling good players to the Sundowner, so there were a lot of those kinds of players in the neighborhood. If they felt their luck was bad at the Sundowner, or they wanted to try something else, they'd fall out across the street, come right over here, and play with us. So competition from the Sundowner pushed us into becoming a full casino.

We began to try to learn the crap game, the roulette wheel, and keno. We'd spend as much time as we could in the pit with John Oliver and our keno manager, and we wanted LaCroix to have that knowledge and Tom Piculas, who was working for us then, too. We wanted everyone on our staff to learn everything there was about a casino operation.

We were being guided and pushed by my dad. He could see that we were doing well and that there was a great opportunity here. He had the vision to see that we could become a fair-sized hotel-casino, and he had a lot more vision than we did. If we had been left to our own devices, we might have just stayed small and run this successful, little casino.

I would come down to the Sands at ten or eleven in the morning every day. I had a little office upstairs in the casino building, with a part-time secretary, and I'd dictate letters and take care of whatever business had to be taken care of, and then I would visit the other properties that we had, and I'd try to see my dad. We'd have lunch together lots of times. After that I would spend the rest of the day pretty much on the floor of the casino. If I had phone calls, I'd take them on a phone in the pit. We also had one hanging on the wall by the registration desk, so I could conduct business and still be out there on the floor, interacting with our customers. I could watch our help. I could pay attention to the pit.

In addition to this, three to five nights a week, I'd work the swing shift from 6:00 pm to 2:00 am. I'd work in the pit with another pit boss who was experienced, or I would even work shifts by myself when it was slow. Sunday night was a slow night, so some Sundays I'd just run the pit. I had a lot of confidence in our crap dealers—I really didn't know that much about craps, but John Oliver had hired them and said they were trustworthy.

I'd spend time in the pit kind of acting as a box man, trying to learn the odds and trying to learn the game, but I never did get to where I could actually deal craps. I did it on occasion when things were slow, but I never became an expert crap dealer. Same way with roulette. First ball I ever tried to spin on a wheel went clear across the room! I limited myself to stacking chips on a roulette wheel when we were busy.

There were a lot of days that I worked fourteen or sixteen hours. I got carried away. I'd go home at one or two or three in the morning, and I'd be back in the casino at ten. I worked six days a week and took most Sundays off. My friends and I owned a boat together, and we liked to go water-skiing, so we'd go to Pyramid Lake with the boat and spend all day out there on Sunday. However, there were times when we were so busy that I'd come to work at ten or eleven o'clock Saturday morning, and we'd stay busy until three or four in the morning. By that time I hadn't eaten anything, and I was hungry, so I would decide to grab a bite to eat and then go home.

I'd sit down in Denny's to have something to eat, and by the time I got through eating and talking things over with the bosses, we'd start to get busy again, because a lot of people like to get up early. On many occasions I didn't get home until Sunday afternoon, somewhere between 1:30 and 3:30. I missed some water-skiing because of that . . . but the biggest result was that I wound up getting a divorce.

All of our dealers were females, except for the crap dealers. In our experience, the luckiest dealers that we had, and the best dealers, were the ones that we taught and broke in ourselves, and so it became our habit to hire inexperienced dealers that were probably not any older than twenty-one or twenty-two. We hired pretty nice-looking girls, attractive girls, because that was good for business—many of our customers were men, and they liked to play with attractive young ladies. We trained these young women to deal the way we wanted them to, and they were beholden to us, because we gave them the opportunity to make a lot more money than they'd ever made in their lives.

When you had a pit full of attractive girls, and your wife knew it, and you were spending a great deal of time there, and you had a strong rapport with these girls, and you were working such long hours, it really wasn't good for a marriage. I separated from my first wife in the 1973 to 1974 time frame. I had two children at that time that were still very young. One was around eight or nine, and the other thirteen or fourteen, so I kept trying to make a go of the marriage. Even though we lived separately, I refused to get divorced, because of the children, and because I still cared for my wife. I wanted to try to make the thing work, but it didn't work out. Eventually, my wife got an attorney and divorced me. It was a thing that happens to you in the gaming business. The gaming business is just hard on marriages. That's all there is to it.

12

Liquored Up

IN THE 1970S we opened a liquor store on our property. We were aware that many people came to Reno for other reasons besides gaming, or they made trips that were combination trips—they wanted to gamble or go to Lake Tahoe, but another thing that many wanted to do was to buy liquor. Liquor was priced much cheaper in Nevada than it was in adjoining states, especially Oregon and Washington. British Columbia had a forty-ounce limit on how much alcohol you could take back across the border, but many of our Canadian customers didn't care. They'd take back several cases. The only time they got caught was if they were stopped at the border, but very few people ever got stopped.

Many people would drive to Reno, stay here and gamble, and then buy several cases of liquor before they went home. A lot of people (we later learned from talking to our customers) would come down with shopping lists from their friends. They'd drive their pick-ups down with a camper on the back, and they'd load up with liquor and take it back and re-sell it to their friends. My brother thought that if we had our own liquor store, it would help our business, and it would be another reason for people to come here.

We started out by bringing in case lots, putting them on the floor of the cocktail lounge area, and selling liquor by the case, not by the bottle. Business boomed. We had wholesale liquor deliveries here daily, and we really started selling! We'd have a display with several cases of different kinds of liquor. Vodkas were very popular, and the least expensive vodka was the thing that sold the most. So we would shop around the distributors and find the least expensive vodka and maybe mark it up 5 percent, or sometimes we even sold it at cost for a loss leader. We tried to break even on the sale items and then make some money on the related stuff.

Our gaming revenue took another jump because of the liquor business, and it helped our hotel business, too. It became a pretty important thing to us, even though we didn't make any money in the liquor business itself. However, we did run into some difficulty:

We had a group of Native Americans come down from Washington. They had smoke shops and sold liquor on their reservations in the Seattle area. They used to come down here and buy whole truckloads of liquor from us, and we'd charge them whatever our retail price was, and they'd pay us in cash. We were aware that they were reselling it, but we'd checked with our attorney. He'd told us that as long as we were not acting as wholesalers, as long as we were selling that liquor to them at the same price we sold it to everyone else, we were within our rights to do so.

This was good business in the casino as well, because when the Indians came down here to buy liquor, they would come in a group of ten or twelve people and stay around for several days, and they gambled a lot. We also found that people from their tribes and related tribes would come down on their own, and, because they were making a great deal of money on this smoke shop and liquor store, the tribal members all had considerable funds. They liked to gamble, and they became very good customers of ours.

The federal Bureau of Alcohol, Tobacco, and Firearms was investigating Indians' sales of liquor and cigarettes on reservations, and on one occasion they followed our customers when they brought down a couple trucks to buy liquor. They got the whole transaction on film—where we loaded their trucks out in the alley, and so on and so forth. Then the federal government charged us with selling liquor without a wholesale license. We had to go to court, and we were fined because of it. We had to talk to the Nevada gaming control board, and we told them that this didn't have anything to do with our gaming business. We had not done anything that Gaming considered reason to fine us or terminate our license, but we did have to stop selling liquor to these Indians.

We continued about our business, selling liquor to anyone else that came through. Eventually, we partitioned off a portion of the cocktail lounge and made it a liquor store. We leased that portion of the building to a man named Collins and sold him the business and the inventory, and he ran the liquor business for several years. We were glad to get out of running the business. It had been a lot of effort, and we weren't making any money on it—the money we were making was from the gaming end of it. Collins had to be real competitive on his prices, because the liquor business was very competitive.

13

1978: Taking a Chance on Expansion

NINETEEN SEVENTY-EIGHT was a major turning point in the history of Reno gaming, with the opening of the MGM, the Circus Circus, the Reno Sahara, the Money Tree expansion, and the Comstock. That was a diverse group of casinos. The MGM had a thousand rooms, and it was by far the biggest casino in Reno. It was outside of downtown, and the only other big operation that was successful outside of Reno at that time was John Ascuaga's Nugget in Sparks. (The Peppermill was growing, but it was still small. The Atlantis had yet to open.) Boomtown was open, and it was doing well, and you could say that they were outside the downtown area, but it was a little different—they pretty much lived off the highway and truckers. They had a special clientele that they catered to. Those truckers wouldn't have been business for Reno, anyway, because they couldn't park their rigs in town. So they were a little different case.

Dick Graves, when he opened the Nugget in Sparks, originally with a little coffee shop and so on, was probably one of the smartest men I've ever met. He could create promotions in the gaming business as well as or better than anyone I've ever known. The other thing that he had was good food. The little town of Sparks had nothing in the way of gaming until Graves started his Nugget, but it's grown to a big operation.

The Nugget was already doing well, when along came MGM, built this huge thing out there all by itself, and put in a lot of convention space. From my observation, what happened to MGM was they were used to doing business in Las Vegas, but it's entirely different to do business in northern Nevada than it is in Las Vegas—was then, and still is. I've seen this happen in other casinos here. You need to be more personable. You need to have a closer contact with your customer. You need to be not quite so splashy, not quite so dramatic as they are in Las Vegas.

MGM was a huge departure from what existed in Reno at the time, and many of the customers that came to Reno and tried out MGM did not go back there. They came back to those of us that are still successful in Reno, because they didn't like that Las Vegas atmosphere. That's one of the reasons they were coming to Reno in the first place. A lot of those people had money to make a choice—they could have gone to Las Vegas or Reno, and they were coming to Reno.

The fact that MGM was willing to come to Reno and spend hundreds of millions of dollars caused other people in the gaming business, people like Circus Circus and Del Webb, who built the Sahara, to say, "Hey, Reno may be a place where we could do well." There was a lot of opportunity here, and the Sahara and the Comstock and Circus Circus opened in this same period.

It was unfortunate that everyone opened at once, because there was some fallout from that. The tremendous amount of casino space and gaming positions and rooms that were added to the market all at one time created a difficult situation. You had all this added capacity, but you didn't have the advertising and introductory promotions that should have been done at the time, because some people thought all you had to do was open your doors, and you'd do well. So the little places—the Comstock, and the Money Tree were the two smaller places that opened up—simply said, "Well, we'll just open our doors, and we'll be OK."

Because of Reno's red line, most gaming people felt if you were going to be in the gaming business, you had to be in downtown Reno, or real close. The Comstock and the Money Tree folks felt they had to be in downtown Reno; and indeed, up till that time, that was certainly the case. But the large casinos had tied up a lot of downtown land, and it was difficult to buy a piece big enough to build a casino that had the amenities you really needed to be successful. Even Del Webb's Sahara didn't really have enough room to build the casino they should have built to be successful. Small casinos like the Money Tree or the Comstock didn't have a big selection of restaurants, and that was another reason why people wouldn't go to those places. Maybe they'd go to the MGM or one of the larger places, Harrah's or Harolds. All this is hindsight, of course . . . .

Parking became a very big issue. The Money Tree had no parking at all, and the Comstock had parking only in the basement of their place, with not enough spaces, and the Sahara the same thing. The Mapes also was experiencing a problem because of parking. The Riverside had changed hands two or three times, and they also had problems with parking and with being an old facility. Parking became important because, with all these casinos opening up in 1978, the business became highly competitive; whereas, before this time it had not been. Now you had this added capacity in the market, but you probably had about the same number of people coming to Reno that you had before. People make choices, and when you had a difficult time parking some place, you went somewhere else.

Slowly, the gaming business was gravitating to the northern end of the city, whereas the former center of gaming was somewhere around Second and Virginia. The Sands was probably one of the factors that made it move. Then Circus Circus and the Eldorado opened up on the northern end of town, and, like ourselves, they had some parking. But these other places that opened, except for the MGM, really didn't have the proper kind of plant that they should have had. They needed more restaurants. They needed parking. They needed more room, and, ultimately, that's why they failed.

In the long run, the 1978 expansion probably was good for Reno. In the short run, it wasn't. There were a lot of casualties.

Las Vegas has never felt that they had to cater to the customer. Their high rollers, yes, but as for the average guy, they felt he was privileged to come into their casino, really. MGM brought that philosophy with them to Reno, even though they hired a lot of local Reno people. They didn't want their dealers talking to people. They wanted them just to do their jobs and go on their breaks and come back and keep to themselves, keep their mouths shut and pay attention to their dealing.

Customers in northern Nevada, both locals *and* tourists, were simply not used to that kind of thing. They expected to see smiles and friendly faces, and they expected pit bosses to walk over and talk to them. The Las Vegas style is to have the pit boss stand out in the middle of the pit with his arms folded and a big frown on his face. It worked down there for them, and it still works, but it just didn't work in Reno.

Essentially, you had three Las Vegas operations in Reno. You had Circus Circus; you had the Sahara; and you had MGM. The Sahara, to my knowledge, never made any money. After it became the Hilton, Ferenc Szony, the man who is president of our company, ran the place, and he made money over there, but he was the only one. The MGM lost money for years—that's one of the reason's they sold it to Bally's. Bally's didn't do any good over there either. That's the reason they sold it to Hilton.

The big Hilton out at the old MGM property made money only when Ferenc left the downtown Hilton, the Flamingo

Hilton, and went out there. He turned the place around. Ferenc got them back into the convention business. Even though they had a large convention facility, and they could do well, their main concentration was gamers and high rollers, and that just didn't work. When they got back into their convention type of business, they made a profit. Of course, they had to spend a lot of money. Ferenc spent sixty million dollars when he was out there—new restaurants and additional convention facilities.

The biggest problem out there is that the casino is so huge that you've got to get several hundred people in it before you look busy. Ferenc had to figure out a way to lower the ceiling and try to compartmentalize the casino area so that in certain areas it looked like you had business. He created some new restaurants to bring people in. He brought a couple of franchises in, and we've done that here at the Sands. There is a place for those franchises, and they help. You can't rely on franchises, but if they bring people in, they help.

The Hilton has 2,000 rooms now that have to be filled. It's a challenge, and the conventions have become their mainstay. The Sahara didn't have that kind of a chance, because they had very little convention space—they just didn't have the room for convention space, so they left it out of the building. I think they've only got ten or twelve thousand square feet, which is nothing for a hotel-casino. Even in our case, we've got seventeen or eighteen thousand square feet, and we never even thought about being a convention hotel.

In the first few years they were open, the newer major casinos weren't making any money, and yet the smaller casinos were being knocked out of business. The large casinos had huge overheads, so even when they stole a lot of business from the little guys, they weren't able to make money. In the short run there was a lot of dislocation and a lot of problems.

The King's Inn was a smaller casino that didn't have the proper plant, and management wasn't good, and they didn't last very long. But while they were operating, we experienced somewhat the same situation with King's Inn that we had with the Sundowner. Their slot floor was not well organized, and they had a lot of Aristocrat slot machines on it, as well as Bally's. People were unhappy with the Aristocrats. And they only had one restaurant and did a poor job in the food business. We began to experience more growth once the King's Inn opened. The King's Inn and the Sundowner were a great help to us, because they brought that many more people to rooms within a very short walk of our casino.

When all this was happening—the smaller casinos were closing, et cetera—we did all right. The two Christianson brothers from Los Angeles had been acquiring property behind the Sands along Third Street with the idea of building a motel. Then they changed their minds, and in 1977 they put the property up for sale. It was a sizeable piece of land, in the neighborhood of two hundred by two hundred feet. Their realtor told us that the property was for sale, and we already knew we needed to expand or be stuck with a little casino.

We bought the property from the Christiansons. That gave us a huge piece of land adjacent to our motel operation, but not adjacent to our casino, so we had to decide what we were going to do. The project that we envisioned was the biggest thing that we'd ever tackled. We felt we could support another three hundred hotel rooms and a casino of fifteen or sixteen thousand square feet more than we already had. We thought we could compete in the Reno market because of our management style and our operational policies, even though there was a glut of rooms and more gaming than the town could support.

The question was: how were we going to finance a project like that in light of what was happening to other casinos in Reno? Fortunately I made the acquaintance of Art Wood, a

The Sands grew up just to the west of the downtown gaming core. It occupies a sizeable piece of land. (The location of the property is indicated by the arrow.)

man who, after my dad, is the second smartest man I've ever
known. Wood was an accountant who came to Nevada from
Oklahoma City, originally, to get a divorce, and he was successful in several different businesses.

Art had secured financing for the Marnell-Corrao Construction Company when they built the Maxim Hotel in Las
Vegas. It was off the Strip, but they had designed it, built it,
and they were operating it successfully. When I made approached Marnell-Corrao about doing our project, I indicated that I didn't have the financing. They introduced me
to Art Wood. I gave Art our statements and showed him
what we had done and how we operated, and he became
convinced that we could be successful.

Because Art had always been successful in his projects,
he could give us entre to the highest levels of First Interstate
Bank. He knew everybody from the top right on down. He
took my dad and me to the Las Vegas offices of First Interstate, where we talked to the president, and Art convinced
them that we had a good project. All we had to do was come
up with a million dollars in cash, pay off the land, and then
they would loan us five million dollars. With that, Marnell-
Corrao told us we could build our 300-room tower and our
casino. The building would have two restaurants and about
seventeen or eighteen thousand feet of convention space,
plus the same amount of casino space, and we had enough
land for surface parking.

We began construction in 1978, and it took us about a
year to build the place. We had had to scratch around to get
the million dollars together, and that's when we sold the Crest
Apartments and picked up three hundred thousand dollars.
After we got the million put together, Art Wood, through a
leasing agency, got us a deal to acquire all our slot machines,
furniture, and fixtures on a lease-purchase kind of a contract.
We put very little cash up. We made payments, and at the

end of the time period, we paid the leasing agency a dollar, and everything belonged to us. Art had created a very advantageous financing package for us.

Art insisted that we get a competent controller for our business. We had a bookkeeper, and we had an accountant, but Art knew that we had to do better than that, because he came from an accounting background himself. So we hired a controller, and he really didn't do a good job for us. Fortunately, Art realized very quickly that he was not doing a good job, so we got rid of him, and, with Art's help, we hired someone else who did much better. We eventually hired Dave Wood (no relation), who became our chief financial officer once we went public—he was our controller prior to that. Dave Wood is still our chief financial officer.

We got Dave when the Gaming Commission required us to get an audit by an outside accounting firm. We retained Barrett and Smith to do it, they sent their man Dave over, and he asked so many penetrating questions that he became difficult to deal with. He knew his business, and he was relentless. Finally, I told everybody, "This fellow ought to work for us. We need him on our side." We hired Dave Wood, and we haven't been sorry.

14

"Canadian Friendly"

WITH OUR ADDITION of 300 rooms, we became a 400-room property. It was important to fill those 400 rooms, because, if the hotel was full, our gaming would do well. The package business for gaming operations and charter air tours was in its infancy. Harolds Club had a good package. Another that the chamber of commerce had put together was sold by Durkee Travel in conjunction with United Airlines. It was the major, all-inclusive package coming into Reno at the time, if not the only one. Jud Allen, executive director of the chamber, told me it would be a good package for my new property to get into, and that was the first all-inclusive package that I became a part of. They needed hotels, and because I had a brand new one, and my rooms were larger than almost anyone's in town, we did very well in that package. Reno has always had about 60 percent repeat business, and so it didn't take long for word to get around that we were new, had nice, large rooms within walking distance of downtown, and had our own casino.

I knew Vern Durkee, of Durkee's Travel Agency, very well. We played handball together, and I learned about the workings of the package. Essentially, Durkee was a wholesaler. He had a block of seats on United Airlines flights coming into Reno from different cities. Most were from the West Coast at that time. United was flying from Seattle, Portland, San Francisco, L.A., and, I think, Denver. On their flights that were routinely not full, they would give him a deep discount—late night flights, for example, or flights during mid-week, and if he took more seats, he'd get a deeper discount per seat.

Just as Vern could get cheaper seats from the airlines during the week, he could get cheaper rooms from the hotels, because mid-week was when our hotels had a lot of empty rooms. It was really a tailor-made kind of thing for Reno—when the airlines needed the seats, we needed the rooms; and when they didn't need them, we didn't need them, because we had all this drive-up traffic coming up from California on weekends.

Vern would put his profit in the price, so if a package with rooms and seats on the airline cost him a hundred dollars, he'd put twenty-five or thirty bucks in the price for himself, maybe more. But it was an attractive package, even if it cost a hundred and thirty or forty or fifty bucks, because it was a good deal all the way around.

Eventually, other wholesalers decided to come into Reno. There was a big one from back East named Funjet. A guy by the name of LaMacchia was one of the leaders, and he still operates that business. LaMacchia was working with United Airlines and Western Airlines, running packages to Las Vegas. I flew to Wisconsin and talked with him. I had my brochures and showed him our place. I got him interested, and within a few months of our opening, I started our Funjet package. It was the same kind of deal Durkee had, only we were getting people from the Midwest. It was one of the first efforts Reno made to try to tap that big, Midwestern market that Las Vegas had had all to themselves.

Almost simultaneously with the time we opened, a gasoline shortage hit the country, and that stopped cross-country auto traveling almost dead in its tracks. So here we were—just opened 300 new rooms, and our cross-country travel had dried up. Fortunately for me, a man named Devereux came to see me about putting together a charter air flight from Vancouver, British Columbia, to Reno. He had an option on a lease for a Boeing 737, and he wanted a place for these people to stay in Reno. I had never participated in anything like this, but he showed me how it was done. It was set up on what they call a twice-a-week rotation. A flight would come down on Sunday night, and it would land at the airport, and they'd bus them right over to your hotel. Then the plane would pick up a load of passengers that they'd brought in on the previous trip, and they'd take them back to Vancouver. So every Sunday night and Thursday night they'd bring down a new load and take the people back that had come on the previous flight. You'd have more natural demand for the weekend package, but you could push people into taking that four-day package by selling it for the same price as the three-day weekend flight. We'd give Devereux some really good rates for a weekday, and then we'd get better rates from him for the weekend.

Devereux brought down a full load the first time he came, and it looked wonderful to us. Right at a hundred people, a full load was about fifty hotel rooms. Most of them would be couples, and they all liked to gamble. That's what they came for. Maybe they'd see a little entertainment, but a lot of those people never even left our casino. They were just wonderful business.

The problem with Devereux was he was a slow pay. [laughter] I started out by saying, "You have to pay me in advance," because I was pretty leery about this whole thing. I'd never had any experience with it, and I thought, "Well, if I'm going to sit around here and hold fifty rooms for this guy, and he doesn't show up, then what do I do?" So it went along that way for awhile, and then one day he sent a flight down, and he had neglected to send a check. So I called him on the phone, and I said, "What's going on here?"

He said, "Oh, gee. I just forgot. It was an oversight."

Well, this kind of thing sort of snowballed and kept going, but it was in our slow season, and these people were, for us, pretty good gamblers. They weren't $500 players, but they were $25 players, and for us that was good. As a matter of fact, we liked $25 and lower players, because they didn't give us any trouble. We beat them. They couldn't win. They didn't have the bankroll we did. So it worked out great, and they liked our place.

We understood Canadians. In those days they hardly ever tipped, so initially we had a hard time with our dealers, but John Oliver was great about that. He started our people out right, and that was another reason we liked break-in dealers: they weren't used to making a lot of tips. Canadians, if they gave you a buck, they really thought they were doing something. A lot of times they'd tip fifty cents or nothing at all. The break-ins weren't used to making tips, so Oliver told these people, "You just smile and be nice to people, and eventually we're going to teach them how to tip." That's exactly what happened, and they're much better tokers today than they were then.

At any rate, I might not get paid for these rooms, but these customers were good for our casino, and my rooms would have been empty, anyway. So I just went along with Devereux and waited for the money, and then a lot of times the check would bounce. One time I flew up there on his charter to see him, because I hadn't been paid for two or three weeks, and when I went to his office, he was very nice to me. He took me to his chief financial officer, a Chinese fellow, and they wrote out a check for me, and I said, "Look, this is all well and good, but is there money in the bank?"

And they said, "We'll just call the bank and let you talk to somebody."

So I took up the phone, and the guy said, "Yes, that check will clear."

So we went out to dinner, and the next day I flew back to Reno with the check in my hand, sent it to the bank, and it bounced! [laughter] By the time I got to the bank, not only were there not enough funds, but it needed two signatures and only one of those guys had signed it. I knew that old gag. It had been pulled on me many times before, but this guy was a salesman. He was a soft-soaper, but he was having more problems as time went by.

One thing led to another, and eventually Devereux's package business wound up in the hands of Canadian Airlines. After Canadian took over, they began to fly bigger and bigger airplanes. We were getting more and more people, and we had to furnish more and more rooms, and we couldn't furnish all of them. So I went around to some other hotels close to us and procured rooms. Canadian would send me a list of requirements for rooms, and I'd take what I wanted, and then I'd farm out the rest of them. I was using the Colonial across the street. It was brand new at that time. I used the Hilton, the Comstock, and one or two other places.

For a few years I controlled the room end of the business in Reno for Canadian Airlines, and it worked out well for both of us. I'd help them negotiate the rates for these other places, because I knew when the slow seasons were and when they could get better rates and so on. So the thing really grew.

Right after we opened our second tower, Canadian Holidays, with our help on this end, began to fly a DC-10 to Reno. We were the first, and, I think, the only, charter airline that ever flew a DC-10 into this town. Then we flew 747's for two or three years. The DC-10's would bring around 380 people at a time, and the 747's would bring about 450, so you had a lot of rooms on those planes. Silver Wings was flying a much smaller plane at the time, probably a 737, so Canadian Airlines had a real hold on the market, and the

Sands became synonymous with Canadian Holidays in the Vancouver area, because we were one and the same, really.

One of the things that I negotiated out with these charter people was that they would do the advertising for the package, but I reserved the right to see their advertising and to help them decide where to place it. We'd do things like give them a special rate for Easter, because Easter was a hard time to move people. We'd do a special gamblers' flight on a real slow time, like the end of the month. (The end of the month would always be slow, maybe because government checks and welfare checks come out after the first of the month. The last few days of the month, a lot of people are short of money.) So, we'd look ahead and find these soft spots and plan different promotions. Our room occupancy was 90 percent because of those charter airlines coming down here, and that's damn good in the industry.

We were probably getting fifteen to eighteen percent of our total business from Canadian Airlines charters, and thirty to thirty-three percent of our *total* business was Canadian business—that would have been the Super Tour and all the other tours that we had. We got established in Vancouver well ahead of any other hotel-casinos in Reno. I saw to it that the ads that Canadian Holidays placed up there always had our name prominently displayed, and it worked well for them, too, because we had a nice hotel.

We had a first-class hotel. Canadians enjoyed staying with us, because we were "Canadian friendly." As a matter of fact, we used to take their money at par, whatever the exchange rate was (usually below the American dollar), and that was a really big deal. It cost a little, but it was well worth it. We learned what Canadians liked. They liked tea and toast for breakfast, so we had a little special in the restaurant for them, our "Canadian breakfast" special. One of the complaints you'd hear from them all the time was, "Well, I went down to so-and-so, and they didn't have any tea." [laughter]

The Canadian dollar started to drop in the mid-1980s. Up until then, it was usually within four cents of the American dollar. Then they had some problems in Canada, their dollar fell, and we couldn't absorb the difference. Then, we'd give them a special discount on the exchange, so they'd gain a little bit, but we began to get competition around town. Cal-Neva started to ape what we were doing, so if we were at 10 percent, they'd go to 8 percent. They were tough. They pulled a lot of our Canadian business out of here.

The Canadians got to where they'd take advantage of you. They'd come down, and they'd just change that money at the casino and stick it in their pocket and walk out. Currently, the Canadian dollar is down to sixty-seven cents, and that's one of the reasons that Canadian business has really dried up. Besides the casinos that are now up there, and all the other things that are happening, the declining value of the Canadian dollar has really hurt gaming business in Reno. In 2001, our Canadian business is 12 or 13 percent, as opposed to the 33 percent that it used to be.

We still fly this charter, but it's no longer owned by Canadian Holidays, and we only get fifteen or twenty rooms off that charter. Indian casinos in Oregon and Washington have hurt the Canadian business, also. And there's some gaming in Vancouver, as well. It isn't much, but it's year round, and it's right in the city.

The way it developed was Calgary and Edmonton became the Vegas market, and Vancouver became a Reno market . . . although Vegas made some big inroads up there, too. For a time, with Canadian Airlines, we had to resort to a two-drop kind of thing—when we were flying those big planes, we sometimes couldn't fill them, so they'd sell some seats to Vegas. They'd have to sell a sufficient number to justify the plane dropping a load in Reno, going to Vegas, dropping a load, and then turning around and doing the same thing going back. We did that, and I worked with the Westward Ho there on that kind of a situation.

15

Franchise Food, No Entertainment

OUR SO-CALLED "RESEARCH" led us to believe that we could run a casino without entertainment, thereby doing away with that overhead. We knew that for many, many years Harolds Club had done it, although later they did have entertainment. Cal-Neva has almost never had any entertainment, and they were very successful . . . and we were copying Cal-Neva in a lot of other ways, too. We gave out as many free drinks as we possibly could—anybody that was gambling didn't have to buy a drink. That's pretty normal these days, but back then, it wasn't.

We built our business around keeping overhead as low as we could. If you didn't have entertainment, it was a cost you didn't have. If you didn't have a marketing department, which we did not, that was a big expense eliminated. So we succeeded for many years without entertainment. But the business changed so much and became so competitive, that we in the late 1990s we started putting entertainment in. When the Silver Legacy opened up, a whole lot of things changed in Reno gaming.

Entertainment is not nearly the drag it used to be, because almost all places now practice what they call "four-walling." They charge admission now, where years ago, it was either free, or you just bought a drink or had something to eat, and you saw the entertainment. Now the entertainer gets the ticket revenue, and the hotel-casinos get the drink and food revenue. All the casino has to do is furnish the room and do the advertising. Whatever tickets they sell, the money goes to the entertainer, and that absolves the casino of paying the entertainer. That's really about the only way you're able to get big-name entertainers nowadays.

In the entertainment business now—because of television and these big shows where they pack in a lot of people in places like Lawlor and big exhibit halls—an entertainer can work two nights and make as much money as he used to make in one week. It's hard to get entertainers to come in and work a whole week, and when you do, it's very costly.

Four-walling has taken over the entertainment industry, but from the customer's standpoint it's not nearly as attractive. In the old days, when you used to go to the Riverside Hotel, you'd have a nice dinner, and you could sit around the table. You weren't jammed in there! [laughter] You paid for your food, and the price wasn't exorbitant, and you had great entertainment. I don't go to shows anymore, because I don't like the idea of sitting there all jammed in. It's just ridiculous. But the public has gotten used to that, because they can't find it any other way. They don't have a choice, if they want to see those entertainers. We don't have that kind of facility at the Sands, so we're not going to have big entertainment.

We now have three food franchises in our property. We have Tony Roma's, we have Arby's, and have a Mel's Diner. We had Winchell's Donuts, but we did away with the franchise. We had learned how to make donuts just like Winchell's does, so we still produce the donut, we just don't have to give Winchell's the override. We don't have a Denny's, anymore, and we also got rid of Baskin-Robbins . . for the same reason that we got rid of Winchell's. We also got rid of Orange Julius. We had a snack bar and a donut shop, and we wanted to start a bingo parlor, so we moved our snack bar over to where the Orange Julius was. That gave us space for a bingo parlor, which has been quite successful.

With Denny's, we found that they satisfied the food requirements of our customers, and we didn't have to run the food business. Almost all casinos lose money in their food operations—that's been true from day one, and it's still true, and because we'd had the positive Denny's experience on East Fourth, when we went into the casino business, it was our deliberate idea to leave our food to franchises of restaurants that were well known all over the country. But it wasn't that easy.

In planning the Regency Tower, which we opened in 1979, we hoped to get a food franchise or two to come in, but we learned that franchises were leery about coming into gambling places. We had to have a restaurant, so we put in a coffee shop and got someone else to operate it. It took me years to convince any franchiser that a casino would be a good place to have a franchise.

Our coffee shop, the Palm Court, was located on the second floor. We ran the snack bar on the ground floor, opposite the casino, because we had to have some kind of food facility where we could send our customers to get a sandwich if we wanted to comp somebody. We had a comp setup with the Palm Court operator, as well, but we had to pay him, and it was not as good a situation as we wanted. He didn't do very well up there, and within a year and a half or so, we had to take over the operation of the Palm Court.

I was not successful in attracting a franchise operation until we opened the Empress Tower in 1984. The first one, which we had to buy ourselves, was the Baskin-Robbins. We always wanted the franchise holder company to either operate the restaurant or franchise it off to a third party. When we couldn't do that, we would buy the franchise and operate it ourselves, but we tried to keep removed from the food business as much as we could.

The Baskin-Robbins parent company did not want to operate a Baskin-Robbins store, and they couldn't find a franchise holder to take one in the Sands, so we bought a franchise and operated it. We put it right on the casino floor. In the beginning, it was a wonderful thing. We had some of the biggest days that a Baskin-Robbins store ever had when we first opened, because it was a real novelty. People were buying ice cream, playing slot machines . . . they were dripping ice cream all over the place, but we were just happy as hell to clean it up!

Shortly after that, we bought a Winchell's Donut franchise, and we had the same experience as with Baskin-Robbins. We operated the Winchell's Donut Shop, and it was a great success. Fresh donuts in a casino were very novel. We made money with them. Even though it was a food business, it was one which was much simpler to operate than a coffee shop.

When you bought a franchise, you got a set of instructions in minute detail. We could take untrained people, and, because their job procedures were broken down into such small segments, we were capable of running the operation, even though we didn't have much food experience. We learned the manual ourselves and then trained our people. We did try to hire an experienced person to head the operation—you tried to hire somebody from another franchise that had experience. We were fortunate enough to get some of those people, and we had one running our Winchell's and one running our Baskin-Robbins.

Tony Roma's was very reluctant to come into a casino, but I felt that Tony Roma's would be a fantastic addition to our hotel-casino. (As a matter of fact, it was and still is. It's a big hit.) We bought the franchise for Tony Roma's. We couldn't get it any other way. Fortunately, Tony Roma's is operated much like a fast-food operation, with only a limited number of items. When you have a limited number of items, a restaurant is a whole lot easier to run. You can break your jobs down into simple, little tasks (except for the guy who actually cooks the meat), because you got this manual to go by. Not only have you got a manual, you got all these big pictures, and you put them up on the wall. Therefore, we can hire a lot of non-English-speaking people, which, nowadays, is a big advantage, because most of the people that are looking for jobs in the food business are immigrants, and they don't know the language. You just give them the pictures and tell them, "Here's what you got to do."

Our Mel's Diner is a company store. In other words, we don't operate it, and I'm happy for that. Mel's pays us a floor rent, and instead of us paying a percentage to the franchise holder, Mel's is going to pay us a percentage of their gross business. We get a rent plus an override after they reach a certain level. That's the same deal we worked out with Arby's. Our Arby's is a company-owned store, and they pay a floor rent and give us a commission.

Either way you do this franchise thing, it's a tremendous advantage in costs in a hotel-casino, and it worked out for us just as we envisioned it. Not only do they give you the instructions, but they also send inspectors around on a periodic basis, and if you're not doing things the way they want you to do them, they correct you. They show you how they should be done, and it's really good for us, because we want them to be run in the proper manner. If we fall down in the management—which you do, no matter how hard you try—then somebody from the company comes in and helps you. They also have mystery shoppers that come around and purchase a meal, and they make reports. Most of those companies really keep close tabs, and it's good for us, because it keeps us on our toes.

If you have an outfit like Arby's or Mel's Diner, they're sitting there paying rent, giving you a percentage on their override, and you don't have a thing to worry about, as far as the food business goes. But if you get a poor manager, and the quality of the operation goes down, it reflects on the hotel-casino, because they're in the Sands. You get the blame if the franchise doesn't perform well.

Another franchise in the Sands is Pizza Hut. We had to buy that franchise and operate it, but it's a real simple operation. It's a Pizza Hut Express, so we only have six different kinds of Pizza. It's a great little operation, and we do very well with it.

We set the pace with food franchises in casinos in Reno. I am proud of that. We were copied, and the sincerest form of flattery is to be copied. The big guys copied us . . . . But I think it's run its course. What seems to be more popular to-day are hotels that have developed a great food department on their own, like the Nugget or the Eldorado. Now, these big, new, billion-dollar places they're building down in Las Vegas are bringing in the famous names like Wolfgang Puck and Emeril.

When Ferenc Szony, our CEO, was at the Reno Hilton, he brought in Johnny Rocket's, which is pretty much the same thing as a Mel's Diner. It's a 1950s kind of operation, and they did really well there. Ferenc was sold on the franchise idea. He converted the Hilton's big coffee shop into a Chevy's Mexican restaurant, and that's almost unheard of. He got them to sell breakfast, and it worked out very well for him. The Hilton used to lose lots of money in their coffee shop, but since he converted it over, Chevy's pays the Hilton rent, so they took that loss and turned it into income. The customers are just as happy, and that was the theory that we used here for so many years.

16

From Arm Wrestling to Cribbage

IN 1979, when we built the Regency Tower, one of the things we did to fill those rooms was to bring in different kinds of events at slow times. We started arm wrestling competition the first winter after we opened the Regency Tower. We had a couple of people working for us that were arm wrestlers, and it was Jerry LaCroix's idea that we try the arm-wrestling competition. We slated it for the first or second weekend of January, because January is usually one of the worst, if not *the* worst month of the year for the whole town. It wasn't real big when we started—we had, maybe, a hundred and twenty people. We rented only forty or fifty rooms, but since we were probably running at a thirty or forty percent occupancy at that time, that represented a 10 percent jump. We also had some people walking around the place.

There were arm-wrestling competitions around northern California, Oregon, and Washington, and we put out handbills at them to let people know about the Reno competition. Reno worked really well, because people knew they could gamble a little bit while they were here and have a good time. We didn't make a lot of money with it, but it showed us that we could bring people in at a slow time.

One of the two arm wrestlers that worked for us was a woman. Her name was Pam, and she became the northern California champ. We'd sponsor her to go to these tournaments, and she'd help us advertise by wearing a Sands T-shirt. The arm-wrestling tournament eventually drew three or four hundred people, at least. I think we even hit five hundred one time. There wasn't a lot of money to be made, but it really filled our place up, and we made it look lively. We cast around for other things, and I think the next competition we hosted was a nine ball (pool) tournament. Later, we had eight ball and nine ball, both.

We were still running the El Rancho on East Fourth Street and doing the same thing there that we were doing at the Sands. We catered to what we called commercial people during the week, and we went to the local businesses and talked to the secretaries and the sales managers, and we even gave commissions to people that would send us business. A lot of salesmen coming into Reno drive in here from California, and we got a lot of those people to stay with us. We gave them a good room rate and tried to take care of them, and we were very successful at it.

Two of the men that stayed with us for many years were Gene Stary and Hank Pericle. They would come to Reno once every three weeks and stay for four days. Pericle sold welding equipment, and Gene sold auto parts. Gene and Hank got interested in competition for pool players. They developed a handicap system and a rating, like golfers are rated, and they gave each player a handicap. They put this system in effect in a large number of California and Oregon pool halls, and they began holding little tournaments in these pool halls. The players would come in, pay a little fee, and get into the tournament. Everybody could play, because they were all handicapped, so a poor player could compete with a good guy.

Gene and Hank started talking about doing a pool tournament in Reno. Gene said, "You know, if you guys put up five thousand bucks, that would be *huge* for a prize, and we could get you four hundred players."

I said, "That sounds like a great deal to me." All we had to do was figure out how to get the tables. Gene had a supplier that decided it would be good advertising for his tables, and then he knew another guy that sold the cloth that went on the tables. Gene worked out a deal where we got the tables at a real good rate, and then somebody else furnished the balls. The big ballrooms that we had could hold fourteen to sixteen tables, but they were really jammed in there. Later on we cut down the number of tables. We had two rooms, one on either side of the hall.

Gene ran the tournament, and Hank ran the scoreboard. It was a big success from the start. We held our first pool tournament in December, because the first three weeks of December, before Christmas, are just as bad a time as January. Even the weekends are slow between Thanksgiving and Christmas. Gene said, "You're not going to get a lot of people unless you do this thing on a weekend, because these people all work, and they just can't come up here." So we scheduled our first pool tournament the first weekend of December, and it was a big success. We drew four hundred people, or so.

These were people that were gamblers, and there were even some hundred-dollar players in the group. In this pool business, most of the players don't have a lot of money, but there's guys that back them because they're good players. If you saw the movie *The Hustler*, the one that Paul Newman played in, you know that a backer will find two or three good pool players, and he'll back them. And, of course, there's a lot of side bets made on these guys, and so we did get some pretty-good money players.

The guys liked to gamble, and our pit play just sky-rocketed. Real quick, we went to a whole-week tournament (we found that players would take a week off from work), and we included two or three different kinds of games. We had eight ball. We had nine ball. We had some other kind . . . three-ball, I think. I never did get the hang of it.

Paying off a winner in one of our pool tournaments.

I was so happy to have all these people around that I wasn't paying a lot of attention to the pool tournaments. I was down at the pit, that's where I was! They were tough players, so a lot of times they'd beat us—I mean, they weren't easy, because they were gamblers. But it was great business to have in December.

Then, we decided that we could hold two tournaments a year. We held our second one right after Memorial Day, because, historically, as soon as Memorial Day ends, Reno goes into a real slump for two weeks. We planned a pool tournament for as soon as the Memorial Day crowd left, and that worked very well for us, too. We've had those tournaments for twenty years, and they still bring a lot of people, and we still make a lot of money with them.

Gene and Hank still run the tournaments for us. Any number of casinos in town tried to steal those tournaments away from us, but because of the rapport that I've developed with Gene and Hank, and because we've known each other for so many years, no one's ever been successful in doing that.

Arm wrestling, after fifteen or twenty years or so, just sort of fell apart. I don't think anybody else picked it up—it just died out.

Once people discovered that we were doing these tournaments (and we were the only ones doing tournaments at this time), we would have people come to us and say, "Look, how about doing a tournament for us?" We did some bridge. Bridge wasn't a real big success. We did it in December, and we tried it in November, but those people really aren't big gamblers. That led us to cribbage.

Barbara Woodward was selling banquets and meeting space and so on for us. She took over a lot of the details of putting on tournaments. She was my right-hand person in the tournament business, and she was out there actively calling different associations and raking people up. Our cribbage tournaments started when Barbara got together with Bill Irons, a local World War II vet and a cribbage player. Bill had done a few local tournaments around town, so Barbara asked him about doing a regional cribbage tournament.

We do about three cribbage tournaments a year now, but we are in danger of losing the biggest one. We do the national tournament in the last week of January, first week of February. Cribbage players are gamblers. We get a lot of hundred-dollar players in our cribbage tournament—a lot for us. We've got one fellow that comes from Milwaukee, and when he doesn't show up, you can see it in the drop. This guy's name is Warren. We pay his fare out here, and he's got a standing invitation to come out any time he wants. He never rests. He says, "I can sleep when I get home." So he's a great player. Cribbage has been really good for us.

From cribbage we got to shuffleboard, the indoor, table-top variety. We have two types of shuffleboard tournaments. We have what's called the bar shuffleboard, which is a shorter table—same rules, but it's simply just a shorter table, developed for bars that don't have room for a long table. We have one of those tournaments, and we have a regular shuffleboard tournament that uses the longer tables. There's a shuffleboard association, and we've got an arrangement with them. We put up the prize money, and they bring in the tables, set them up, and take them down. They're pretty good gamblers, too. They're not the hundred-dollar players, but they're OK, and they like to drink a lot. Most shuffleboard players learn their game in a bar, so we sell a lot of booze! [laughter] It's been real good.

Scrabble is good for us, too. Barbara raked up the Scrabble people. Now, they're not gamblers, but we bring them in at a slow time, and they fill up the rooms, and they stay right here. They don't go anywhere else. They eat here. Whatever gambling they do, they do right here, because they're really into that Scrabble game.

Barbara is good at talking to people, and she is really aggressive at that. She eventually got married and had two children, and she didn't want to work full time, but we made an arrangement that we contract this work with her, so she can do a lot of this work at home and take care of her two little children. Barbara was also instrumental in developing the Reno balloon races. She and Candy Pearce came up with the idea with one or two other people.

Bill Robinson, the fellow that ran Canadian Holidays, was a balloon enthusiast, and when he learned that Reno was talking about doing a balloon race thing, he really got excited about it. He'd bring down two or three plane-loads of balloon enthusiasts from Vancouver for the Reno balloon races. They came down for the first one, and they really helped make the Reno balloon races. He made sure he had room in the luggage hold to bring a couple of Canadian Holidays balloons to fly in the Reno balloon races. It was a big party week.

The first two or three years of the balloon races, they'd show up here on a Thursday, and it was a party until they left on Sunday night. In those days we'd go to Sierra Sid's in Sparks to buy propane for the balloons' burners, and we'd buy tanks of compressed air from Sierra Oxygen. Then we'd have to rent a couple of trucks and put the balloons on them and the baskets and the oxygen and the propane. We'd spend all night Friday getting all these preparations made, and then it was time to fly. [laughter] So in the first two or three years of the balloon races, we all flew without any sleep and plenty of booze.

They always break out champagne at the end of a balloon race, and anyone who has gone up for the first time gets champagne poured on his head. I went through that initiation, and we really had some fun times. The balloon races just grew and grew, but when Robinson left Canadian Holidays, they quit bringing down their balloon. By that time, Barbara had raked up a guy in Idaho, whose name is Curt Pengally. He owns his own balloon, loves to fly. We hang our Sands banner on his balloon. We sponsor a balloon every year. It's been a great promotion, and Barbara had a really big hand in that.

We have chess tournaments. They come every year in the off season, so we fill up a weekend there. We did have backgammon in here for a time, but it didn't do that well, and I'm not quite sure exactly what happened. I think that was a promotion that was stolen from us by Hilton or somebody

"... we all flew without any sleep and plenty of booze."

else. Backgammon was one of the very few promotions that we were not successful with.

Another promotion we have is darts. A man named McNamara, executive secretary of the National Dart Association, contacted us. So we set up a dart competition, and it's a good tournament. Dart players usually learn to play darts in a bar, so they drink a lot, and gambling and drinking goes together. They're not big players, but we're filling up rooms. One of the things that we tell these guys is, "Look, you got to come here. We want you." They're happy to get somebody to put up the prize money that they never had before, and to come to a place that we turn into a dart player's hang-out when they're here. They meet all their friends here, people they know from other places and from their work.

Our first tournaments were played with what are called "hard-tip" darts, which I didn't know at the time. A guy called me up one day and said, "I want to do soft-tip darts."

I said, "Well, what the hell is that?" [laughter]

It turns out that a soft-tip dart is what you throw at an electronic board. They have a soft tip on them, and you throw them at this board, and wherever they stick, the machine brings up a score for you. So, now we have a soft-tip tournament, too.

We also have a bar table pool tournament. Bar table pool is played on a much smaller pool table—usually, they're coin operated like shuffle board tables. There's an association of players that specialize in bar table pool. We had an inquiry about that, and Barbara handled it, and we have those people in here for a tournament once a year. It's mildly successful. We don't turn out as many people as for some other tournaments, but again, these people learned to play this game in bars, so they're our kind of customers.

Many people that come for these tournaments come to Reno at other times during the year, and when they think about Reno, they think about us. Tournaments have always been one of our mainstays. It really isn't a big percentage of our total business, because we bring them in at a slow time, but what you need to look at is what we'd have in here without those people. We're not going to bring them here in the middle of August or the middle of July, because we don't need them. If they want to come then, they'll just have to go somewhere else.

17

Going Public

DOWN THROUGH THE YEARS, my father was very active in the stock market. He bought stock in a lot of different companies, because he was a speculator. He'd buy and sell, and he got familiar with a large number of public companies in the country. Because of his vision and his experiences, he felt that if we ever had the opportunity to go public, it would be a wonderful thing for the company. He never dreamt that this would happen, because in the climate that he was associated with, small companies like us normally didn't get to go public, but it would be a great source of financing, and financing was always a very difficult thing for casinos to obtain.

Even the banks in Nevada didn't want to loan you money, and for many years, until Harrah finally broke the line, they *wouldn't* loan you any money. We had to resort to all kinds of strategies . . . like for example, we'd build a hotel and leave the ground floor empty, and we wouldn't tell them we were going to put a casino in. We'd say, "This is just a hotel." So we'd have to do a pro forma statement and show them that the hotel would stand on its own and make money. They really knew what we were doing, but as long as we could show them that we could pay the debt service with just the hotel revenue, we would get the financing.

If you were a public company, you had other options open to you. You could float bonds. You could sell stock, and you didn't have to be dependent on local banks. (There weren't any out-of-state banks that would do financing for you either.) One of the reasons that Vegas grew so fast and so well is because they had access to Teamsters Union money. The Teamsters had huge pension plans, and they loaned money from them to the hotel-casinos, because some of them were mobsters and had been in bed with those casino owners for a long time. The only Teamster loan, to my knowledge, that was ever made in Reno was to the Riverside Hotel.

The first public gaming company was Harrah's, and they went public in 1971. When that happened, we knew it could happen for us. The next one was IGT, and so we began to think about it, but we weren't yet big enough. When we built the Regency Tower in 1979 we had 400 rooms, and when we finally started the Empress Tower in 1984, we had a story to tell. That's what you need when you do a public offering. You got to get people to believe that you're going to grow, that you're going to prosper, and your stock price is going to go up. So we had a story—we were getting ready to build another 280 or 300 rooms and grow to 700 rooms.

I'd gone to military school with Drake Delanoy, who became a lawyer for Bill Raggio in the district attorney's office. He had gone on some of those raids on Joe Conforte's houses of prostitution when we used to pick up those trailers. Later, Drake moved to Las Vegas when a law firm there offered him a very lucrative position. Drake's law firm represented the Golden Nugget, which was Steve Wynn's first place, and Clyde Turner was the liaison between his firm and the Golden Nugget. Clyde was the chief financial officer of the Nugget when the Golden Nugget went public. (They were, I think, the third gaming company that went public.)

Drake, Clyde Turner, and another lawyer from Drake's firm bought a condo at Lake Tahoe right next to the Hyatt on Lakeshore Drive, and Drake would come up here quite frequently. We'd go waterskiing together. I began to talk to

Clyde about the feasibility of taking my company public, and Clyde said, "Sure. Let me see your last four or five year-end statements." I gave him the statements and brought him down to Reno and showed him the property. He said, "I think you can do it. You got a great story to tell. It would be wonderful for your company, and you could raise a lot of cash. The value of your ownership of this company will probably increase five-fold."

I began to look for an investment banking firm that might be interested in taking us public. We were still pretty small, but there were three gaming companies that had gone public, and their stock was doing well, so there was an appetite out there for more gaming companies. It was a good time, so I started to make the rounds.

The way it shook out, it was going to be about a fifteen-million-dollar stock offering, and the investment bankers that had taken these other companies public were not interested in a deal that small. Eventually I was sent to a firm in Los Angeles, and they wouldn't do the deal, either. But they hooked me up with a fellow that worked for DLJ (Donaldson, Lufkin, and Jenrette). I talked to the Los Angeles office, and then I was to go to New York and talk to the people in their headquarters, and by that time it looked like it was a doable thing.

Clyde and everyone else advised me that I needed to hire somebody who had had experience bringing a company public, so before I went to New York, I hired Jon Bengtson. Jon was working for George Drews at IGT then. My friend, Chuck Zeh, a lawyer here in town that I used to play handball with, introduced me to Jon, and Jon was ready to leave IGT. Jon had been working for Harrah's when they had their public offering. He'd earned a master's degree at Stanford in business administration, and he had a minor in accounting. Harrah's had hired George Drews from an investment banking firm to help them in their public offering, and so Jon began to work with George, and he worked directly with George Drews in the Harrah's public offering.

When Si Redd, who owned IGT, decided to go public, he hired George Drews from Harrah's to help him in his offering. George brought some of his staff along with him to IGT, and Jon was one of those folks that he brought over there. So Jon had two public offerings under his belt by the time I started talking to him about it.

Jon fit right in with our company. Jon is a man that gets along great with people. He's a wonderful people guy, and he's smart and intelligent. The first thing you have to do when you go public is sell yourself to an investment banking firm. In order to do that, you got to talk their language, and I definitely didn't talk their language. Without Jon, I'm sure we would not have been able to accomplish it.

Essentially, there are two kinds of offerings; they're called a "guaranteed" offering and a "best-efforts" offering. If you can get an investment banking firm to do a guaranteed offering for you, it means they believe in you to such an extent that they'll buy whatever stock doesn't sell on the public market. In other words, if only half your stock sells, they'll buy the rest, because they believe it's a good investment. Usually, when an investment banking firm thinks you're that good an offering, your stock is over-subscribed, so they don't have to buy any.

Other firms that might not be as professional, or might not believe in you so much, do a best-efforts offering. On that basis, nobody guarantees you're going to sell all your stock, so you might go through that whole procedure—and it's costly—and find out you don't sell enough stock to do you any good. I knew nothing about these things. I had to learn from Jon and Clyde Turner.

We hoped DLJ would do a guaranteed offering for us, but before they would give us that kind of guarantee, we had to educate them in our business from scratch, and that took time and effort and expense. We had to bring them to our property, and they spent many days and nights with us learning our business. They couldn't afford to take the chance that they'd be hoodwinked or that they didn't really have the whole story. (You see that nowadays in these "dot.com" public offerings. They're in such a rush to do it that they don't get the whole story, and there may be some shadows in the background that they don't know about.) DLJ sent two investment bankers out, and they spent two or three months here. One was a man named Oliver Cromwell. Fred Cohen, from the law firm of Latham and Watkins, represented us, and Doug Tanner represented DLJ.

Investment bankers are very quick and sharp. You don't have to tell them something more than once, and they really learn fast. They knew our business as well as we knew it by the time they got through. They did a narrative so it would sell on Wall Street, and then they took it back to their bosses and said, "Well, here's what these guys are doing. We think it's going to be a good stock and make money, and here's why we think we should guarantee it."

Those bankers all get a piece of the action. They get a salary, sure, but they make their real money on a piece of every offering. They're out there hustling like hell, working long hours and weekends, because they get a pretty good chunk when a place goes public. The higher the stock price you get and the more stock you move, the more money they make. They even get some shares at no cost to them, which they turn around and sell, and they make money on those. That's part of the deal, and they're up-front about it.

When DLJ decided to take this project on, they didn't tell us that they were going to take us public. They said, "OK, we'll spend some time on it. You will pay all our expenses." We paid a hefty fee up front, and then we paid for everything associated with their study of our business and the eventual issuance of stock; but it was still a period of six, eight months that were tied up in the project, and that's why a small offering is difficult to get financed. They could do the same amount of work for a $150 million offering, so I'm not sure why they decided to take us on. It may be because we operated so very differently from other casinos of the time.

The report to the main office spelled it all out: how we had started our business; the fact that we didn't have entertainment to pay for, where most other casinos did; the fact that we didn't lose money on food—we made money on food. (Other casinos—and they looked right at Harrah's—all lost a lot of money on their food operations, and their entertainment costs were very high.) When they did pro formas on our company, it turned out that we had like a 35 to 38 percent profit margin, and that was a huge margin. One reason we were able to keep our costs so low was that we didn't have to hire upper management. We had myself and my sister and Dave Wood and Jon Bengtson. (My brother got sick in 1981, and after that he didn't work anymore.) The guys who studied us could go back to New York and say, "Look, these guys got a 38 percent profit margin! And they're getting ready to add another 280 rooms, so their revenues are going to go up."

We showed steady growth right from day one. When I read things nowadays where people like Amazon.com say, "We're losing money for the first three or four years . . . ." Well, I just have to laugh. We *never* opened a business that lost money from scratch, except, maybe, the Lovelock Mercantile Company. We even made money in Mississippi for the first few months. And in all of our expansions—every time we'd add a new tower or add a new portion to our complex—we made money from day one.

We looked really good, and DLJ said, "OK. We'll do it." But the thing about a successful public offering is, you've got to hit the market at the right time. There has to be an appetite for IPO's, Initial Public Offerings. When we went public, there had already been three successful gaming offerings, and it was our good fortune that everybody was anticipating that the next one would be as successful as the others, even though it might be a little smaller.

DLJ finally said, "OK. We'll do this, but there's one more thing you got do, and that is what's called a road show." It's important in stock sales to sell institutions (pension funds or retirement programs, primarily) on buying your stock, and the way you sell institutions is you go out and call on them and do a "dog-and-pony" show. So Bengtson and I and the investment banker, Oliver Cromwell, did two or three trips around the country.

We were successful in our efforts. Our initial public offering was two million and some odd shares at twelve bucks each. The institutions helped us out by buying a lot of our stock, but if institutions own too much of your stock, you don't get much "float." You don't get much trading in the stock, and that's not good, because you need a certain amount of trade volume. That might have hurt us a little bit in the beginning, but our stock never did drop below twelve dollars . . . or if it did, it wasn't by very much.

After we built the Empress Tower, our stock really began to climb. We eventually did a two-for-one split. The old price was, I think, twenty-eight dollars, the highest we ever hit. With the split, the stock wound up at fourteen dollars a share after the split—but there were four million some odd shares, and *that* stock went up to twenty-two dollars. Unfortunately, it's now three dollars! [laughter]

Our operation, unlike many other casino operations, had never had to borrow money to get through a winter. We always made sure we had the cash to get us through. Even so, going public made our financial position much more secure than it had been. We now were largely free of having to go to banks and lenders for funds, but we were still dependent on them when we had capital projects to do.

February 1, 1985

1,000,000 Shares

THE SANDS REGENT

Common Stock

Price $12 Per Share

Copies of the Prospectus may be obtained in any State from such of the undersigned as may legally offer these securities in compliance with the securities laws of such State.

Donaldson, Lufkin & Jenrette
Securities Corporation

Bear, Stearns & Co.	Alex. Brown & Sons Incorporated	Hambrecht & Quist Incorporated
E. F. Hutton & Company Inc.	PaineWebber Incorporated	Prudential–Bache Securities
L. F. Rothschild, Unterberg, Towbin		Salomon Brothers Inc
A. G. Edwards & Sons, Inc.		Oppenheimer & Co., Inc.
Thomson McKinnon Securities Inc.		Tucker, Anthony & R. L. Day, Inc.
Advest, Inc.	Butcher & Singer Inc.	Interstate Securities Corporation
Ladenburg, Thalmann & Co. Inc.		Legg Mason Wood Walker Incorporated
Moseley, Hallgarten, Estabrook & Weeden Inc.		Neuberger & Berman
Wheat, First Securities, Inc.		Herzfeld & Stern Inc.
Josephthal & Co. Incorporated		Scott & Stringfellow, Inc.

We used the money from our public offering to retire our debt, and so here we were, essentially a debt-free company with cash in the bank and a great cash-flow. Our cash-flow was probably fifteen, sixteen million dollars a year, and so money was no problem at all. We just had to spend it and invest it wisely. That was a big change, and that was really one of the major reasons why we went public. It raised our stature with the local banks, as well. The fact that we were a public company made it easier for us to borrow from them. As a publicly-traded gaming company, we were part of an elite group. Our employees from the bottom up—the porters, the maids, and the line people—would tell people that we were a public company. It made them proud to be a part of our company, and it was good for our esprit de corps.

My sister and I and our board of directors and our executives, Bengtson and Dave Wood, also had that spirit. I felt really good that we were able to accomplish a goal that Dad had set years back. It made me feel that I had done something worthwhile and important that was durable and lasting.

In 1987 the Sands Regency was named by *Forbes* magazine as one of the top 200 small businesses in the United States. That was as big an accomplishment in my mind as our going public. *Forbes* monitored all the public companies through information they received from the SEC. Some of the key things that they looked at were how much debt the company had in relation to its income and what its executives were getting paid. In a lot of instances companies overpay their CEO, their chief financial officer, and other executive positions, in relation to how much money the company makes. In our company, we were always very careful, because we didn't want our employees or the public to think that we were lining our own pockets with big salaries when maybe we didn't deserve it. So our salary ratios were low, and that was an important thing as far as *Forbes* was concerned. We were also paying dividends on our stock. Many companies don't pay dividends. We began to pay dividends to our shareholders, because when we were doing well, we thought the shareholders should benefit. Our PE ratio was excellent, in the four or five range, which is very good for a public company.

We came in at number 107 out of 200 companies on the *Forbes* list. I had no idea. I got a call from the *Reno Gazette-Journal*, and the reporter said to me, "Do you know that you've been named on the *Forbes* 200 list?"

I said, "I don't even know what the *Forbes* 200 list is."

He explained it to me, and so I went out and got a copy of the *Forbes* magazine, and, sure enough, there we were! There has not been a gaming company listed since, nor was there one prior to that. We still hold the distinction of being the *only* gaming company that ever made that list.

The SEC stipulates that prior to going public you have to disclose how much stock the original owners are going to keep and how much they're going to sell. They want to know who's going to control the company and how they're going to control it. They have special regulations for companies that are closely held. (My family owns 46 percent of the Sands Regency stock.) You must have at least two outside directors on your board, and your board must have at least seven people—and the larger your board, the more outside directors you must have. They want outside directors to be people that have no stock in the company and people that are familiar with the industry and/or have had experience with public companies before. We had to find some people and name them before we could go public. One we chose was Maurice Sheppard, who'd been president at Harrah's and was retired. During the time Jon Bengtson was at Harrah's, he had worked for and with Maurice. Maurice became very helpful to us.

Maurice Sheppard came up through the ranks at Harrah's. I think he started either in the cashier's cage or in the accounting department, and eventually he became president of Harrah's. When he came on board, he looked over our accounting department and our cashier's cage and gave us some tips—he found some weak spots, showed us where we could do some things better. He reviewed some of our employees and talked to them, and he found some that were not doing their job as good as they could have. He was instrumental in helping us find other people, so we were able to build a good, strong cashier's department, as well as strengthen our accounting department and our procedures. Harrah's had been very strong in security procedures, and we borrowed a lot of things that Harrah's did, things that Shep knew about. He went above and beyond the call of duty. We only paid him to be a board member, and this was really not his function, but that's the kind of guy he was. He wanted the company to succeed. He was willing to put in time and effort, and he'd give us all he had, even though it wasn't required of a board member.

Maurice was on the board for many years. He finally quit when his health began deteriorating. It was a great loss. He was somebody that we could talk to, because almost any incident that we had, or any problem that we had, Harrah's had faced many times before, and he gave us insight into how Harrah's had solved those problems . . . not that they were right every time.

The other outside director on our board when we went public was Jack Stratton. We were neighbors when we were kids, and I knew Jack and his brother down through the years. Jack was always an honest, straight-forward guy who spoke his piece, and he knew his business.

Jack started out with the Nevada Tax Commission, which was the entity that originally collected gaming taxes. When the Gaming Commission and the Gaming Control Board were formed in the 1950s, Jack transferred over to the control board, and he was with them about twenty-five years. He had recently retired from the control board about the time we went public, and so I asked him to serve on our board. He graciously agreed.

Jack was another fellow who went out of his way to ensure our success. On his own volition he monitored our compliance with Regulation Six, the regulation that pertains to the protection of company assets. Regulation Six is all about the security of your bankroll, and that's important to the casino, as well as being important to the state. Jack picked up some weak spots that we had and showed us where we could do things better. It was good to have him in our board meetings. He was experienced in the regulation of gaming, and he could help us head things off. Consequently, we never got into trouble with Gaming (the Gaming Control Board), and we were never fined. (Actually, we were involved once in a money laundering incident, where we didn't report a $10,000 transaction—one of our cashiers didn't follow regulations.) Our relations with Gaming have been excellent all the years we've been in business, and one of the reasons was that Stratton was on our board.

Stratton and Sheppard left the board at about the same time and for similar reasons. Joe Fanelli replaced one of them. Fanelli was a man who'd had years of experience working in food service at Harrah's. Food is always a difficult thing, and Fanelli was instrumental in getting some good chefs for us that had worked for him. He helped us in our buying procedures, too. He showed us how we had been negligent in not inspecting the food that was coming in. Once you get a reputation with your wholesalers that you'll accept whatever they send you, then they'll have a tendency to send you whatever they have. They keep the better stuff for the guy who checks and inspects it.

We hired somebody who inspected everything when it came in, and we weighed everything. That was another thing we hadn't been doing, and Joe said, "It's important that if you order thirty pounds of stew meat, you weigh it when they bring it to you, because they might give you twenty-eight . . . or they might give you thirty-two. We found that was happening, and a lot of it was just human error. The guy that put the meat together just threw it on the scale and didn't pay that much attention to it, and so it was a pound or two off. It doesn't sound like a lot, but you have to control your food and labor costs to succeed with a restaurant.

Now as one of our outside directors, we have Lou Phillips, who worked for Harrah's for many years and actually ran their casino at Lake Tahoe for four or five years. He has the Harrah's chair up at the University of Nevada now, and he's one of our outside directors. The other one we have is a man named Larry Tuntland. Larry was with the local First National Bank (which eventually became FIB, which then became Wells Fargo) for many years here in Reno. Then he was transferred to Las Vegas and worked there for years. We feel fortunate to have those two folks on our board. Jon Bengtson is still on, even though he doesn't work with us anymore, and my sister, my son, Dave Wood, and Ferenc Szony make up our board. That's been our board now for two or three years.

18

Employee Loyalty

WE BEGAN PROFIT SHARING and pension plans in the middle 1960s, and here's how they came about. My dad had a friend, Chris Georgiadas, who sold life insurance. He was a Greek man from *Zákinthos*, who had lived in Reno and worked for New York Mutual Life Insurance, then had moved to southern California. My father had stayed in touch with him.

At the time my mother passed away, Chris put us in touch with a law firm in Los Angeles to handle her complicated estate. (She died without a will, and there were a lot of tax issues.) As I was the executor for my mother's estate, I traveled to Los Angeles quite frequently. I'd usually see Chris when I'd go down there.

Chris not only was helping people with estate planning, he was also doing pension and profit-sharing plans for different businesses. He showed us the advantage to such plans—they gave employees an inducement to stay with their employer. We decided to start such a plan for our people.

After an employee had been a certain time in our work force (I think it was six months before you were eligible), the company would begin putting an amount equivalent to 10 percent of his salary in the pension plan and 10 percent in the profit-sharing plan. The employee didn't have to put in any at all, but he had the option to do so, and some of our employees did. My father invested that money in conservative investments, which he didn't care to do for himself; but for the plans, he thought that was the thing to do. He bought a lot of utilities, for instance, and over the span of the years that the plan was open, those utilities probably quadrupled in their stock prices, because it was a period of growth in the country.

It took our employees a little while to realize what was going on. One wouldn't really see the growth until after he was in the plan for a few years. After you were in the plans for ten years, you were fully vested—if you left after ten years, you got everything that was in your plan, both the money that the company put in and the earnings from that money. If you left any time within the first ten years, then it was pro-rated. For example, if you left after five years, you only got half the money in the plan and half of the earnings, and the other half was distributed to the rest of the people in the plan.

It was a great incentive, and we built a very loyal force of people, especially in middle management. (We didn't really have any upper management, because we did that ourselves.) We had many happy folks who stayed with us fifteen or twenty years.

One night I was on my way home. It was late, and I was exceeding the speed limit by quite a bit, and I'd had a few drinks. A state trooper stopped me. I gave him my license, and when he read my name, he said, "Are you the man that owns the El Rancho Motel on East Fourth Street?"

I said, "Yes."

He said, "You're going to follow me to make sure that you get home and that you don't get in an accident. My mother worked for you folks for eighteen years." His mother was Marian Donnelly, our housekeeper over there. When she retired she got a big pension for a working person. He said, "I think you guys have done a marvelous thing for people."

Pension and profit-sharing plans weren't heard of back then in our business. From our standpoint, however, the plans were deductible, and since it was a high tax bracket we were in, much of the money that we put into the plans was paid for by the government. Another thing is that my brother and sister and I were all employees in these companies, so we also participated in the plans. It was another way for us to get money out of the company without having to pay big taxes.

We carried that plan over to the Sands when we opened up, and we kept the plan until the late 1980s, when we suffered a spate of lawsuits. One of the things that they were suing us for was that we were terminating people in order to get them off the plan, so that we ourselves (the Cladianos family) could benefit. It was a spurious charge, and it was never proven to be true. But in order to protect ourselves at the time and to stop people from suing us—because we had to go into court and defend ourselves on each one of those lawsuits—we fully vested everybody in the plan, no matter how long they had been there. (We said, "OK. Everybody is completely vested, just as if they were here at least ten years.") Then we liquidated all the investments of the plans, and we paid off everybody. I've sorely missed those plans ever since, because we used to have a great deal more loyalty than we do now. However, since we developed a bonus system for our middle managers and upper managers to sort of take the place of that plan, it's helped a lot.

Our bonus plan is based more on profitability than the length of service. We do have a little length of service plan where anybody that's been with us for a year gets a bonus, and those are for line employees. After one year, you get one hundred dollars twice a year; after two years service, employees get two hundred dollars twice a year; after three years, etc. . . . We give people that bonus as long as they work for us, and it kind of works like the pension and profit-sharing plan. In some ways it's even better, because they get the money right away. A lot of people in this business are shortsighted. They say, "I don't want the money when I retire. I want it now." So that works out, in some cases, even better than pension and profit sharing.

My father had several employees who stayed with him for many years. Gladys Cox started with him when he was on Lake Street. She was his first bookkeeper-secretary type person. She moved with him when he built the El Rancho Two on East Second Street; and when he sold the majority of his slot route, she moved out to the El Rancho Motel on South Virginia Street as secretary-bookkeeper until she became ill and had to retire. Gladys was a very loyal, hard-working employee. She learned the motel business with my dad—neither one of them knew anything about it when he bought the place. She wound up being the manager, really, right under my dad's supervision.

When Gladys left, Dad hired a lady named Etta Kruckow. Etta came from the Lovelock Mercantile store. She was a bookkeeper-secretary in Lovelock, and when my dad finally disposed of the store there, he moved Etta and her husband to Reno because she was such a loyal employee and such a good, hard worker. She went to work when Gladys left, and my father got her husband, who was a pharmacist, a job with Hale's Drugstores through his friend, Clarence Hale. (Etta's husband had worked in the pharmacy for my dad in Lovelock, as well.)

When Etta left, Dad hired a lady named Ruth Blanchard, and she took over the job that Gladys and Etta had had. She turned out to be a very loyal, hard-working employee, and she was with us for many years, as well. Eventually, we wound up with the executive secretary that we have now, Teri Wallace, and I think we've been blessed. These women have been the mainstay of the administration of our business and a tremendous help to myself and my father through all the years.

Other folks that that did wonderful jobs for us and were very loyal include a lady named Tina Kopp, who still works for us. She runs our health club, and she's probably worked for us for forty-five years or so. She started as a chambermaid at the El Rancho on East Fourth Street, shortly after we opened in 1954. Eventually she became our head housekeeper—she ran our chambermaid crew. When we converted the El Rancho to a weekly rental operation, we moved her to the Sands, and she became the head housekeeper here. When she lost a part of her leg, and her ankle and foot were amputated, she couldn't work for a few years, but we kept her on the payroll. She now works for us running our health club. When Tina Kopp left, we hired Marian Donnelly to be our head housekeeper, and she was also an extremely loyal person.

Cheryl Jensen has been with us for many years also. She started as a reservations clerk for us in 1979 or 1980, became our hotel manager, and worked for us until just last year. She was a loyal, hard-working person. David Wood, our chief financial officer, came to us in 1980 or 1981.

Mickey Meredith was a room clerk that worked for my dad at the El Rancho on East Fourth Street, and she worked for a short time at the El Rancho on South Virginia Street. Many times, my father tried to get her to become front desk manager, but she refused. Mickey was a hard-working, loyal person, but she didn't want the responsibility. She was middle-aged, and she just wanted to work for a salary and not have to be concerned about any administrative duties.

My brother developed a bad cardiovascular condition in his right leg, and in 1981 he had two or three operations to open the arteries. The doctors told him it would be best if he stayed off of his leg. He was really our principal pit and slot guy at the time.

When my brother had to quit working, it created a little hole in our operation, so we hired a guy named Bruce Dewing as our assistant slot manager, or something like that. He had started in the industry at the Mapes Hotel, probably as a change person, but he advanced quickly, because he wanted to learn. The Mapes transferred him to the Money Tree when it opened, and he worked there as a mechanic. He also worked as key man and learned how to do slot percentages. Bruce was probably in his thirties when we hired him, and we always liked younger employees.

Youth worked great for us in a lot of cases, but not necessarily in all cases. In room clerks and housekeeping, we found middle-aged ladies to be our best employees. And we had a number of dealers that were middle aged, and eventually we had pit bosses and shift managers that were middle-aged ladies.

At the time we hired Dewing, we also hired our first hotel manager. (Up until then my sister and I had done the hotel managing.) I hired a man by the name of Mike Pickens, who had worked for a few big hotel chains, so he had good experience. Pickens took a little of the load off me by running the hotel, and Dewing stepped in to help fill the role of my brother.

Pickens and Dewing became close friends, and Dewing made it his business to learn the hotel operation. He wanted to learn about operating the hotel so that someday he could be of greater help to the company. I thought that was a good idea, and I began to introduce Dewing and Pickens to our wholesalers, our charter operator, and the Canadian people. It took a little load off of me, because if one of those people called and I wasn't available, they had somebody else they could talk to.

Pickens was smart and knew the business, and he was hard-working, but it seemed that he had an alcohol problem that he couldn't beat. Eventually, I had to let him go, but by that time Dewing had learned quite a bit about the sales and marketing of the hotel. My sister was doing the actual running of the hotel, so we didn't need any help there. Eventually, we made Dewing our general manager.

After my brother left, the pit more or less returned to me. I worked a lot in the pit, and Dewing knew the two major parts of our business, the hotel and the slots. We always were essentially a slot house, but we did make money in our pit. We certainly never chased high rollers around, but because of the people we'd hired, starting with Oliver and the people that he brought in, we always had a good, efficient pit operation, and we ran right at a 20 percent win.

Dewing did a good job for us, but there were some things we didn't see eye-to-eye on. Eventually that led to my letting him go. We had just agreed to disagree, and I gave him a letter of recommendation when he left.

Carrol Rippy started our keno operation for us. Carrol had been in the business for many years, came from the Palace Club, and he *knew* the keno business. He did a good job for us, and when he left, his assistant, Don Byerley, took over. Don became a very good keno manager, actually better than Carrol. He was a department head whom I could depend on to be innovative, and he spent a great deal of time going around town looking at other keno games, looking at different tickets, working out the percentages on tickets to see if they'd be a good ticket for us to try, watching to see what was popular in town, and going to Las Vegas on his own to look at keno operations down there.

For a small game, our keno game did very well. And as far as I know, it was operated honestly . . . I don't think we were taken off any more than usual! [laughter] You can't ever think that you're not going to get hurt there once in awhile, but Byerley ran a good game for us for many years. He was also a great addition to our executive committee, because not only did he pay attention to what keno was doing, he would also watch our competition to see what other promotions were going on in their pits and slot areas.

Unfortunately, Don's wife became really ill, and Don was torn between his job and his wife's health, and he eventually left us. We appointed his assistant, Carol Wilson, whom he trained just like Rippy had trained him. She's now our keno manager, and she's doing a good job . . . so all of this came down from Carrol Rippy.

19

In the Pit

WORKING IN THE PIT is a unique experience. When I first got involved with live gaming, I didn't believe there was any such thing as luck—it was just something people talked about. But when you spend years in the pit watching people gamble and seeing what occurs, you have to think that there certainly is luck in this world. People will come in who know nothing at all about gaming, and they'll consistently do things wrong and yet win. On a twenty-one game they will consistently hit eighteens and nineteens and come up with twos or threes. That's a highly stressful situation for a pit boss, because one of the things you're concerned about is whether everything is on the square.

In the gaming business, if everything is on the square, in the end the house is going to win. It's up to the pit boss to determine whether everything really is on the square. When you see a customer who almost appears to know the next card coming off the deck, or what the next roll of the dice is going to be, you say to yourself, "Well, how could this happen?" You begin to look for something that may not be quite on the level—a move that doesn't look like a normal move by a hand or an arm.

Most of the time, everything really is on the square. So you stand there watching your dealers get whipped horribly, and you're worried about the results of your shift. Everybody that runs a shift always keeps in his mind how much his shift is going to drop and how much they're going to win or lose. When people come in and beat you unmercifully, you know that you're going to wind up losing, no matter how the other games are going. You might have a $70,000 drop and still lose $40,000. It's a highly stressful job. And most of the people that did that job when I used to do it would smoke a great deal and would drink a lot of coffee, and that made it even more stressful. Physically, it's a demanding job.

When I first started doing pit work in the little casino, I used to deal when a dealer took a break. One night a couple came in that had been drinking heavily. We had a twenty-five dollar limit game, and before I knew it they were winners—two or three thousand bucks. I had used all my dealers; I'd changed decks; I had done everything I knew to change our luck. I'd asked the dealers to stand on one leg. I'd sent them to the restroom and told them to turn their pants around. Finally, I said, "If anybody is going to lose any more money in this place, it is going to be me!" So I went in and started dealing to these people, but it was one of those cases where they just couldn't do anything wrong. That was the dumbest thing I could have done. I wound up losing about eight or nine thousand bucks that night on a lousy twenty-five dollar limit table. [laughter] All during this time, I am trying to figure out what kind of edge these people have. But I am sure they didn't have an edge—they were just lucky! That is the frustrating kind of thing you face.

Wayne Stokes was a local man, and it seemed like every time he came in, he would beat us. We looked at Wayne Stokes every way we possibly could. He lived in Reno, and everybody knew him. We asked around and found that other places didn't have that experience with him, but when he came into our place, he just beat us. I came close to asking Wayne Stokes not to ever set foot in our casino again . . . but everything told me that he was as square as we were. Eventually, Stokes lost his whole bank roll at some other place—we never got a chance to get even with him. We had a lot of smaller players like that.

The few times I gambled, more often than not, I was unlucky. No matter what I did, I lost. I believe in luck, and a lot of people in our business are like me. Sometimes you'll change dealers, or you'll change decks, or you'll tell your dealer to stand on one leg, and then things change, and you say, "Well, it worked!" But we don't really know whether that's why it worked or not.

Certain dealers were consistently more lucky than others, and some were not. We pretty much always found that break-ins were luckier than experienced dealers. When we had a player that was betting some serious money, we would try to put our lucky dealer in there. You couldn't really blame the dealer if she was losing—she was just doing her job. You were there looking at her, and you could see that everything she was doing was fine, but it just seemed like she was unlucky more often than some other dealer was.

Managing a pit is challenging, and every time you turned in a winning shift, you felt good about it. You felt like you had accomplished something. That's what kept you in there doing it and kept you interested in what you were doing. Fortunately, you usually had a lot more good shifts than bad shifts, but when things went bad, it seemed they all went bad. If the blackjack tables were losing, than the crap tables lost; and then somebody would hit you on the wheel; and then the whole house would collapse. [laughter]

Because we were only going to have a 20 percent win, we expected some people out there to win, and that was fine—as a matter of fact, we wanted to keep our customers happy. But you were torn between two conflicting goals, really: you had to beat some people, because you had to turn in that winning shift; but you didn't want to beat *everybody* that walked into your place, because that would be bad for business. You had to send out *some* happy people.

In the years when I worked in the pit, when everything was going along pretty smooth—and the house was winning some money, but not a great deal—you sort of got into a rhythm, and there was kind of a hum throughout the casino. It made you feel that everything was wonderful. Much of the time that's the way it was, but every once in a while, the roof would fall in, and the hum wasn't there anymore. Anybody that's been in the business and worked on the floor has experienced that kind of thing.

In the end, the customers *always* lose money. The house wins for two reasons: it has the odds going for it, and it has the bank roll. The house can outlast losing streaks, whereas when the customer's luck turns, he doesn't have enough money to outlast a losing streak. Yet, I'd see these people that work for me go right out and start playing the minute they got off shift. I guess they thought that they were going to be the exception to the rule. [laughter] If anybody knows anything about gaming, it's those people that work in gaming and sit there watching it all day, day after day after day. For them to go out and gamble their money away until they have no more is ridiculous.

There was so much stress on pit bosses and shift managers that a lot of them had health problems. There was heart trouble; there were early retirements. But some stayed with it for the long haul. There were individuals that were able to live through it, but whiskey and cigarettes killed a lot of those people. At the end of a shift, you really needed a drink, and most everybody I knew had one as soon as they got off shift. Many times those few drinks led to a few drinks too many. I was fortunate that I never became addicted to alcohol, but many people in this business are, and many have a problem with nicotine.

We always gave our employees a free drink after a shift, and we allowed them to gamble in our house, just not in their own departments. The pit, for example, could play the slots, and the slots could play in the pit, and so on. We changed our policy a time or two, but we found that when we stopped our employees from gambling in our casino, they just went right across the street and gambled in the other guy's casino. We couldn't stop them, so we thought, "Well, we'll just stop them from gambling in their own department." That way they wouldn't be gambling with some dealer that they knew, so there'd be less chance for collusion.

My experience has been that people are going to gamble—you can't stop them. It's just like people that drink and smoke. Until people come to an understanding, like I did. . . . I quit smoking twenty years ago when I finally realized that it was going to kill me, and I cut way back on alcohol for the same reason. I never really had a gambling problem, but I could have easily wound up with a drinking problem.

When you, as a shift boss or pit boss, are getting your brains beat out, losing right and left, if you're going to do your job right, you make the customer believe that you're not "sweating" the game. You can't let the customer know what's going through your mind, and that's quite a balancing act, because you're walking around in that pit, watching your money go out the door. The customers are all having a good time, and they want to talk to you, and you want to be nice to them, because that's your job.

Customers prefer to play in a place where people don't sweat the money—where if you beat the house, the house is still nice to you. We succeeded in creating an atmosphere where our pit bosses didn't get all upset and allow the customer to see that we were having a difficult time because we were losing money. I think that was another important part of our success.

20

Too Old, Too Slow, Too Litigious

OUR PIT SUPERVISORS were old-timers that had been in the business for a long time—John Oliver was responsible for hiring most of them. John had brought in old-timers who knew the business well, who knew the mechanics of the game, who could tell if the house was being cheated, but who didn't understand what we called the "new ideas of gaming." They were the kind of guys that used to stand around with their arms folded, and a smile never crossed their face. We brought those people in and told them that ours was a different house. Yes, they would have to protect our games. Yes, they had to make sure that we weren't being cheated, either by our employees or by our customers; but they had to act as public relations people, as well. They could not just stand in the middle of the pit and glare at everybody. When we'd find a fellow that couldn't work that way, that just couldn't change his ways, we'd have to get rid of him.

One of the things we tried to do in our pit, and one of the reasons we were successful and made money, was that we tried to get a lot of hands out. The more hands you get out, the more money you're going to make, because you're going to have more bets. Now, there's a limit—you can't rush your players too much—but a good, efficient dealer can move a game along and get those hands out and make the house more money.

A man named Charles Kennelly worked for us many years as a pit boss, and eventually I made him our pit manager. He was doing a good job. Then he hired a man by the name of Don Dennis, and Dennis had a difficult time trying to change his method of operation from the old-timer's ways to what we wanted him to do.

Sometime around 1987, Kennelly decided that there were two dealers that weren't able to do what we required of them with the speed of their game. Firing somebody is a difficult thing to do, however, and many people duck the responsibility and assign it to somebody else when it's really their job. Kennelly never wanted to fire anybody. Don Dennis had been made our swing shift manager, and Kennelly told him these two ladies had to be let go. Don didn't feel the way Kennelly did, but Kennelly directed him to do it.

I was not aware that Kennelly and Don had had these conversations. It was a Saturday night, and I came in and walked the pit for awhile and then sat at a dead game and talked to Don and Chuck. When the shift ended, I left.

Don had told the two dealers that he wanted to talk to them. They waited outside the pit, and he walked over and said, "I'm going to have to let you two ladies go."

They said, "Why?"

He said, "Well, you're just too old and too slow."

One of them knew that this was way out of line, so she flagged a couple of our other employees and asked them to stand there for a minute, and then she looked at Don and said, "Would you repeat that please, so these other folks can hear it?"

Don said, "You're fired, because you're too old and too slow." So the two ladies had their witnesses.

I didn't know all this had happened. When I came to work Monday morning, I was told that these two ladies had been fired because they were too old and too slow. Immediately, I called our lawyer, Chuck Zeh, who was with the firm of Leeder, Sferazza and Zeh. He had started out working for legal aid, so he had represented a lot of these folks on the other side.

Chuck said, "Send telegrams to those two telling them that they're on the schedule. Give them a date to report back to work. Tell them to ignore whatever happened to them on Saturday night, that the company still wants them to be employed." So we did that, but they didn't answer the telegrams, and they didn't show up for work when we had them scheduled. (We had scheduled them right away, on Monday or Tuesday night.)

One of the fired dealers had gotten in touch with a lawyer, Erica Michaels, and her partner, Warren Goeddert. Michaels advised them not to report for duty, that she would file a lawsuit. So within a week or two, they had filed a lawsuit against the company alleging that they had been fired because of age discrimination.

We felt that we had done everything in our power to reverse the terminations, that it was not a policy of our company, and that we were not guilty of age discrimination. We had innumerable other people who worked in the same department, on the same shift, that were older than these ladies. We didn't fire them, and more importantly, we didn't hire younger people to replace the two who had been fired. The people that eventually replaced them were as old, or older, than they were. If, in fact, we fired people because they were too old, and then hired somebody younger, we might have been guilty of age discrimination; but we were not, in our view.

We felt comfortable that we had a good legal position, but it's always easier to settle these matters than it is to go to court. You don't like the publicity; legal fees are usually heavy; and a lot of time is spent getting ready for trial. So we attempted to settle these cases. All the time we were trying to settle, we continued the invitation to these ladies to come back to work, but to no avail, and they were not interested in talking to us about any kind of settlement. They and their lawyers felt that they had a great case and could not only prevail but exact punitive damages from our company. Punitive damages can be a very heavy penalty, because when damages are assessed, the plaintiffs can bring forth evidence of how much the company is worth. The whole idea of punitive damages is that they need to hurt the company, so you might take 10 percent of its worth, or 20 percent. That would be a pretty big hit for a $50 million company, and that's what these people were thinking about. That's why we couldn't settle.

We prepared for trial, because it appeared there wasn't any way out. We deposed a number of our dealers that were over the age of forty or forty-two. When you get over that age, then you are considered old enough to be eligible for a possible age discrimination suit if you are terminated. We had many dealers and other employees that were of that age, and we deposed them, so we could prove that age discrimination was not one of our methods of operation. Don Dennis was also deposed, and in his deposition, Chuck Zeh got him to say on the record that he had not used age as a criterion to fire these two women. He said he felt they were stale in their jobs and weren't producing, but age was not a factor.

There was a huge volume of work to do to prepare for the trial, which Zeh was going to try alone. Fortunately, our insurance company was involved, because those were the days before there had been a lot of these lawsuits, and insurance companies had not yet excluded these kinds of suits from their policies. In other words, they would pay on these kinds of claims, and they would pay on punitives, as well. We were insured, and the insurance company was paying for our legal defense.

It was a jury trial, because plaintiffs had asked for one, and during the trial they called forth me and Kennelly, Don Dennis, Bruce Dewing, Jon Bengtson, and most of our executive staff. They grilled us about how we felt about people over forty, whether we intended to do this, and so on. They also brought up the matter of our pension and profit sharing plan. The plaintiffs had been with us for several years and were about to be vested in our pension and profit sharing plan when they were fired. Their contention was that one reason we fired them was that we did not want them to be vested in the plan, because then their unused contributions would be split among those people that were still part of the plan. The executives, because their pay was much higher, were a big part of that plan, and that was one of their big arguments, which they thought they could make stick.

Initially, the trial did not go well for the plaintiffs, and their testimony was not good. It looked like we were going to be able to win that lawsuit. Obviously, they thought so, too, because they went out and hired a very fine trial lawyer. They even got a recess, as I recall, because when they brought in the new lawyer, he had to be brought up to speed. His name was Peter Durney, and he was a very eloquent, young, forceful attorney, who was experienced. When he took over the trial, things changed and went the other way. A pivotal factor was that Judge Schouweiler mysteriously sustained an objection to our getting it on record that Don Dennis had sworn he had not fired the plaintiffs because of their age. Durney swayed the jury, did a great job, and the jury brought in a verdict that we were guilty.

They awarded the two ladies about $1.6 million, which was reduced on appeal to about $300,000. The court dismissed the punitive damages, because we had done nothing wrong, but because these ladies had been out of work for two years or so, the court agreed that they should be compensated for the tips and pay that they had lost. I think they also gave them some money for the shame they had been through because they had been fired and so on.

The insurance company paid the awards, and they paid all our legal expenses. However, it had been a big drain on our time. It was an important case for us, and we had to do a lot of work on it. Mr. Zeh did a great job for us. We hired a lady, Fran Forsman, a lawyer in Las Vegas who specialized in this kind of work, and she did the argument for us at the supreme court level. There were briefs as well as oral arguments at that level. Zeh wrote the briefs and the argument, and we won that lawsuit.

We had fired Dennis and then filed a suit against him. Then he counter-sued us for age discrimination! [laughter] That's what happened, but the whole thing was settled out of court. The insurance company paid Dennis a few thousand bucks, and he dropped the suit against us, and we dropped the suit against him.

There's a lawyer in Reno who specializes in termination lawsuits and harassments: sexual harassment and sexual discrimination, age discrimination lawsuits. He became interested in our company because of the dealers' lawsuit and thought that maybe there were other opportunities to sue us. So my understanding—I don't know this for a fact—is that he began to investigate the company to see if he could find some potential clients. How it came about that he represented some of our employees, I am not sure, but it did come about. He filed several lawsuits on behalf of some. One was a law-

Chuck Zeh (right) did a great job defending us against possibly ruinous suits.

suit that had to do with our bartenders . . . . We had bartenders suing us. We had cocktail waitresses suing us. We had our sales manager, an attractive thirty year old lady, suing us, and maybe one or two other people.

In this period our human resources director left our company and went to work for the lawyer representing these people. We don't know this for a fact, but we have to assume that she gave the lawyer several leads on disgruntled employees. He would go after these people and talk to them about hiring him to sue us, leading to some kind of settlement, because he usually settled out of court.

We had several different things going on at the same time. The bartenders sued us because they said that we didn't allow them to take the breaks that they were entitled to by state law. They were supposed to have a break in the morning and a break in the afternoon, and they said that we told them they couldn't have their breaks. In actuality, what really happened was this:

When bar poker machines first came on the scene, bartenders found that their tokes were heavier than before, because people had money in their hands, and if they won, they'd tip the bartender. Bartenders were very happy with the bar pokers. As a matter of fact, they were *so* happy that they didn't want a relief bartender coming in and giving them a break, because they felt that while they were gone the relief bartender would get a few tokes that would rightfully belong to them. So they talked our bar manager, Vic DiMaggio, into allowing them not to take their breaks. Now, they'd take a break if they had no players; but if they had players that were toking, they'd stay. [laughter]

Nonetheless, a group of them got together, and this attorney filed a lawsuit that claimed we had not given them breaks. When the suit was filed, I brought Vic in my office and said, "OK, what's going on here, Vic? Tell me about this."

He said, "Here's the deal. Here's what happened: they didn't want their breaks."

I said, "Well, that's fine, Vic, and when the time comes, you can testify that they did this on their own accord."

Well, I believe Vic was subject to a great deal of pressure from the bartenders, because he knew what the real story was. Whatever the reason, he quit and got this lawyer to file a suit against us on his behalf. It wasn't wrongful termination, because he quit on his own; but sometimes they'd sue you for wrongful termination, saying they'd been harassed so bad they had to quit. We wound up settling for $30,000 or less.

Then we had a suit by a cocktail waitress. Then we had the head of our sales department, a lady around twenty-eight or thirty years old that claimed sexual discrimination and wrongful termination, as well. The cocktail waitress had been with us for quite awhile. She was in her thirties, and she worked the pit most of the time. As in any organization, especially in the gaming business, we had male supervisors who would treat females differently than males. They might allow the female employee to do things they wouldn't allow males to do, because the age-old sex thing was there. Maybe they were thinking if they did some favors for a female employee, the female employee might do a sexual favor for them. There was a lot of this going on between the pit supervisors, the pit manager, and the cocktail waitresses, dealers, and bartenders, and so on. No more than is normal in casinos, or maybe even any other kind of business. I think this is just a normal . . . . Women were sometimes given better stations or better schedules or better sections to work, and they were allowed to do things that the guys couldn't do.

In the suit by our cocktail waitress, she pretty much got what she wanted. We had a period of time there when we were talking about new cocktail waitress uniforms. Uniforms were important to cocktail waitresses, because their tips could depend on their looks and their revealing costumes or uniforms. It was important to them to have uniforms that revealed their legs and a lot of their breasts and so on, because they made better tips. Well, the cocktail waitress who sued us got in an argument with our seamstress because she didn't like the uniforms we were proposing the cocktail waitresses wear. She made many trips downstairs to the seamstress's office and got in a big hassle with her. Her pit manager and some of the other pit people protected her and didn't reprimand her for this kind of activity. Somebody at the executive level finally became aware of this hassle and the fact that she was being treated differently, the fact that *she* was taking a lot on herself. She was trying to get the seamstress to make uniforms the way she wanted them, rather than the way the company had instructed the seamstress to do it. So she was fired.

She hired the same lawyer as the others and filed a lawsuit against us alleging everything under the sun. She claimed she'd been sexually harassed by my sister's husband, who worked at the Sands for many years and never had a problem in that regard. It was simply a red herring; that was never true. And Dewing and I and any number of other people . . . .

The case went to trial—she wouldn't settle. It went to trial before judge Robin Wright, who had recently been elected to the district court. The case dragged on for years, with the cocktail waitress changing attorneys and so forth, and finally it ended with her being awarded $250,000. Then Charles Zeh threatened to appeal to the state supreme court, and the plaintiff accepted a smaller settlement. Our insurance company paid the settlement and our lawyers' fees.

The bartender cases were filed as a class-action suit. Then we had two or three dealers that filed suits. We had a couple of maids that filed. All these cases were pretty much going on at the same time, and a lot of this, we're fairly sure, was the result of the fact that our former personnel manager had left us and gone to work with the attorney who was filing them. He represented all these people.

The bartenders' suit was filed as a class action, but we filed a motion to split the suit into individual suits, each bartender against the Sands. Our legal advice was that we could better defend the suit if it was individual cases, because then we could deal individually with each bartender and make a settlement with each one. One guy might settle for ten thousand; the other guy might want fifteen or twenty or something. Anyway, we won that motion, and we got rid of the class-action suit.

With the bartenders, the issue was how much time had they really worked when they should have been on a break, and whether, in fact, they had really told DiMaggio they didn't want that time off. Unfortunately, we found out that the company was in the wrong even if they had told their supervisor that they didn't want their breaks. It was up to the company to make sure they took their breaks, so the company was in violation. What essentially happened was, we took each bartender, calculated how long he worked, and negotiated with him about how many breaks he'd missed. Then we paid them for the time that they had worked when they should have been on break. Most of those cases were settled for somewhere between five and ten thousand dollars apiece.

The attorney for the plaintiffs in all these cases made every possible effort he could to implicate me personally (or Bruce Dewing, Jon Bengtson, Dave Wood, or my brother-in-law) in a termination case. He dug into every possible thing that he could. He hired investigators, and he finally found out that I had been court-martialed when I was in the army. He spent two or three hours talking to me about why I was court-martialed in a deposition. And at the end of the deposition, I said to him, "Jack, you're in real sad shape if this is all you can find that I've done wrong in all these years."

One of the things that happened is that the lawyer alienated a lot of our employees. A lot of our employees didn't like the idea that he was suing us every day. It wasn't good for our business.

We had a lot of bad publicity that came out of the litigation. Probably worst of all was testimony from a cocktail waitress in the famous "penis colada" case. She told the court that when a customer was dissatisfied with his drink, and she brought it back to the bar manager to mix him a new one, he'd pour a drink and stir it with his penis and send it back to the customer. That testimony came out in one of those trials.

In the paper you'd see articles about this suit and that suit and the other suit. Fortunately for us, we didn't do a lot of local business. If we had been a hotel-casino that did a lot of local business, it would have hurt real bad. In our case, it didn't bother us that much, but we were members of the community, and everybody knew us, and we didn't feel good about that.

We took a lot of criticism. Plaintiffs' attorney just loved it, and he kept after us and kept after us . . . but one of the reasons he couldn't find much of anything bad is because a lot of our employees came to our defense. The lawyer and his investigators and our ex human resources director were talking to our employees and trying to dig up dirt on me and our executives, and many of our employees got disturbed about that. They viewed that as an attack against our company, and that helped us a great deal. Other cocktail waitresses testified for us in the case of the one who had brought suit, and that's pretty much unheard of. Usually, when something like that happens, employees don't like to testify against each other.

If any good came out of all this litigation, it was that we had been involved in a couple of landmark cases that established some important precedents. In the case of the two women who had sued us for age discrimination, the Nevada Supreme Court established that where there is a liquidated damages provision in the statutory framework, such as the Age Discrimination in Employment Act, an employee is limited to liquidated damages and cannot obtain punitive damages on top of them. The rationale was that Congress had spoken on the nature and quantity of relief that might be obtained, and thus had established limits. In this case, the available relief expressly did not include punitive damages.

The other landmark case within this flurry of litigation involved the state's "at-will" doctrine regarding lawful termination of an employee's services. ("At-will" meant essentially that an employee could be terminated without cause, at the will of the employer, so long as no law was broken through the action.) We fired a woman who worked for us as a tour bus coordinator or something like that; I can't remember why we fired her, but we did. She then sued us on the grounds that our employee handbook contained language that protected her from at-will termination. When the case eventually reached the Nevada Supreme Court, the court ruled that the mere fact that an employer has an employee handbook does not, in and of itself, alter the at-will employment relationship. Furthermore, the court concluded that there was no exception in the Sands's handbook to the at-will employment relationship, and that the handbook was in general so vague that no employee could use it as a defense. I think the case pretty well established that Nevada employers need not be concerned that in-house procedural handbooks somehow give their employees protection against at-will termination.

21

Multi-venue?

IN MAY OF 1990, the Dynasty Tower opened. It had 260 rooms, giving us a total of 940. We built that tower so that we had a porte-cochère that opened up on Fourth Street. That was the first direct access that we ever had to our property off of West Fourth Street. Before we built that tower, we had a driveway from Fourth Street to our lobby area, but the new tower extended our entire image right up to West Fourth Street. We immediately noticed a big increase in business, and some of it was local, because we had a bigger presence on Fourth Street than we had before.

Until we built that tower, during our busy times we found ourselves short of rooms. We had to cut off the sale of our packages in some instances, because we couldn't provide enough rooms. We had to curtail some of our bus charters, because we were at a maximum. Until we opened that tower, we had six hundred and some odd rooms, and between the packages and the tournaments and the buses, we were running 95 or 96 percent occupancy. That was why we could add 280 more rooms and fill them. As a matter of fact, we maintained that middle nineties annual occupancy rate, and we had additional casino space on the ground level.

One factor in our continued success was that airline deregulation went into effect. About thirteen airlines flew into Reno, some them regional ones. We gave Royal West Airlines a big block of rooms.

They flew in from Southern California and Arizona. They were only around for a couple of years or so, but we became their principal package hotel, and they sold a lot of low-cost tours, and they helped us a great deal. Of these airlines flying into Reno at that time, many were coming from the East Coast. TWA, Northwest, and Delta had a lot more flights than they do now. Our big supplier was FunJet, out of the Midwest. There were a lot more seats coming to Reno, and, because of deregulation, fares were very reasonable. That helped a lot of hotel-casinos in Reno, but it probably helped us more than anybody, because we were so big in the package business.

Because of the extra rooms that we had, we could also do more bus business. Bus operators would tell us how many rooms they needed on which dates, and we'd take whatever we could handle. If we couldn't take them all, we'd go out and find rooms for them at other properties. When we had that position with the bus operator, he gave us first call on rooms, and we controlled the rate, so that also helped us a great deal.

We also began doing convention business. We became known in the military reunion business, and in the 1980s you began to have the forty-year reunions of people that had been in the Second World War. Barbara Woodward, who did a lot of our tournaments, and Bill Irons, a veteran of the Second World War who is still doing some cribbage tournaments for us, got involved in one or two reunion groups. We were probably one of the first casinos to aggressively market those reunion groups. Reno was a fairly easy sell for reunion groups, because a lot of them liked going to gaming destinations.

We had 15,000 square feet of meeting space, and with our little sales department, we started to cultivate sales to regional groups. We belonged to the Sacramento Sales Managers Association, and when they'd have their monthly meetings, our sales department would go there and meet with them and get leads. A lot of California groups like coming to Nevada.

In those days, the downtown casinos pretty much didn't go after meeting groups. They were interested primarily in gamblers, and they overlooked this segment of the market. Until the Legacy opened, conventioneers were a bad name in some of the downtown casinos. But because we were one of the largest hotels, and we had meeting space, we weren't quite as busy as some of the leading casinos, and it worked for us. Conventions were actually discouraged by many casinos. That was an unfortunate thing that happened in Reno, but now it's changed, and conventions are encouraged.

In Sparks, John Ascuaga decided that, because of his location and the fact that he had to compete with Reno, conventions would be his niche. The only real convention hotel in Reno was the Hilton, and even the Reno Hilton for a long time discouraged conventions to go after gamblers. John Ascuaga realized that there was a big need out there, and that he could fill it, so he built a big convention facility, and it's done relatively well for him. If we had a bigger facility, we could have done better ourselves, but with the facility that we had, we did pretty good. Everything went fine for us until the Silver Legacy opened.

Conventions, reunions, tournaments, bus tours, and airline packages account for about three quarters of our business. We also get a certain amount of local business and what we call F.I.T. business—free, independent travelers. A lot of that is people coming in from California, Washington, Oregon, or Canada.

In 1952 the Sands Hotel in Las Vegas opened, and my dad and I went down there for the opening. It was as big an event then as when the Bellagio opened recently, and we went there to see it. I thought I was in the presence of greatness when I saw that place. I said to my dad, "If we ever open a casino, we ought to use a lot of the ideas that these folks have here." When it came time for us to build our hotel-casino, we had a long discussion about whether we should name it the Tropicana or the Sands, and we eventually settled on the Sands, because we liked the logo better and it was a shorter name; it was easier to remember, easier to put up on signs. We actually copied their sign—the sign that still sits out on Arlington Avenue is a smaller version of the sign that the Sands had in front of their place in Las Vegas.

We actually named our place the Sands Motor Inn, because at first all we had was rooms, and the Las Vegas Sands never bothered us. Nobody ever said a word. So we got known as the Sands. Well, in the early 1980s, Howard Hughes bought the Sands in Las Vegas, and after a year or two we got a letter from his law firm in saying that we were using the name in an unauthorized fashion. We were shocked. We went to our attorney, and there was a question about whether or not Hughes had the right to force us to quit using the name. We negotiated a deal with Hughes's people—we added the name "Regent" and called it the Sands Regent, and that satisfied them. They let us keep the signs that we had, but any new signs and any new printing that we did, we had to add the word Regent.

We thought we were over that problem. Then, about the time we went public, or just after we went public, we got a letter from the Regent Hotel chain. [laughter] And the Regent chain had pretty much the same thing to say to us as Howard Hughes. They said, "You can't use Regent. That's our name, and we got it registered." I didn't want to go to court. I've never wanted to go to court, and it was easy enough for us to change our name to Sands Regency, and that satisfied them. The public corporation that we registered with the Securities and Exchange Commission is stilled called the Sands Regent, however.

All the Regent people were concerned about is what we were advertising ourselves as being. Their story was, "Well, suppose we come to Reno and build a Regent Hotel?" They never did.

In the late 1980s and the first years of the 1990s, it became apparent to me that our business was not going to continue to be as good as it had been in the last several years. The signs were in our monthly, quarterly, and annual statements. One of the major trends that I picked up was that for several years we had been unable to raise our average room rate. (In our business we call it the ADR, the average daily rate.) In business, even a minimal two percent increase in costs, or inflation, on an annual basis means that unless you're able to raise your prices or increase your revenues more than that, you're falling behind. What I saw, and I'm sure other people in business in northern Nevada saw this too, was no increase in ADR.

We had an abnormally low ADR, anyway, because our business was based on a very reasonable rate for our rooms, the idea being that if people stayed with us, they gambled with us . . . or at least we got two shots at them: in the morning when they got up, and in the evening when they came back to their room.

We had built our business on the idea that you could stay with us for less in a superior room close to the other downtown casinos. Overall, you'd have the best value in downtown Reno. When the other hotel-casinos didn't raise their rates, we couldn't do so and remain competitive. With our package and our charter tours, we were in the same situation. In order to fill our charters, to be the lead property, we had to have the best value for the money. We *had* to maintain low room rates, and we were charging thirty-one to thirty-three dollars a night. Costs were creeping up, but hotel revenues were stagnant.

Gaming revenues were fairly stagnant, as well. We were getting into the multi-coin machines and poker machines, which have a lower hold percentage, so our gaming revenues were still somewhat stagnant. Another thing was that wages were creeping up, and we were caught in that squeeze. We were not keeping up with annual inflation; or, if we were, we weren't doing any better than that. We were still very profitable, but we did see our profit margins going down.

Another thing that was happening was that there were other states in the United States that were opening up gaming. The Indian casinos had just started, and we could see that Nevada no longer was going to have a monopoly on gaming. We had lived with Atlantic City for many years, but Atlantic City didn't hurt northern Nevada at all, because it was far enough away that it had no effect, but now there was a different situation, and from what we could learn, it looked as if several states were going to have gaming.

One day I had lunch with Jon Bengtson, probably in 1990 or 1991, and Bengtson said, "Where do you think gaming is going to be in ten years?"

I think I responded, "You know, gaming's going to be all over the country. So what should our company do about that?"

In our board meetings and with my family and my executives, we had long discussions about the matter, and we decided that we had different courses we could take. One would be to just sell the company and get out of the gaming business. Another would be to *aggressively* stay in the gaming business. We, at that time, still had no marketing department, still had no slot club, still had no computerized system to recognize our best players. We were still relying on the old shotgun approach where we tried to be nice to everybody and hoped they would all came back. That was no longer working too well. Our competition, especially the Eldorado, were taking away some of our better customers. We found that even the Nugget in Sparks was taking away some of our good customers.

In consultation with our investment bankers, DLJ, we decided that it was time for us to exit the business, but that first we should maximize the stock price for our shareholders and ourselves. DLJ laid out a plan for us. That plan was as follows:

The most successful publicly traded gaming companies at that time were multi-venue operations. And if you had operations in three or four states, the market liked that even better. The plan that DLJ laid out for us was that if we could acquire at least one other operation, preferably in another state, then there was a very good possibility that we could do a secondary offering. In that secondary offering, my family and I could divest ourselves of a large portion of the stock that we owned in the company. We might become minority shareholders or sell out altogether, depending on which family members wanted to be out and which ones didn't.

I still wanted to work in the business. I still felt that I had something more to contribute. I didn't want to retire. I didn't really want to start a new career. I was in my early sixties, and I never had any desire to retire at sixty-five, like a lot of people do, but some of the other members of my family would have been happy to sell out. We had a loan from First Interstate Bank (FIB) that the family had taken out to maintain control of the company, and with this secondary offering that we wanted to make, we could have paid FIB off. Then we, as a family, would be free to do whatever we wanted with our shares.

We talked a great deal about being more aggressive in our business, and what that would entail, and hindsight says we undoubtedly should have done that, but it would have meant we'd have had to hire a marketing director, and we'd have had to start a marketing department. We'd have had to put a slot card system in—all things that eventually we did, but at that time we thought, "Well, let the new management do that kind of thing." That wasn't our style of operation.

We began to look for opportunities. In May of 1992 the Sands made an offer to IGT to buy the Silver Club, the Treasury Club, the El Capitan, and the King's Inn Casino in the Bahamas. The story with that transaction was that IGT had co-signed on mortgages for Karl's Silver Club, the Treasury Club, the El Capitan, and the King's Casino. The man that was running those places, Roger Elton, had trouble paying IGT, but IGT didn't want to foreclose, because they didn't want to be in the casino business—they didn't want to be in competition with their customers. When he couldn't keep up payments, IGT wound up with his Silver Club and other properties. They wanted to get out, so they were casting around for somebody to buy these casinos.

IGT also had somebody who was talking to an Indian tribe in Iowa, and they told us that this Indian tribe had the ability and the approval from the Bureau of Indian Affairs in the state of Iowa to open a casino. The casino that they were going to open was about eighty miles north of Omaha, Nebraska, and it would have been the only casino that was in operation in that area at the time. (It was the Kickapoo Indian Tribe. I thought that was a joke, but it actually was Kickapoo.)

The way IGT presented the deal to us was, "You take over the mortgages on these properties here in Nevada, and we'll give you this Indian casino." Well, we didn't really want these properties, especially the Silver Club. We didn't like the Silver Club, and we didn't like the Treasury Club. The El Capitan was OK. (The El Capitan's always made money. It's the only casino in Hawthorne, and it still makes money.) But we thought if we could get that Indian casino in Iowa, it might be worth taking on these others. We didn't have any idea what was going on in the Bahamas or wherever the King's Inn Casino was.

It appeared that the Indian casino was the big prize at the time, so we flew back there and opened up conversations with the tribe. They had an old building where they were running a bingo game, and they wanted to convert it into a slot emporium. It looked like it was pretty well located, and we could have put five or six hundred slot machines in that hall, so that was the basis of the whole deal. We were trying to wrap up our deal with the Indians, and we were dealing with the state of Iowa, as well, to make sure that we'd be able to operate. They had a Racing and Gaming Commission in Iowa, and we determined that the licensing procedure wasn't going to be very tough, because we were a public company and were licensed in the state of Nevada. At least, that's what they told us. Then we got our first taste of dealing with Indians.

It's not that Indians are difficult, so much as it is their way of doing business is altogether dissimilar to our way of doing business. Each Indian tribe is a sovereign nation, so it's like dealing with another country, except you're dealing with the chief and the tribal council. There's a lot of turmoil and turnover, at least with the Indian tribes that I've heard about and the ones that I've negotiated with, and I think we may have gotten caught in that kind of a situation.

We had about three different meetings with the chief and some of the executive officers of the council, and we'd hammered out a memo that outlined all the facts, and we had an agreement. We were going to remodel the building, put in 500 slot machines and give them a percentage of the profits. After we drew the agreement, we faxed it to them and talked to them on the phone. They said, "OK, we're ready to sign. There's only two or three little problems that we're sure we can iron out."

So we told IGT, "Fine. We get these guys signed up, we'll go for this deal." IGT was really anxious to do this deal, so they flew us out there in their jet, and we had an appointment with the chief for eleven o'clock in the morning. When we landed at the closest airport, we drove to the tribal headquarters and told the receptionist we were there, and she said, "Fine. I'll tell the chief, and I'm sure he'll call you."

We sat out there for about an hour and a half and didn't hear anything from the chief. I finally went back to the receptionist. I said, "You know, we've flown all the way out here, and the chief said he was going to talk to us so we could wrap this thing up today. We'd really like to get out of here this afternoon so we don't get stuck here."

She said, "Well, I'll go tell him." She came back, and she said, "He suggests that you go have lunch." [laughter]

So we went and had lunch. Then I went back to see her, and I said, "What can you tell me?"

She said, "He's busy."

The long and short of it is, we sat around there for about four hours that day, and they never called us. We didn't know exactly what to do, so we told the receptionist, "Look, we're going to get on the plane and fly back to Reno. When the chief gets ready to talk to us, he's got our phone number. Have him call us."

We came back, a few days went by, and nothing happened. We tried to call the chief. He was unavailable. The upshot of the whole thing was we never heard any more from the Indian tribe, and IGT kept bugging us about doing the deal with them. We wouldn't. We told IGT, "Look, the only reason we got involved in this deal is because of this Indian casino." IGT found somebody else to buy their property, and the Indian casino, we understand, never got off the ground, for whatever reason.

But, there was an unforeseen consequence of that Kickapoo deal. Carter Lake, Iowa, is a suburb of Omaha, right across the Mississippi River. Carter Lake was kind of in a no man's land, because the river had changed course there, forming the lake after which the town is named, so Carter Lake could decide which state they were in, depending on what they wanted to do.

While we were going back and forth with the Kickapoos, Jon Bengtson introduced us to a man that he had met when he was with IGT selling gaming machines. He put us in touch with the mayor of Carter Lake, and the mayor took us to the state Racing Commission, and when we talked to them, it appeared as if we could float a casino on Carter Lake. We made a deal with the mayor and city council, and we talked to a ship builder in Texas that had a ship we could buy. It was like a river boat, probably 200 feet long, but we figured we could get about 400 slot machines on it, and everything was going along great. Then there was an election, and the mayor lost. The new mayor was against gambling and talked the city council into canceling the deal. That was the end of our Carter Lake deal. [laughter]

Then we looked at a casino in Wendover. Even though it was in the state of Nevada, Wendover is really an altogether different market than any other place in Nevada. After talking to DLJ about it, they felt that there was a possibility that a Wendover casino might work, but they still preferred an out-of-state casino, so we passed up a very good opportunity in Wendover. It was the Nevada Crossing, the one that Bob Berry had started. It was a truck stop with a casino and a little motel.

Actually, a lot of the reason we passed on Wendover was my fault. I looked at that operation, and I said, "There's no direct flight to Wendover." It was an eight-hour drive across the state to get there, or you had to fly to Salt Lake City and drive for an hour. It was a limited market. Salt Lake City was the only place you could look at for business, and if you did get more competition there, it would not be a good opportunity. What eventually happened was that they did not get more competition, and the place that we were looking at buying expanded and prospered. The truck stop was rebuilt and more rooms were added; so, as it turned out, it was a very bad mistake on our part that we didn't go into that project. It would have worked . . . but this is all hindsight.

We looked at one or two other opportunities. There was a river boat that was going to be moved to Sioux City, and we looked at that, and we made an offer on that, but we couldn't make a deal with those folks. There were other possibilities that failed to pan out.

Then, late in 1992, we were approached by Stanley McDonald. He and his son owned the Copa, a dockside casino in Gulfport, Mississippi. (Mississippi permitted that kind of gambling.) The Copa was a converted cruise ship that no longer had power and had been towed to Gulfport and moored at the dock as a floating casino. Si Redd had once unsuccessfully operated the ship as an offshore casino.

22

Down in Mississippi

STANLEY MCDONALD had a deal for us. He'd been a stockholder in our company for several years, and our company had been paying dividends and doing very well. His stock had been going up, so he had every reason to believe that we were good operators. He wanted us to go in with him on his dockside casino, the Copa. His offer seemed almost too good to be true, and we should have realized that it wasn't. Here was our dream. Here was what we wanted. We needed a venue in another state, and this man walked through the door and had this thing ready to go.

Rick Carter and Terry Green were to be his operators. They'd been born in Mississippi. They'd had experience operating an offshore gaming ship. Although there wasn't any licensing procedure for that, there was every reason in the world to believe that those folks could get licensed in Mississippi.

When McDonald sat down and explained the whole deal, he said that he wanted a partner. The word "partner" really grated on my nerves, because my dad had said many times, "You don't need partners." That was a big hump for me to get over, to decide that our company should be a partner, but our thinking at the time was, "Well, this is all part of our grand exit strategy to enhance shareholder value in the Sands. We're going to get this casino open. It's going to do well. It's going to complement our income. Our stock is going to go up. All our shareholders will benefit by getting a huge increase in the stock price. The Sands will have a huge increase in earnings. We're going to do a secondary offering. We're going to pay the bank off. We're going to be free to start divesting ourselves." At any rate, I insisted that the only way that we'd go into the deal was if we ran it, if we controlled it.

We didn't argue much about the money. McDonald told us that he would sell us 40 percent interest in the project for $6 million. He would agree that that $6 million would be used only to finish out the casino remodel on the ship, and that we could direct the casino remodel and build the casino the way we wanted it, because we were going to operate it. We probably could have shaved some money off of that, but our key aim was to be in control.

So we worked out a deal with McDonald where we'd be the managing partners, and we'd run the business, but on any other major decisions, we'd have 50 percent of the vote. For example, if it came down to selling the business or moving the ship somewhere, some major decision like that, then he had an equal vote to our vote, but we were to be allowed to run the business as we saw fit. On that basis, I agreed to the partnership.

We knew what was going on in gaming in Mississippi, and it looked like a tremendous opportunity for us, because at the time there were only four casinos in operation on the Gulf Coast. The Mississippi Belle was run by a man that had been in the restaurant business in Texas, who had no casino business experience at all. He came there because Carter and Green had told him what a great opportunity there was there. He had a little river boat with very low ceilings. It was smoky and crowded, and by no stretch of the imagination was it any kind of a casino; and yet, people were lined up, actually paying an admission fee of a few dollars to go aboard the ship to gamble.

Each ship had its own complement of passengers that could be allowed, and the fire department was counting the people getting on board. They were only allowing a certain number of people on. Then if five people got off, they'd let five more board. On a Saturday night you had a line a block long, and the other three casinos were the same way.

Another casino was the President Casino operated by a man named Connelly. He had operated passenger ships without gaming up and down the Mississippi River, so he knew the passenger ship operation, but he knew nothing about gaming. He just took one of those river boats and brought it down there, found a site, docked it, put some slot machines on it, and it was just like the Mississippi Belle.

A third casino operator was a man named Goldstein, who had also been a river boat operator like Connelly, and whose operation was similar to the Mississippi Belle. He called his operation the Isle of Capri.

The fourth operator was Marlin Torgeson. Marlin operated the Casino Magic. After Marlin lost his contract with the Indians, he was looking for another opportunity. He felt that gaming was going to be legalized in Mississippi, so he bought an old, small-boat harbor that was in bankruptcy and was located way back at the end of a bayou at a place called Bay St. Louis, fifteen miles west of Gulfport. This harbor was connected to a series of bayous that eventually reached the Gulf, but it was way back in the swamps. In order to get to this operation, you had to drive down some little, old, two-lane road that had no curbs and gutters. The main virtue of his operation was that it was the closest casino to New Orleans.

When we went down there with Loran Schmidt, he took us back to show us Marlin's operation, Casino Magic. I couldn't believe a man would have the nerve to go back in the swamps like that and spend millions and millions of dol-

lars, but he did, and it turned out that he was extremely vi-
sionary. He was the first operator, to my knowledge, to build
a casino on a barge. As a matter of fact, he floated four barges
back in there, tied them together, and snugged them right
up to the shore. Because it had been a small-boat harbor,
they had a bulkhead built along one side of the harbor, and
he just tied these barges right up to this bulkhead, and when
you walked in, you had no idea that you were on anything
that floated.

Marlin's casino was a prototype of what happened in
Mississippi. Most all the other casinos copied him. You'd put
a building on land. You walked into that building, and it was
like a big entrance hall, and when you walked from that building onto these barges, you had no knowledge that you were
on a barge. The knowledgeable folks knew that you were on
a barge, because there was a ramp there, because of the tide.
This ramp went up and down, but it moved very slowly, so
you didn't notice it. So when they tied those barges to the
land, they looked just like casinos look in Nevada.

Jon Bengtson and I went down there with Bengtson's
friend, Loran Schmidt, and we spent three or four days, and
we came away with our mouths hanging open. All they had
there were quarter and dollar slot machines. No nickels. No
dimes. There wasn't any table game less than a five-dollar
minimum, and most of them were ten, twenty-five, hundred-
dollar minimums.

It occurred to us that possibly there were going to be more
casinos, so we tried to figure out how many casinos were going to be allowed there. We knew a couple of folks that worked
for the Mississippi gaming commission, that had previously
worked for the Nevada gaming commission, and so we talked
to them, so that we could get all the knowledge that we would
possibly need before we went into business down there. They
identified for us a total of eight sites on the Gulf Coast that
they said were all the possible sites that could ever, ever be

developed as floating casinos under the regulations. After we acquired ours, there were only three more sites left. A total of eight casinos in that area, within a two-hour drive of 30 million people, sounded just fine.

We then looked at the seven-year lease that the McDonalds had with the port, because the port was going to be our landlord. One of the things we found that disturbed us was that it was a standard lease that was used for other purposes besides casino ships, and it had a clause that gave the port the right to move our ship after seven years if their maritime business required it. That bothered me, so we talked to the port director, and the port director said, "Don't worry. We have never moved anyone."

We talked to Carter and Green's lawyer, a man by the name of Hugh Keating, who had helped negotiate that lease, and he told us that, yes, it's true they had that clause, and it was also true that that clause could not be changed. But in all the years the port had been in operation there, they'd always lost money, and there wasn't any reason to believe that the port would want to fool with somebody that could make money for them. Not only was our lease over $41,000 a month, if we had any month that we took in more than $2.5 million gross gaming revenues, then we would pay them 5 percent of anything over that. With approximately eight hundred slot machines and twenty-four table games, including craps and a couple of wheels, in that 30,000-square-foot casino, our forecast was that we would do somewhere between four and five million a month, average; and because for the first seven years they couldn't move us, the risk appeared to be very small. So we agreed to accept the lease like that.

We made our deal with McDonald, and we actually signed it on New Year's Eve, 1992. Our conversations with Gaming down there led us to believe that there wasn't going to be any difficulty at all with licensing for anyone concerned, especially Carter and Green, because they were born in Mississippi, and as far as we knew, had never been involved in any activity that would warrant them not being licensed. It never occurred to us that they could not get licensed. It was a lapse, no doubt, in our judgement, but we felt that speed was important, because these four other casinos were doing so well, and we wanted to be one of them. We even felt that our forecasts were low, from looking at what the other casinos were doing. So speed was what we were interested in.

Another thing that was attractive about Mississippi was the cost of construction labor. They were paying carpenters twelve bucks an hour. In Reno we were paying thirty-five dollars an hour. Plumbers and other building trades, such as electricians, were getting wages in Mississippi that corresponded to the carpenters' wages, so the cost of construction was extremely reasonable. We ran a crew twenty-four hours a day to do the remodeling on the ship, because we could hire people to work the other two shifts for the same wages that we hired people to work the day shift. There wasn't any differential between shifts, and there was lots of labor available. We thought we'd be open for business by May at the latest, maybe even April. The only other casino that was scheduled to open that year was the Grand Casino in Gulfport, which was on the port property just west of the two piers, up on the highway.

The downside to the Copa was that we were way out on the end of the east pier, and customers had to wind around through the port and go through a gate with a guard to get to us. The guard didn't stop you or anything—he was just there; but it did discourage some people from driving in. And entry to the Copa was very poor, because you had to drive around a lot of trucks.

The main business of that port was bananas. The two big banana companies, Chiquita and Dole, were the main users of the port. They brought bananas up from Central America, loaded them on trucks, and the trucks then transported them to wherever they were going. So these refrigerated trucks were parked all over the port. The big truck parking lots were very unsightly. The Grand, because it was on the west end of the port, didn't have that problem. It was bad for our business, but it appeared as if we were going to do so well for at least two or three years that it was worth the risk.

The Mississippi project was so important to our company that I decided that I would move there. I'd recently married my third wife, and we had a child in 1991. Nevertheless, we moved to Gulfport so I could push that operation and get it open as soon as possible. It would be worth millions and millions of dollars to us to get the thing going, and rather than trust somebody else to do it, I thought that it would be best for me to be there. Jon Bengtson and Dave Wood were left in charge of the Sands. Actually, Bengtson pretty much ran the place. My son was working under Bengtson, and he was picking up more responsibility all the time. Also, Bruce Dewing was still with the Sands, and those are the folks that I left in charge.

I was probably the one in our company that knew the most about construction. I knew nothing about ships, but the structural stuff had all been done. It was now the finishes, and that was important. We had to lay out the count rooms, the executive offices, the restaurant area, and things that I was familiar with doing. The McDonalds had an architect who had experience doing passenger liners. He had done work for them when they had the Princess Cruise Lines. He also had done a lot of private yachts and was a qualified architect.

The casino looked very, very nice. The McDonalds had given the architect his head and let him do pretty much what he wanted, but my style was to work a lot closer with architects and the construction crew than the McDonalds had ever worked, and probably closer than most people. I wasn't there very long when I found myself in conflict with both the contractor and the architect.

We had our offices in a building at the end of the east pier that we were leasing from the port. You just walked out of the office and went across the pier, and the ship was right there. So we were on site, and I began to take part in construction meetings. It appeared to me that we were spending money needlessly in certain areas, so I put a halt to it. Well, the architect got ahold of McDonald, and then they got ahold of me, and we had our first "bust-up," you might say.

I said, "The deal we made is I'm in charge down here, and this is the way I see it, and this is the way it's going to be."

The next little problem that we had right in the beginning was I got a call from Immigration. They said that the Swedish structural engineer working on the job didn't have a green card, and if he continued to work for us, we were going to be fined. I was familiar with the green card situation, because we have all these people that work for us in Reno that are from Central America and Mexico that have to have green cards. So I knew what they were talking about. I got ahold of this fellow and said, "You have a green card or not?"

He said, "No, I don't have a green card."

I said, "Well, how is it you're here in this country?"

He said, "I don't know. You'll have to ask the McDonalds."

So I got hold of Kirby McDonald, and he said, "We'll fight the Immigration Service. We want this fellow here."

I said, "Look, I don't have time to be doing things like that. You ought to go out there and fire him. I'm not going to have this guy on the job, because I don't want to be fined." So I asked the Swede to leave, and the McDonalds became disturbed over that, and we didn't really get off to a good start. I brought in a guy we had worked with before to finish the job.

Kirby McDonald was associated with a company called Ogden Services. Ogden Services' principal line of business is furnishing all the foodstuffs, the labor, and the material for oil platforms. Kirby wanted us to contract with Ogden to do that same kind of thing for our casino down there, and I told him that I didn't think we needed Ogden's services—we had experience doing that in Reno for many years. But I didn't want to be at cross purposes all the time with our partners, and I knew that it was going to wind up hurting the operation if we were arguing with each other about every issue that came along, so I finally asked Bengtson to work with Kirby, and we hammered out a contract with Ogden.

Ogden furnished a lot of our foodstuffs and the plates and dishes for the restaurant that we were going to have, which really was just a glorified snack bar. Later on we did build a buffet restaurant, but in the beginning we started out with just the snack bar. We also contracted with Ogden to run our human resources department. The best deal we could strike with Ogden cost us forty or fifty percent more than if we would have done it ourselves, but in order to maintain the best relations I could with the McDonalds, I agreed to it for a twelve-month basis. At the end of that twelve months, we'd examine it, and if it was costlier, then we could get out of the deal. I thought, "Well, OK, for the first year, in order to get this thing opened and get going, instead of having a lot of problems, I'll do it like that."

In seventy-eight days Vic Tilly completed the remodel. That was by working around the clock, six days a week. The cost was much lower than it would have been in Nevada, because the labor costs were so much lower, but it chewed up most of that six million bucks that we had given McDonald. There would have been a great number of cost overruns, but after I got there, I started changing things, and it came in right about where we thought it was going to come in. That was in April.

Earlier we had filed our applications with Gaming in Mississippi. Bengtson and Dave Wood and I were the responsible people that had to be licensed. We hoped that the Mississippi Gaming Commission would pretty much rely on the investigations that the Nevada Gaming Commission had done and not go through the whole rigmarole all over again, and we had indications that that's what they would do.

Well, by April there had been a big exodus from Gaming. In Mississippi (unlike Nevada) you could walk out of the Gaming Commission and join a gaming company the same day. All the people that we knew in Gaming when we went down there went to work for private gaming companies, and Mississippi was having an awful time filling their Gaming positions.

The man that wound up running Gaming was somebody they brought in from another state, who had been a racetrack regulator and really knew nothing about gaming. Many of the people that investigate you for being licensed had been hired away, as well. They wound up using some ex-Mississippi state troopers for investigators, and, unfortunately, our investigations fell to one, a man named North. He or some member of his family had had some difficulty with Carter and Green, and I think it had something to do with a bankruptcy. North made it his business to do whatever he could to keep Carter and Green from getting licensed.

We didn't know at the time what was going on. All we could get out of Gaming was, "Well, you know, we're working as hard as we can, as fast as we can. You're going to get licensed. Things are coming along." Then they ran across the fact that I had been court-martialed in the army, and even though I was licensed in the state of Nevada and had been for many years, they made an issue out of it. The investigator called me and discussed the matter, and it appeared that he wasn't going to license me because of my court-martial. We were in an awful fix, and it just made us sick, because we could see all these other casinos making money hand over fist.

Well, we got over my licensing problem, but it added another thirty to sixty days to the procedure. The attorney that was representing the Copa knew an attorney who practiced law in Gulfport and had been in the Judge Advocate General's Corps in the U.S. Army. He knew the army regulations, and so we hired him. After some research, he convinced the Mississippi deputy attorney general that was handling gaming matters that just because I had had a court-martial in the army didn't mean that I had committed any felony. So eventually I got licensed.

By that time it was June, and Carter and Green still hadn't gotten licensed. There had been another change in the directorship of the Gaming Commission. We eventually got a sit-down meeting with this new man, and he told us that it appeared highly unlikely that Carter and Green were going to get licensed; or, if they did get licensed, the procedure was going to take another eighteen months. That was a disaster, of course.

Things had come to a head. We needed to get Carter and Green out of the business so we could go forward; but when we negotiated our deal with the McDonalds, we had agreed that we wouldn't try to buy the stock of any shareholder in their company. Since they had a closely held company, they didn't want an outsider being able to buy Carter and Green's stock . . . which would have been the right move for us to make—just buy their stock and get them out of there. Carter and Green were in the driver's seat. They had stopped our whole operation, and they were very difficult to deal with, but the McDonalds just didn't want to pay them what they wanted.

The negotiations between the McDonalds and Carter and Green took the whole summer. It wasn't until sometime in September that the McDonalds and Carter and Green reached an agreement that allowed the McDonalds to buy them out for some cash and a series of notes that were to be paid off over a few years. No matter how hard we argued and how much we pleaded with the McDonalds, we couldn't get them to do it any faster. I'm still puzzled as to why it took them so long. They were really penny-wise and pound-foolish. I know that Carter and Green were irresponsible in their demands, but the five casinos that were in operation at this time were doing so well that the McDonalds would have made it up, even if they would have had to pay them a little extra money. But it was just not in their nature to give in. They cost us millions and millions of dollars . . . and themselves, too, as far as that goes.

In the meantime, we had brought our key people down to Mississippi and had begun to train dealers. There was a shortage of housing down there on the Gulf Coast, so it was a lot easier to hire and train people that were already living there, rather than bring somebody in. You'd bring some key people in, and then you'd train slot mechanics, dealers, and other folks that you needed for your operation.

We had a casino manager named John Brevick, who had worked at the Reno Cal-Neva for many years. He was already there when we came on board, and we kept him. We set up a pit in the building where we had our offices, and we trained dealers. But there was a problem: we'd get these people marginally good enough to deal, and when they felt that they were competent enough, they'd just run off and get a job. So we just kept on training dealers. We must have trained half the dealers down there on the coast! [laughter] It was costing us money.

Our deal was that once the ship opened, if we had a short-fall or needed extra cash, the McDonalds would have to share fifty-fifty—but first we had to get the ship opened. What had looked so promising was becoming a looming disaster. I found myself in *the* most difficult position I had ever been in in my business life, and I wasn't handling it very well. So I prevailed upon Jon Bengtson to go to Gulfport and run the operation there, and I moved my family back to Reno. Jon did a better job of holding things together there than I would have done. It was good of Jon to go down there and do that, because summer down there is like being in a steam bath all the time.

I had worked out some marketing ideas when we knew that we were going to go into business in Gulfport. Our plan there was based pretty much on what it was here, and that was buses and airplanes. There was a brand new regional airport in Gulfport, about three miles from the ship, and they had a new terminal that had second level loading for at least six airplanes at the same time. Boeing 737's and the other normal jet airplanes that all the airlines flew and the charter people flew could be handled out of this brand new terminal. No major airline was flying in and out of Gulfport, so it was a beautiful setup for charter business.

The Canadian Holiday Company that I dealt with in Reno had a very extensive charter operation from eastern Canada to cities in Florida. Through Bill Robinson, the man that I had done business with in Reno, we began working on an arrangement with Canadian Holidays to fly people directly from Toronto, Montreal, and so on, to Gulfport.

We had no rooms, but there was a string of motels up and down Highway 90 right close to our ship. Those folks had been in a depressed state of business, and we had done some preliminary work and knew we could line up rooms for the charter passengers. We had to put everything off when we couldn't open, but the charter business looked like it held a lot of promise if we could get it going.

We felt we could get side trips out of the hundreds and thousands of people that Canadian and other charter people were flying into Florida. We could sell an add-on package to all those people that were going to Orlando and Fort Lauderdale, and if we had a charter operator that could fly them from Florida over to Gulfport for a couple nights, it would be great. We tentatively set that up with Canadian and a couple of other operators, so it looked real promising—if we got open.

Another thing we did was contact Frontier Travel, which is owned by a man named Lippencott. Frontier is one of the biggest movers of bus passengers in America. We made an agreement with Lippencott that he would furnish us with bus customers, and we'd pay him a commission. We gave him an office in the complex that we were renting from the port. He put his own phones in and began to line up buses, but we had to send them to other casinos, because we couldn't take care of them.

When we finally got open and got into the off season, we needed buses badly, and I wasn't satisfied with what we were getting from Lippencott, so I instructed our general manager to go into the bus business ourselves. Then we got into a lawsuit with Lippencott . . . but it was important to do that to get that business. I still to this day never understood why Lippencott wasn't able to produce. He does so well up in the Reno-Tahoe area.

We opened the thirtieth of September, 1993, and we should have opened no later than May. So we lost that summer when there would have been no more than five casinos open. Just to give you an example of how it could have gone, there was a casino called Splash that opened in Tunica, about thirty miles from Memphis. After a week or two, Gaming closed them down, because they couldn't count the money fast enough. When Gaming showed up over there, they found rooms full of uncounted money, mostly coins, so they closed them, brought in a "Big Eight" accounting firm, made them count everything and start over again. Then they let them reopen.

The Grand, right next door to us, was a huge operation. Lyle Berman owned it. He really knew his stuff, and he had the land and the room and the money, and he opened up with 2600 slot machines. He did the same thing that Marlin did in Bay St. Louis. He tied four barges together, and then he built a sea wall, tied the barges up to this sea wall, and built an entrance building on land, so it looked like you were walking into a Nevada casino. He had two floors and a huge parking lot out in front. He hit the jackpot.

We were paying $18,000 a month all the time we weren't open. And we were paying wages to key people and training dealers, so by the time we opened, we had invested eight or nine million dollars in the place.

When we opened, we were ready to make some money. We had 840 slot machines and twenty-four tables, and our slots were all quarters and dollars, like everybody else at the time. But we quickly found out that it wasn't going to work. Within a few months after we opened, at least four other casinos opened. We had been told that there could only be eight casinos licensed in the area, but there was a tremendous amount of pressure on the state government of Mississippi to create new sites, so they gave in. Eventually, there were fourteen casinos where we thought there would be no more than eight.

There was a big bay called Back Bay, and it was supposedly off limits. One day we woke up, and the Gaming Commission had decided to allow casinos in Back Bay, so three casinos opened there. The center of the casino business in the Gulfport-Biloxi area is in Biloxi, because the shrimp-boat

"When we opened, we were ready to make some money."

center was in Biloxi, and that's where there was a chance for them to build more casinos. Gulfport really only had the Port of Gulfport and one centralized shrimp-boat harbor that the port ran; and that's where all the shrimp boats were parked, so there wasn't room for a casino there.

The port authority of Gulfport had a big change during the first few months that we were there. When we came, a man named Bill Edwards was the port director. He was the man that Carter and Green and McDonald had negotiated a lease with. Bill Edwards had seen the port lose money for many years. At every legislative session, the port used to have to go to Jackson, the state capital, and ask the legislature for more money. Edwards was sick and tired of doing that, and he was on the verge of quitting, but when he found that the Grand and ourselves were going to pay him the kind of rent that we were forecasting, he knew that he didn't have to go to the legislature anymore—his port could make money.

It was Bill's idea to turn the port into as many gaming sites as he possibly could, and he drew up plans in that regard. He talked to Carter and Green about it, and he talked to us, and our initial reaction was that we thought that it was going to be bad for us, because it would be too many sites, too many casinos. Then we began to think that it would be a good idea, because we'd create a center, and, as we knew in Reno, people like to move from one casino to another. So we think if Bill Edwards had been able to follow his plan, we would have been much more successful. Instead, the port authority, a five-member board with Bill as the executive director, decided that they wanted to make the Port of Gulfport as big a commercial port as New Orleans or Mobile. When they got this promise of money coming in from gaming, their thinking was not to create more casino sites, but to create a bigger, better port. So there was a tussle going on between the authority and Bill Edwards, and they fired him.

We got caught in the middle of that argument and lost and didn't even know it was going on until later. They then hired a new director from the West Coast. His name was Anthony Terroamina, and they gave him instructions that the port was to grow—not gaming, but the port. He came up with the idea that he would develop the port into what's called intermodal transportation, or container shipping. This intermodal plan required that the site the Copa was on be eliminated. They began to try to get rid of us even before our seven-year lease was up.

Probably the worst situation that we had was with their Gaming Control Board. (They called it something else, but it was akin to Nevada's Gaming Control Board.) They had three commissioners. One of the commissioners was a man named Ingram. (They called him Captain Ingram.) Ingram had an interest in a stevedoring company that did business on the port, unloading mostly bananas. It was to Ingram's interest that the port lean in the direction of being a port and handling freight so his stevedoring company could get that business. It took us awhile to figure it out, but we came to believe that Ingram would do everything in his power to keep us from being successful.

Shortly after we opened—and I'm fairly positive this was at Ingram's instigation—the Mississippi Gaming Commission retroactively decided that all casino barges and ships had to comply with a regulation stipulating that ships must be anchored to withstand 155 mile per hour winds. A couple of decades before, hurricane Camille had come ashore in the Gulfport area and actually thrown some ships across Highway 90; but those vessels were, to my understanding, somewhere in the hundred-and-fifty to two-hundred-foot length. All the casino barges and ships in Mississippi waters in 1991 were much bigger than that. Our ship, for example, was 500 feet long. But Gaming just said all the dockside casinos had to comply, period.

The barges had a much easier time of it than we did, because they were anchored in very shallow water. Most had a draft of only about six or eight feet, and they pretty much were in water of eight feet. The truth is that a lot of those barges just sat on the bottom! [laughter] But some of them had six inches or a foot of water underneath them. Our ship had a draft of twenty-eight feet. The port had dredged a channel out to thirty-two feet, and that's how we were able to get the ship in there. Where we originally anchored on the end of the east pier, we were deep enough, but we had to dredge out our permanent anchorage.

In order to comply with this regulation, we consulted two or three engineering firms. The best that they could work out for us was that we had to have three anchors on each side of the ship and one in front and one in back, and they had to be out on an angle that put them beyond our leased area. The port, because they saw that this was a way to get rid of us, wouldn't give us the right to put these anchors in.

They caught us between the regulations and our leased premises, and it was a deliberate act on their part to get us to leave.

Gaming drew an arc six hundred miles south of our site. Any tropical storm or hurricane that came within this arc forced us to call two tugboats from New Orleans to come to Gulfport and stand alongside to tow us out of the harbor if Gulfport were threatened by the storm. We were forced to retain the services of a tugboat company in New Orleans. Those tugboats cost nine hundred bucks an hour apiece, but every time there was a hurricane in the Caribbean, we had to call for both of them. That's the only way we could stay in business.

Hurricane season runs from June to November, but the bulk of the hurricanes usually come between August and October. September is probably the heaviest month. Almost every year we had at least one, and sometimes two. One year we had three hurricanes. So every time we'd hit one of those, it cost us two or three hundred thousand bucks, and we had to stop operations. No gambling. We were the only ones down there with a ship like this. Everyone else had a barge. This was worse than a thorn in our side—it was almost a disaster.

After we were in business a few months, we weren't making anything near what we thought we were going to be making, and we attributed that to the fact that we had a lot more competition that we had planned on. Also, our location was the worst location on the coast at the time; but I guess we got what we paid for. These other people were spending upwards of a hundred million dollars or so to get good locations and bring in their barges, and we were in there for ten or eleven million dollars. Nonetheless, it became imperative that we get a better location.

There was an area in the port called the Horseshoe, the land between the east pier and the west pier. The port had no use for it, and they dumped a lot of timbers and other debris there; but it was the area closest to Highway 90, and the port had built a road directly from Highway 90 to this site. Evidently, they had planned to develop it at some time in the past, so they had built this wide, two-lane road that could accommodate huge trucks. The lanes were twelve feet wide, but the road was hardly used at all.

In our lease, we had the right to move to this site. In order to dock the ship there, we would have to build a pier, but that was our plan, and the McDonalds agreed that after a year or two, when we had acquired enough money through the operation of the business, we'd move the ship up to the Horseshoe site. The port also wanted us to move there, be-cause if (when) we left, the pier we had built would belong to them. We would have to make it a deep-water anchorage, because our ship drew twenty-eight feet, and if we left, it could be used by the port to bring in banana boats or other big cargo ships. We made an agreement with the McDonalds. They would put up half the money, and we'd put up the other half, and we'd build a pier at the Horseshoe, pave the park-ing lot, and move the Copa there. Then we would be at the end of a road, only about a quarter mile from Highway 90. We negotiated a lease with the port that gave us the road as part of our premises. It included a plot of land where the road met Highway 90 where we could put up a sign. Prior to that, we didn't have a sign on the road, because we couldn't find a location to put one up, but we had billboards along Interstate 10, the main traffic mover east and west. We used the slogan: "Gamble on the only luxury cruise ship on the Mississippi coast."

The ship was an old ship, but it had good lines, and its interior was really nice. We painted it white, so it looked like a luxury cruise ship. Out on the pier at the new site, we built elevators to its main deck. It wasn't like entering a ship— you'd go in a building, get on an elevator, go up a couple of flights to the casino level, and then the elevator would open, and you'd just walk right out into the ship, so it was real handy to get off and on. It was almost as good as the barges. We were limited in our space, however, because at the widest point, our ship was only eighty feet wide, and it narrowed down at each end, especially in the bow.

Our revenues increased at the new location, but not nearly as much as we thought they would. We spent $7.5 million to build the pier. When we started building it, we made two payments to the contractor, then the McDonalds said, "We're not going to help fund this thing, because we don't like the way you operate." (We'd had arguments about a lot of little things.) That left us in a situation where we either had to buy them out, sue them, or go into bankruptcy. So we filed suit against the McDonalds to force them to put up their share of the money, and we discovered that they had made provisions for this kind of a situation. They had set up a series of corporations and partnerships, and they'd insulated themselves from being financially responsible. All we had were two or three dummy corporations or partnerships that we could go up against, who had no assets. We found out in our lawsuit that unless we were able to "pierce the corporate veil," which is a legalism for getting to the source of the money—which is difficult to do—we weren't going to be able to force them to put up that money.

We had a partnership, and each partner is responsible by law for his partner's debts. We had already contracted with Tilly to build this pier, and . . . literally, the McDonalds forced us to buy them out. We had to stop construction until we negotiated some kind of a buyout, and it was a very difficult process. It took several months, because they were unreasonable.

I was fully prepared to put the Copa into bankruptcy, and I hired two bankruptcy attorneys, one in Nevada, and one in Mississippi. I put the Chapter 11 reorganization papers through the bankruptcy attorneys and sent a copy to the McDonalds that told them that this was my answer to their actions, and it brought them around somewhat. We negotiated a deal where we would pay them $3.5 million, which is the amount of money that they had in the deal, giving them $1.5 million of stock in the Sands Regency as part of the purchase price. They also insisted that we buy their corporation, Gulfside Casino, Inc., and if we bought the corporation, we would obligate ourselves to make the payments to Carter and Green that they had negotiated in order to get Carter and Green bought out. So we would have that liability, as well. That was originally $6 million, but probably down to five million by then—they'd made some payments.

I was alone at the time. Bengtson had left me again, because he had an opportunity to do something that was better than what he could do with us, and I had absolutely no idea which way to go. I took my family and went to Maui and sat on the beach for several days and took walks and tried to figure out how to extricate myself and my company from this terrible problem that we had. In the end, because our company had cash, I went ahead with the deal. Our company in Reno was still doing as well as it had before. This was in 1994, and although the future didn't look good, we still had a cash flow of eight to ten million dollars a year. I had to build the pier and move the ship, because I was convinced that we couldn't ever be successful without it.

What finally tilted the balance for me to go in that direction was that I had just completed negotiations for a sale of property just north of Circus Circus on Virginia Street, property that my father had begun to acquire in the 1960s, when he was thinking about building a casino there. We had never done anything with it, and we had practically a whole block between Sixth and Seventh Street, and between Virginia and Sierra. When the Legacy project was put together, Circus Circus felt that they needed additional garage space, and I was able to complete a deal with Clyde Turner, who at that time was president of Circus Circus. I sold that property to Circus Circus for $6 million cash.

We could have had a huge tax bill on the sale, because five million of it was capital gain, and we would have had to pay 20 percent of that as tax. However, our tax attorney showed us how to take that six million and invest it in Mississippi, and we didn't have to pay that 20 percent tax. So, partially because we had that $6 million sale, and we needed to save the tax on it, I decided to go ahead with the project in Mississippi. That meant, with all of our costs and expenses combined, we were by then into the project for about $24 million.

We weren't doing as well as we should have, so Bengtson, while he was still down there, hired a man named Dennis Connally, who did a very creditable job of managing the place for us. Also, I finally broke down and hired a marketing director, Neil Narter, who'd been in the marketing department at Fitzgerald's. Even before we bought out the McDonalds, he got a good bus program going for us. We never did get our air charter off the ground.

We decided that we had to be a local casino. It was very hard for us to appeal to tourists, because there were all these other casinos on Highway 90 and in Bay St. Louis. Our whole thrust, except for the buses, had to be towards local people. Neil understood that, and he created a number of programs.

Gulfport was an area that had a large number of retired people, a lot of ex-government employees. Mississippi has a number of military installations, and a lot of military people retired there, because it was a very reasonable place to live. Because of all the retired people living there, Neil started some senior-citizen programs, and they helped a great deal.

One of our most successful programs was one where, three days a week, anybody that was fifty-five or older would get a free breakfast. We had enlarged our snack bar dining area, and we had also taken another portion of the ship and put in a buffet line. There was a huge kitchen on that ship, but it didn't meet the code—the ceilings were too low. However, we were able to go out in the community and find restaurants that had big enough kitchens where we could prepare food, bring it on board the ship, and serve it. We contracted with two or three different restaurants, and that's how we ran our buffet. The buffet wasn't costing us any money, and we weren't losing any money on the snack bar, either, so we were able to maintain the food operation.

We used that senior-citizen promotion to get people in. Three or four hundred seniors would come in three days a week. We started serving about eight o'clock in the morning, because most of those people got up early, and a number of them would stay after breakfast. We'd do little bingo games, and we stole an idea from John Ascuaga's Nugget—we did house giveaways, because you could buy a house on a lot down there for about forty-five or fifty thousand. The house giveaways worked out good. We did car giveaways, but the other casinos started to do a lot of car giveaways too, so they weren't quite as popular as our house giveaway.

Neil came up with a program that we've used at the Sands a couple of times, and we're going to continue to use it, and that is the "Bye-Bye Landlord" program. The way that works is, first of all, you have to join the slot club. Then, every time you buy change or hit a jackpot or go to the restaurant or make any number of transactions in the casino, you get a ticket, and that ticket is deposited in a drum, and then there's a drawing. Usually, you have a drawing every sixty to ninety days, and the winner of that drawing gets a year's free rent. We pay a year, up to some maximum amount, or we make the winner's house payments for a year in that program. Neil instituted that program down in Gulfport.

We continued to be harassed. We had a clause in the lease that said we couldn't sit on the bottom. Mr. Terroamina, the new port director, decided that our ship *was* sitting on the bottom. He hired divers without our knowledge to go down and check it from time to time, then he'd come up with a report and say, "On such and such a time, your ship touched bottom, so you're going to have to dredge out from under the ship, or we're going to cancel your lease."

Worse than that, Terroamina would call up Ingram and say, "Look, they're sitting on the bottom."

Ingram would go to the gaming board and say, "Take their license away. They're sitting on the bottom."

So we continually fought that battle. I can't tell you how many times we had to bring in dredging outfits to dredge out under the ship, and they're not cheap. If I remember right, to dredge out from under a ship while it's sitting there cost something like thirty or forty dollars a yard; and if we had to move the ship, we had to close the gaming operations while we moved.

Then they resorted to a strategem . . . . Chiquita Bananas had the pier just to the west of us, and the freighters that came in there to unload bananas had what they call side-thrusters on them. When they'd come up to a pier, they'd get within thirty or forty feet of the pier, and then they'd turn their side-thrusters on. They were kind of like a jet on the other side of the ship, and the thrusters would just push their ship over to the pier, and then they'd tie up. When they used those side thrusters, they would churn up a lot of the bottom; and at Terroamina's suggestion (we believed), they'd come in and use those side-thrusters sooner than they needed to, and we'd get a lot of silt piled up under our ship.

We continually fought that battle. We were getting ready to file suit against the port, and the port knew, because Gulfport was a small community, and you couldn't keep anything secret. So the port beat us to the punch. They filed a suit against us, asking for us to be evicted because we were sitting on the bottom, and various other charges that were not true.

They wanted to file a suit first, because they wanted to get us into what in Mississippi is called a chancery court. A chancery court is supposed to deal only in disputes that have to do with equity, and in Mississippi the judges in a chancery court do not even have to be lawyers. Anybody can run for the office. Through our legal firm in California, Latham and Watkins, we were directing our Mississippi lawyers in how to handle the legal problems we had in Mississippi. We hired Phelps-Dunbar, a national law firm that had headquarters in Jackson, Mississippi, at the urging of Latham and Watkins, because they said we needed good counsel. So we wound up at one time, sad to say, with fourteen lawyers on our payroll because of the various problems that we had with Gaming, with the port, with Carter and Green, and with the McDonalds.

In chancery court the judge didn't care about the law. He just looked at it and said, "Well, this is what I think." Every time we went to chancery court, we lost. Eventually, Carter and Green sued us in chancery court. The port sued us in chancery court. Some subcontractor that did a job for us that we weren't satisfied with sued us in chancery court.

Then the Army Corps of Engineers made us take all our dredged-up bottom to an approved dumpsite, because they said it was contaminated. The trucking company that we hired charged us to take the materials to an approved dumpsite, but they dumped it somewhere else, and the corps found out about it, and *they* sued us. [laughter] Then we sued the trucking company, and then the trucking company sued us, and we wound up in chancery court again! So we had a series of lawsuits to contend with, besides everything else that was going on.

The port won its suit against us in chancery court, but we knew there was at least one way to keep them from forcing us out of there. Our Los Angeles attorneys advised us to put Gulfside Casino, Inc., which was the corporation that we had bought from the McDonalds, into bankruptcy. Going into bankruptcy would keep us sitting where we were until we went through the reorganization procedure, and the port could not evict us, because every time we'd lose a case, we'd appeal it. We thought that once we got up to a court that was run by real judges, we might win one of those suits . . . but the appeal process takes forever. Months and months and months went by, and we were hanging by our thumbs, so to speak.

Once in bankruptcy, we said Gulfside Casino, Inc. didn't have the money to pay Carter and Green, and we stopped paying them what we owed them. They sued us in chancery court. Their note was against Gulfside, Inc., and we had bought out that corporation and put its assets into our entity, Gulfside Casino Partnership. Gulfside, Inc. had no assets, but chancery court still ruled that we owed Carter and Green their money. Not only did we owe them that money, but the ruling was that after we paid all our expenses at the end of every month, whatever loose cash we had, we had to give it to Carter and Green until we paid them off! [laughter]

We resorted to a strategy of charging the partnership with services that the Sands was performing. We also made a deal with the tugboat operator over in Louisiana, and we transferred a million dollars earmarked for tugboat rental to a bank in Louisiana, so we kept from having to pay Carter and Green anything.

There was always something you had to be concerned about, and we spent more time working on all these problems than we did running our business. The first general manager that Jon Bengtson hired, Dennis Connally, wanted to move back to Nevada after he was in Mississippi a year and a half, and Neil was doing such a good job with marketing that I decided to make him general manager. Neil kept the place together for us. He did a great job. Without Neil, we'd have been in bankruptcy. (Come to think of it, we *were* in bankruptcy.) We kind of kept him isolated and tried to keep him focused on running the business, and he reported directly to me. I gave him a lot of latitude. I could see he was doing a good job.

The only good thing that came out of Carter and Green's business was their slot manager, John Mott. He was a very conscientious, hardworking slot manager. He knew the slot business, and he created good relationships with the major slot suppliers, IGT and the other companies down there.

We had started with quarters and dollars, but we had to get a whole bunch of nickel machines in there and get rid of most of our dollars, because with our local play we needed mostly nickels and quarters. We didn't have a lot of video machines, and as videos became more popular, we had to bring in video equipment. So we had this huge shift in the gaming area.

We also had to cut down the number of table games, and I think we wound up with about sixteen rather than twenty-four. We had to lower our limits, and we had to get rid of John Brevick. John and I had several disagreements, because he felt that we should be aiming for high rollers and we should have high limits. Well, it just wasn't going to work. I was sure it wasn't going to work. All the other casinos *quickly* had to shift their whole focus also. It's not a real high-roller area.

I don't know why anybody would take a summer vacation there, but we found that July was our best month. There were two good months down there, February and July—February because of Mardi Gras. Every little town has its own

Mardi Gras celebration, and Gulfport has one. New Orleans has the big one. Fat Tuesday is the biggest day of the year. All the businesses close, and they have a parade down the middle of the main street. Leading up to the Mardi Gras they have these huge parties and dinners. It's just a huge event that we knew nothing about before we went down there, but we took advantage of it. It's great for the gaming business.

In the end we wound up doing twenty-four or twenty-five million dollars a year in gross gaming, but our nut (our overhead) was about fifty thousand a day, so that's a million and a half dollars a month. If we hadn't had to fight all the legal battles, and if we hadn't had Carter and Green to fight, and if we didn't have the problems with the Gaming Commission because of Ingram, we would still be there. It wouldn't have been a really good investment, but we would have made a return on our money. We made a niche for ourselves. It is still one of the best local casinos down there, and they're still doing the same amount of money that we were doing.

We sold out in 1998. New Year's Eve, again, was the day we made the deal. A man named Harvey, a retired air-force general, became head of the Gaming Commission. Carter and Green appealed to him through some friends of his that it was unfair that they were denied a license. He allowed them, even though they were not actively running a casino, to become licensed. Once they became licensed, then we were able to talk about selling the casino to them, because it became apparent to us that our troubles were almost insurmountable. It looked like the best thing to do would be to get out of Mississippi.

23

900 Pound Gorilla

AFTER FERENC SZONY came on board with the Sands Regent, he looked at the Copa and said, "This is not good for the company. It has depressed the stock. It's a no-win situation, and we should try to make a deal with somebody and try to get rid of this thing." So we sold the Copa to Carter and Green. They didn't have enough money to pay for it, but it was obvious to us, because of all the political problems that we had, that local people had to own that casino, so we made a deal with them. They pay us 2 percent of the gross gaming revenues on a monthly basis. They have to send us the form that they file with the state of Mississippi, so that we can verify their gross gaming revenues. We have a minimum payment coming from them of about $8.5 million, based on that 2 percent figure, with a maximum price of twenty million, depending on a certain number of factors. As long as they stay in business, they pay us. Ultimately, it would end once we got $20 million, but it could end sooner.

It just shows you what can happen when you're a native of a state and have access to public officials. Mississippi licensed these two fellows, even though they had no operating casino, and neither Nevada, to my knowledge, nor Mississippi, nor any other state, ever licensed anybody who didn't have an operation! [laughter] So these guys were licensed and ready to go. They knew all the players.

Our original reason for going to Mississippi was so we could have a secondary stock offering of a multi-venue operation. Our investment bankers were telling us a couple of good quarters were all we needed, and we could do an offering. We could get that stock price up to the mid twenties, maybe even more than that, and all shareholders would benefit. That did not come about, because the Mississippi operation didn't do well. If we'd have been able to open in May or June like we planned, we'd have been all right. I liken it to reaching for the brass ring and falling off your horse. [laughter] It was a real shocker to us, and it was so difficult, because we were so very, very close to success.

Sometime in 1993 the Eldorado and Circus Circus jointly announced that they were going to open a project on the land that the Eldorado owned between them and Circus Circus facing Virginia Street, between Fourth and Fifth Street and as far west as West Street. The initial announcement was that they were going to build a themed casino, and it sounded like it was going to be something that would help Reno a great deal. As I recall, the theme was going to be Spanish conquistadors and feature Spanish galleons, maybe something floating in the water, similar to what Steve Wynn had done down in Vegas. Everybody was encouraged, because we could see that Reno was falling further and further behind. Las Vegas was getting fabulous casinos out on the Strip, there was gaming spreading all around the country, and we knew that Reno had to do something to stay competitive.

Our business in Reno had started to erode somewhat, and our feeling was that the big reason was because the town generally was eroding. In our case, in retrospect, what we found out was that our competitors were taking away our best customers. Many of them had put in slot card systems, and they had slot clubs. They were promoting their best customers, and some of their best customers were ours, because a lot of customers are not loyal to just one casino.

We didn't have a slot club, and we were not promoting like other casinos were and identifying our best players, so they were taking our best players away from us. The Eldorado was probably the biggest culprit, but it took us awhile to realize that, because we were so heavily involved in Mississippi. The Copa took my mind away from our situation in Reno.

Looking back on it, we were kind of in a fool's paradise. We kept thinking, "Boy, they're going to build this beautiful, themed casino between the Eldorado and Circus Circus, within walking distance of our place. They're going to create so much business that they're not going to be able to handle it, and here we are, so close to them. It's just got to rub off on us."

Circus Circus was committing three hundred and fifty to four hundred million dollars, and New York New York, a hugely successful casino on the Strip was built for that amount, so we felt that we were going to get something like that here in Reno, and it was going to be great for everybody. Our thinking was, "Let them build that and see how things go, and if it works out like we think it will, then we'll expand our place, and maybe we'll try to turn our place into a themed casino, as well." (We knew that was the direction that the gaming business was going in.)

Then we started hearing that Circus Circus and Eldorado might do some other theme. They weren't sure what it was going to be, and then they began to talk about a mining theme. When I heard that, I said, "Well, that sounds to me like something that's been done and overdone so damn many times. It's just a Western theme." And Western has been just beat to death, especially in the state of Nevada. I was really disappointed when I heard that.

They had started construction, as I recall, before they *really* knew what kind of a theme they were going to have. I can't look into their minds and see exactly what happened, but we were hearing that they had started the foundation, and they were putting the steel up and so on, but they still didn't know what they were going to do.

Building the infamous "skyways" over Fourth Street required special permission from the city. The Silver Legacy partners got their lawyers to work, and they went far back in the city's records. I don't know whether this is true or not, but the story that they came out with, and the city attorney agreed with, was that the "air rights" over the streets around their properties had never been deeded to the city. They argued that the air rights over the streets running between their three casinos, the Tri-Properties, were theirs, because air rights belonged to adjoining property owners. The city attorney bought it, and they got the city council to agree.

The Silver Legacy represented that they merely wanted to build crossovers—they said, "Look, the Sands, the Flamingo, and Harrah's have crossovers." Well, it's true. We have one across Third Street, but we actually *own* the air rights over Third Street.

When we bought the property from the railroad just south of the tracks, they sold us the air rights over Third Street— they owned the air rights over Third Street and over the railroad tracks, besides the real estate. Because we purchased those air rights, we can build across there all we want. So we had paid for our air rights, but the Tri-Properties had not. But that's not the real issue.

The real issue is that the city allowed them to build across the city streets with not just a crossover like we have, or like Harrah's has, or like the Flamingo has. They built over practically *all* of adjoining Sierra Street and Fourth Street. They paid *nothing* for the air rights, and they pay no rent, and they have restaurants, and all sorts of facilities—stores, and what have you. That above-street construction tied all three of these properties together, so once somebody gets into one, it's easy to go from one to another without having to go back out on the street. Studies have shown that the average number of casinos that people visit when they come to Reno is about three, so once they get somebody in there, it almost means that no one else in town gets any of that business—especially in the wintertime, when we need business the most, because people hesitate to go out if it's cold or snowing or inclement weather.

Because the city allowed them to do that, that gave them a clear and distinct advantage over the rest of us in downtown Reno, and it *really* hurt. What hurt even more than that, though, was this mining theme that they came out with. I'm sure they didn't do this on purpose, because they wanted it to succeed even more than we did, but Sam Fairchild and whatever he's supposed to represent—his silver legacy and so on—all just fell flat on its face. The mining rig itself fell flat on its face. If you look at their advertising and promotions, they don't even talk about that anymore. You got to give them credit. It didn't take them long to realize that they were barking up the wrong tree, and they just forgot all about Fairchild and the mining rig.

The Silver Legacy did very poorly when they first opened. When they saw that their themed casino wasn't working, they began to go for whatever business was available, as quickly as they possibly could. What they could snatch quickly was the charter bus business, the charter airplane business, and the package business—all three of the businesses that we depended on for 60 percent of our business.

Here was this brand new place with seventeen hundred rooms and eight restaurants, or whatever they had, and I thought, "Well, they're the nine-hundred-pound gorilla." When they got into that market, it didn't matter what rate they had to quote. They went out and got all that business. If we were quoting, say, a twenty-dollar rate, and they came in at an eighteen-dollar rate, or even a twenty-dollar rate, where are you going to stay? A brand new place, or our place? The guys that operate charter businesses are interested in selling as many people as they can. So if they can come in and offer a customer a room in a hotel-casino that's brand new, for the same price or a lesser price than an older casino, nine times out of ten, the customer's going to take the new one.

I believe our drop in revenue resulted from the fact that the Silver Legacy didn't have a workable theme, and they did not bring any new people into town to speak of. Therefore, all they did was rob the rest of us, and when they did that, every hotel-casino in downtown Reno really felt it.

It took them two to three years or more to figure out how to overcome that, but they finally got into the entertainment field in a big way, and they do have some real good entertainment, which Reno hadn't seen for a long time. They put a lot of extra stuff on weekends that works, but the amount of people that come to Reno today is about the same as it was five years ago.

We've had an erosion of people that come to Reno, because Indian gaming and Las Vegas are hurting us so badly. To counter some of that erosion, the Tri-Properties and the two guys down on South Virginia Street, the Peppermill and the Atlantis, are bringing some new customers in, but Reno still doesn't have an *increase*. So, yes, we've covered the erosion that happened, but we've only come back to where we were. I think we're getting about five million people a year, and that's the same number we've been getting all these years. We haven't made any headway.

When they were bringing this project in, the Silver Legacy people did the same thing that all of us in Reno have done in the past. You work very closely with the city attorney's office to get them on board first, and then you ferret out the councilmen on a one-on-one basis, and you sell them on your project. There's nothing wrong with that, except the council fails to recognize that there's other businesses in town that need to be considered. The Eldorado and Circus Circus have much greater resources than the rest of us, and they directed all their efforts towards that council person to get their project passed. No one is there to represent the rest of the community.

MGM did that, as well. I know this is true, because I've talked to people that were at a meeting held at the Palace Club. (I think Silvio Petricciani knew somebody.) MGM brought Cary Grant up here, and he sat with the city council, and it was a wonderful thing for those guys to be able to sit there and talk to Cary Grant.

What the Legacy did was simply overwhelm the council with "facts" about how this was going to be wonderful. They sold it, and they sold us, too. We said, "Well, this huge, themed casino is going to be wonderful."

Almost everybody was taken off guard by the Silver Legacy's "passageways" over the streets. They didn't really describe exactly what they were going to do. If the council had asked some questions and tried to put some parameters on the thing and were thinking about the rest of the town, they might have said, "Well, look, how many of these are you going to have, and how big are they going to be?" But once the Silver Legacy got their theory across, and the council accepted it, then it was just a question of schmoozing the building department. The city attorney was sold already.

When the Silver Legacy opened in 1995, they quickly found out that their theme just was not working, and they jumped into our line of business—charter planes, packages, and buses. It was very difficult for us to fight back, because, you could only cut your room rates so far. They also had a great advantage in the food business, because they had so many more restaurants than we did.

Once the Silver Legacy got customers into their place, we never saw them at all. Our fiscal year closes June 30, and the year that began July 1, 1995 and closed June 30 of 1996 was the first in our history that we ever had a loss for the year. We lost several million dollars. Before the Legacy opened, we had an occupancy of close to 90 percent, but were down to 82 percent in the year that ended June 30, 1996. Worse than that, in trying to compete, our average room rate dropped three or four dollars, down to around twenty-eight dollars average daily rate. Lower occupancy also made our gaming revenue go down. And then we were caught in this situation where our major competitors had slot card systems and slot-promo programs, where they were marketing directly to their better players, whom they had identified through their slot club.

It became apparent to us that if we were to survive, we were going to have to get a slot card system, begin a customer database, get some of our old customers back, and create new customers. We were going to have to get new business to replace those customers that we'd lost to the Legacy and to Circus Circus, and there was only one type available: that was local business.

It had been my practice in past years not to pursue local business, but now it became apparent that the best source of new customers would be local people. They would be new customers, because we had always had such a low profile in Reno that a lot of local people had never really known we existed. We began to make some moves in that direction as quickly as we possibly could.

We got a slot club established, and we got a slot card system. Those things take time and they're very expensive— you can spend a million dollars or more. Then, once you have everything up and running, you have to build your database, so it's not very effective for quite some time. It takes a while before you can market to those people in your database that are your good customers, and if you wind up with fifteen or twenty percent of the total base being good customers, you're lucky.

One of the things that attracted me to Ferenc Szony was he had done this kind of thing at both Hiltons. He'd started from scratch and developed a local business, so he knew how to do it. Ferenc came to work for the Sands Regent in December of 1997. He and I had long conversations about the problems that the Sands had and how to solve them. We were just being outgunned in the tourist business, and Reno's tourist business was really flat anyway.

Ferenc felt that the first thing we had to do was something I didn't see—that was to "fix" our parking. We had adequate parking in our property, because we've got eight acres, but it was a little parking lot here and a little parking lot there, and our parking garage entrance was difficult to find. We've also got two and a half acres just south of the railroad tracks with a crossover to walk into our casino, but it's really not handy, and it's difficult to find. The public doesn't want to have to look around for things—they want things to hit them right in the face.

Ferenc said, "We have to create a big parking lot, and we have to put it at our front door." Our front door is really Arlington and Fourth Street, and so that meant tearing down those buildings over there, the original motel and the original little casino that we had broken into pieces and leased out: we had a cocktail lounge there, a Blimpies, a liquor store, a Denny's, and so on. It was difficult for my sister and me to swallow, because these buildings were still making us money, and we still had a lot of call for our motel rooms. Many people prefer to stay in a motel. They like the idea of parking their car right in front of their rooms, or the fact that they don't have to go through a hallway or up an elevator. We had a swimming pool there too, and we had customers that had been coming to the Sands for years and liked the fact that their room was adjacent to the pool. It took a great deal of courage to say, "Well, we're going to tear all this stuff down." They were all generating revenue, and we had to really do some soul searching before Ferenc swung us around to his view.

We finally bit the bullet and tore them down. Now, of course, we're happy as hell that we did. Now we have this huge parking lot that's easily accessible, where local people can come in and out. All the advertising that we might have done, and all the ferreting out of our database and finding good customers, would have come to naught if they weren't able to just drive up and park. Surface parking always beats garage parking. You can paint parking garages, light them up good, make wide aisles, and so on, but there's still a great number of people that just don't want to park in a garage, *if* they can park on the surface.

Then we did a lot of direct marketing, where we sent direct mail to our good customers, which is what most major hotel-casinos do nowadays. We'd invite them to special events, and we tiered our customers. We have A, B, and C customers. Our A customers, just like in almost any other major hotel-casino, are comped completely, and the B customer gets a little less, and the C customer gets a little less. We had to develop that whole system, and we had never done that before, but Ferenc had done it twice, once at the Flamingo and once at the Reno Hilton. He had also worked with the Hilton in Las Vegas, and they'd done it, so he had that experience in his background. That's how we slowly began to pull ourselves up by our bootstraps. But our hotel still suffered, because here's this 900-pound gorilla, the Silver Legacy tied to the Eldorado and Circus Circus, with all these rooms, with second-level, block-long bridges.

The City Center Pavilion also helped the gorilla. It gave them a place to do a lot of exhibits and other types of things. It's the building on Fourth and Center Streets. That helped them, because once they realized that entertainment was the way they were going to get people in their place, they began using their Grand Exposition Hall as an entertainment venue and the City Center Pavilion for expositions and other things. Then, as they grew slightly less competitive in room rates, we got some of the room business back that we had initially lost.

The year that ended June 30, 1995, our company showed an eleven million dollar loss, but it wasn't due to business at the Sands in Reno. Our operating profit in Reno for that year was still pretty good, because the Legacy hadn't opened yet. We took that big loss because of Mississippi. The following year's loss was due to losing so many customers to the Legacy and others.

I would like to say that 1995-1996 was the worst year we ever had, but the next year probably was just as bad, maybe even a little worse. We had two *really* bad years. But by 1998 we had started to turn it around. Ferenc came to work in December of 1997, and we showed a pick-up after he was here just four or five months.

24

"Don't Want to be Panhandled"

WE HAVE THIS ongoing problem that just becomes worse and worse. Several years ago John Cavanaugh, who owns the Gold Dust Motel on Fourth and Vine, donated to the Catholic Church a piece of property just to the west of us on Third Street, between Ralston and Washington Street. It's just a couple of doors down from the southwest corner of our property. On that piece, St. Vincent's has built a soup kitchen, where they serve breakfast and lunch at no charge to whoever walks up. All the homeless people in town are fully aware that they can get a free meal there.

We're the casino that's affected the most by what happens when they serve breakfast, around seven or eight o'clock in the morning. There's this huge stream of literally hundreds of homeless people. Some of them are belligerent types, and all of them, almost without exception, are dressed in a fashion that puts fear in people, especially middle-aged ladies, which is a good part of our clientele. They stream down Third Street to the west and line up across the street. Many times the line extends over to our side of the street, and they sit on cars in our parking lot that belong to our guests, and then, after they finish, they stream back on Third Street. It starts again around eleven-thirty or so in the morning, when they come over for lunch. So we have that kind of disruption . . . . Besides that, on the corner of West and Third Street, there's a place that's called the Gospel

Mission, and there they serve dinner, and it's a gathering place in the evenings between four and five o'clock, when the same homeless people gather to eat dinner.

The shortest way for our customers to get to the downtown center is down Third Street, and that means that most of them pass all these homeless people. We have been putting up with this situation for years and years. The council has made several attempts to alleviate this problem, but I don't think it's been uppermost in their minds, to say the least. [laughter] Not only is that bad for us, but it's bad for the whole downtown area, because these people, when they're not walking back and forth to eat or to sleep at the Gospel Mission, are wandering around town. These are the same people that you'll find up and down Virginia Street and on Center Street and along Second Street and sleeping in the parks. It is a problem that has really hurt downtown Reno, and it is probably one of the reasons why the Peppermill and the Atlantis and maybe the Nugget have done so well in locations away from downtown. We have comment cards, and innumerable times people will write on a comment card, "Well, we really like your place, and we like downtown Reno, but we just don't want to be panhandled. We don't like looking at these bums, and we fear for ourselves and for our safety much of the time." So we've lost people, and we continue to lose people to this problem.

We've done everything under the sun, and so have the Hilton and the Eldorado and Harrah's, the Cal-Neva, and other places. All of us have tried in every way we could to get the council to solve this problem, and the council has simply failed. In my view, the reason they've failed is that they just don't have the guts, and they haven't had the guts— not only this council that we have now, but for the last ten, fifteen years. You've got to make a decision that these people are going to be moved to some particular site, and you have to stand the heat of residents of that area of the city, wherever it is you're going to put them, because no one really wants this group in their part of town.

Las Vegas established a facility out in North Las Vegas, about a mile away from downtown Vegas. They bought an old Safeway store that was closed, and they created this drop-in center. They have beds; they have showers; they have telephones for these people to use; they have newspapers there. They can come in and take a shower; they can get some clean clothes; they can call from there and get a job. People that want to help themselves have a place to go for help, because when you think about it, if you're looking for a job, and you don't have a permanent address or a phone number that you can leave, how are you going to find a job?

The business people in downtown Reno have been urging the city to do something like Vegas has for many years, and the city has yet to do it. One reason that this has not happened is the St. Vincent's Society. From what I know, St. Vincent's reports their philanthropy to the Catholic Church, and they tell them how many people they have fed every day; and the more people they feed every day, the more successful they look. They get a good portion of their funding from the Catholic Church.

I've had many conversations with city officials and with the city council about St. Vincent's kitchen. St. Vincent's has been the real stumbling block in trying to get one location where the Gospel Mission would go, where St. Vincent's would go, where you could have a drop-in center, so that the homeless people would have a better facility. They have just simply not cooperated, and if you were going to put this drop-in center some place—Sage Street, or anywhere you want—and you still had St. Vincent's over here, you'd only have the problem half solved. A lot of homeless people simply wouldn't go to the remote drop-in center, because it's easier to walk to St. Vincent's.

The city attorney has been less than helpful in this problem. Her big fear—at least from my observation—is that the city is going to get sued if it takes action. She has always come down on the side of the homeless: "Well, you can't arrest these people. We don't have any place to put them, and we don't want to send them to jail." If we had a drop-in center, it's been her position that the police could insist that they go to the center, and she would give them more authority to do that kind of thing. As it is now, the police usually do not bother these people unless they become really obnoxious. I know they roust them out of the parks once in awhile . . . . and the problem just festers.

Mr. Pilzner, a city councilman whom I backed, promised the business people downtown that he would help with this. We had the Sage Street site for a homeless center, and it appeared that we were going to be able to put that plan together, but we needed the vote of the council. Pilzner organized enough opposition on the council to kill the Sage Street site.

Then there was the Project Restart program. That group was trying to get a drop-in center, and maybe they ruffled some feathers. I'm not quite sure what happened. All I know is that every time you try to put this center some place, the council simply can't stand up to the opposition. They're telling me now that they're going to take another run at the Sage Street site.

St. Vincent's is still as intractable as ever. What I get from third parties is that if they agree to move their facility, they are demanding a brand new kitchen and a much bigger facility. I've offered in the past that if they would move, our company would buy their current property. I also offered a site, the old El Rancho Motel down on East Fourth Street that we owned for many years. I said, "Here, I'll give you this site if you'll just move these people down there." But somebody across Wells Avenue, a Realtor who's had that property for sale for years, went down to the council and told them that he had a big project all set to go there, and the council, just like they did with the crossovers for the Legacy, simply took the man at his word and said, "OK, fine. We don't want to put a homeless shelter here, because it will ruin this big project." The project never happened.

That is an area where this drop-in center would work. In the early 1950s, the first urban renewal area in Reno was bounded by Wells Avenue to the west, Seventh Street or Eighth Street to the north, as far east as Morrill or one of those other streets down there, and Fourth Street to the south. Urban Renewal went in and bought most of that land up. At that time it was a lower-class residential area. There were little homes where people lived, and they tore them all down and put the land up for sale, just like has happened downtown with redevelopment. Eventually, with help from the federal government, low cost housing and stores were built in this area.

Those people that are customers at the casinos in the downtown center that might want to come over to the Sands are intimidated by all the homeless people along Third Street. Once they start walking down this way and see all these homeless people . . . . In many cases we've talked to people who've on other occasions stayed with us, who said, "Look, I was in Reno, and I wanted to come down and see you guys, but when I started walking down towards your place, and I saw all these homeless people and bums, I just turned around and went back."

It's hurt us a great deal with out-of-towners who might want to stay at our place but walk downtown to visit others.

It has also meant less business for us from people staying at other hotels who might otherwise walk over to the Sands to play with us. Fortunately, our local customers are not bothered by the homeless. They can just drive into one of our parking lots or our parking garage and enter our casino without ever setting foot on Third Street.

25

RSCVA: A Creature of the Casinos

JUD ALLEN, who was head of the Reno Chamber of Commerce for twenty-four years, started marketing conventions through the chamber. He made reservations and did a lot of the things on a very small budget, funded only by the chamber of commerce. Jud believed that the use of tax revenues encourages far more waste and inefficiency than when you operate on a limited budget. You've got this flow of tax money coming in, and the issue becomes, "How do we spend it?" Redevelopment, for instance, wound up building that theater on the river that gets fewer people per screen on a daily basis than any other theater in northern Nevada, because they had to do *something*. They fiddled around for so long that, whether it was right or wrong, that they had to spend that money on something. The RSCVA has been guilty of that, too.

Jud Allen knew a lot about what was going on. He was on the city council himself. He was one of those individuals that was a retired person that didn't need the job, that didn't take the job for the money, but he did it, because he wanted to do a good job. Reno was his home. He was a conscientious kind of guy. He's the kind of man you need in these positions that we're talking about, and there's so few of them around. If we could get those kind of people, we could do a much better job in the public agencies.

One of the reasons Reno has been so divided and has not progressed as well as it should, is because the gaming industry has almost never spoken with one voice. When you have a project to do, you're down there talking to those councilmen by yourself. You're not interested in Reno as a community. That's not necessarily true with all of us, because many of us realize that Reno has to do well if we're going to do well. But some people in town don't think that way.

Jud Allen made the observation that when Harolds Club wanted to do something, they thought about the community first. They said, "If it's good for the community, it's good for Harolds Club." But a great many folks since Harolds Club say, "If it's good for *me*, if it's good for my casino, *then* it's good for the community." That's the kind of thinking that has caused the rest of us so much difficulty.

I tried every way I could to create an association that would represent all the gamers in Reno, and we've made a couple of different starts at it. The NRA, Nevada Resort Association, is composed mostly of Las Vegas Strip properties. A few properties in northern Nevada belong to that association, but we never joined. We thought the association just simply wasn't going to do the job that we needed to do here in Reno. So the Northern Nevada Gaming Association was formed, and we got most everybody together to do that. When we began it in the early 1990s, we were trying to create a situation where the industry in northern Nevada would speak with one voice.

There are outlying properties like the Atlantis, the Peppermill, Boomtown, and Ascuaga's Nugget, that are in many instances opposing the downtown properties. For most of our history, all we had was the downtown casinos, with the exception of the Nugget and the MGM. You could set those people aside and let them do what they wanted to do, and then you could get all the downtown people together, and you could deal with your problems.

If I had to do it all over again, I would establish close personal contacts with politicians at all levels, such as Ascuaga did with Laxalt and the Caranos have done with the city council, the county commissioners, and Bill Raggio.

The Reno-Sparks Convention and Visitors Authority, the RSCVA, started out as the Fair and Recreation Board twenty-five or thirty years ago. That's when the room tax was initiated. The legislature gave Washoe County the right to put a room tax in effect, and that money was earmarked for this Fair and Recreation Board. It was a creature of the casinos, and it was one issue where the casinos were somewhat united—they felt that we needed this Fair and Recreation Board to collect the room tax. In order to sell it to the legislature and the residents of the county, the plan was to use the room tax not only for the establishment of a convention center, but also for the establishment of recreation facilities for the citizens of Reno. This was so that you could get the support of the community, but the real aim of the Fair and Recreation Board was to get a convention facility for the city of Reno for the benefit of the casinos. Also, the rest of the business people in town and the rest of the community would benefit from convention business, because when you bring convention business into town, it helps everybody in town.

There was a big hassle about where this facility was going to go, and eventually some deals were made that sort of compromised the thing. Harolds Club owned the land where the convention center is now, and they wanted to get rid of it at a good price; and because Harolds Club had a lot of sway with the council, they were able to sell the property to the Fair and Recreation Board. In order to mollify the downtown interests that didn't want the center way out there, the Pioneer Theater Auditorium was also conceived. There was a building there called the State Building, and I think it was county property. It was pretty old and due to be demolished, anyway; so, as a compromise, in order to get the thing worked out, they built the Pioneer Theater. Supposedly the downtown properties would be able to use that, and then the whole community could use this building way out on South Virginia. The flaw in that thinking, of course, is that at that time there were just a few motels out there, and there were very few rooms. There was nothing out there that could be considered a convention hotel or motel facility. The Convention Center should have been built where the rooms were, and the rooms at that time were all in downtown Reno, almost without exception. And the Pioneer Theater became a facility without parking, which in itself is idiotic!

That is how the RSCVA started. Within a few years, they dropped the Fair and Recreation Board name and took up the name Reno-Sparks Convention and Visitors Authority in order to direct all the money they possibly could towards building and maintaining tourist-type facilities. The Pioneer Theater Auditorium never really helped the tourist business at all, but it was helpful to local patrons of the arts, because they have plays and operas and that sort of thing. Even though parking is nonexistent, it works, because in the evening the downtown area is so dead north of the river that there's usually parking on the streets.

The convention authority is composed of four representatives from the gaming industry and four local politicians. The city council has two people on it; the county commission has either one or two. And then there's representatives from some of the other major businesses in town. The mayor is one of the two that represent the council, I think. So it's a board of eleven or twelve people. They have more political types on that board than business people, but it's really a business that they're running. These people are politicians, trying to do something that they don't really know anything about. That's one of the reasons we've had such an awful record out there.

They didn't get the hall completely built, and it's never been fully utilized. They have some rooms that could service conventions, but if you have a convention big enough to fill that hall, the Peppermill and the Atlantis aren't going to give you enough rooms to take care of these people. So the conventioneers have to stay in some other hotel, some distance away. What's happened is that, generally speaking, the Nugget, the Reno Hilton, and the Atlantis really kind of dominate the business of that convention center. They keep abreast of the RSCVA's convention book, so they know when that hall, or a portion of it, is empty. If one of these operations has a group that they can book, and they don't have enough meeting space or exhibit space, then they use the convention center. There's nothing wrong with that, but it's just not a good situation.

The convention center should be in a place where there's several thousand rooms nearby. Downtown Reno doesn't have much convention space. Because the center is not in our vicinity, when we go out to sell large groups to come to Reno, we have to tell them we're going to have to put them all over town. That means you got to bus people out to the convention center and back.

The absurd Convention Center location was a political decision. We still have a board that really doesn't understand the business. Only three or four people, the industry representatives, on that board understand tourist and convention business. Politicians are concerned about getting re-elected, so they don't want to take an unpopular stand, and you get things like the awful debacle that happened with the bowling stadium.

Hotel and gaming interests on Virginia Street in downtown Reno wanted to see the bowling stadium placed very close to where the major gaming places are, Fitzgerald had some property in that location that he wanted to sell. Our company owned a piece of property just north of Circus Circus, fronting on Virginia Street, almost a complete square block. I offered to sell the RSCVA that property for twenty-five to thirty dollars a square foot, but they bought Fitz's property for paid fifty dollars a square foot, which was an outrageous price to pay.

Unfortunately, the RSCVA has been blessed with a number of seemingly incompetent executive directors. One of them was a man named Milligan, whose experience in running convention authorities was nil. A group of casinos became concerned about Mr. Milligan's ability and about what was happening with the convention authority, so we had a meeting at Bill Thornton's Donner Lake Lodge facility. All the major properties were represented, and some of the minors. As a group, we decided to request the RSCVA board to relieve Mr. Milligan of his duties and find a new director. Most of us just felt that he wasn't the right man for the job. However, Gary Carano said maybe we should not be so rash, even though we had been thinking about it for quite some time.

The Eldorado and two or three other major properties finally decided they wanted to give Milligan another chance. They saved his job. Well, we know what happened: Milligan was the director when the bowling stadium was built, and some of these major properties wound up with free advertising signs in it, as well as other perks.

Milligan was one reason we had such a huge cost overrun in the property. He's the one that approved the wine cellar, the cocktail lounge, the private meeting room. He worked in conjunction with the architect, Mr. Wilday, to put in all the frills that we didn't need. The budget practically became unlimited—no one watched the extras. It was Mr. Milligan's job to do that, but one thing lead to another, and we had huge cost overruns. And not only that, but the facility isn't even finished. If you drive over there along the tracks, you'll see the exposed beams that are coming down from the second floor. They simply ran out of funds, didn't even finish the facility.

Finally, the community became aware that much of what had happened there was the fault of Mr. Milligan and the RSCVA boards, because they did not oversee the architects, and they did not pay any attention to the cost overruns and the change orders that were signed. Too late, we finally were able to rid ourselves of Milligan, but the job was done then. That's not to say that the bowling stadium is not good for Reno. It is. Unfortunately, it cost twenty or twenty-five million dollars more than it should have, which is money that the RSCVA could have spent in other places.

After Milligan, we had a guy in there three or four months, who went right to work taking men and building materials out to his house, and he began to build a deck around his house. [laughter] He didn't waste much time at all. He reminds me of Phil Keene, but he was quicker than Keene. He didn't last long.

There were several people in there between Milligan and Keene. One had been with Western Airlines. His big idea was to do a sales blitz on southern California. It was a huge market, but Los Angeles has always been a Las Vegas market, and it was not a good idea for us to try to compete against Las Vegas when our air service was not as good, when it was more expensive to come to Reno than it was to go to Las Vegas, and when the perception was that all you had in northern Nevada was the same thing you had in Vegas, just casinos. Why should you go to Reno? It was a complete waste of money. But for a couple of years the convention authority wasted hundreds of thousands of dollars trying to market southern California, and that didn't work.

This is what happens when you've got an RSCVA board with no business people, no tourist-oriented people. The majority of the members are politicians that really know nothing at all about what we're talking about and what ought to be done. They're easily led, and in spite of the fact that you would think that they would listen to the business people and the tourist people on the board, it appears that what's uppermost in those political minds is whether they're going to get re-elected or not. They're concerned about how they're going to be perceived by the public, instead of trying to make hard decisions as to where and how this money should be spent and what we should do to further the tourist industry in Washoe County.

After Kevitt's short tenure, Fred Boyd took over as temporary executive director while the RSCVA board conducted a search. They hired a firm to find a qualified director, and whatever they paid them was a complete waste of money. You would think that if you hired a search firm, you'd come up with decent finalists, but the candidate that the RSCVA board picked was Phil Keene, and he lasted only a little more than two years. He was being paid more than $150,000 a year, and after his first year there he got a fifteen or twenty-percent raise. Phil, as we know now (and many of us suspected this shortly after he first came to work), probably took the job just for the pay. At least, that's my view of it. Then he began to charge things on his credit card.

The RSCVA under Milligan's tenure had built a wine storage room in the bowling center, where the temperature is maintained at a certain level. They bought thousands and thousands of dollars worth of fine wines, justifying it by saying they were going to entertain group meeting planners and try to sell them on the fact that Reno was a good place to bring their business. Probably, what really happened was that most of the wine was used by Milligan and people like him for their own purposes. Keene fell right into place and decided that that was something that he wanted to do, as well.

One thing the RSCVA did was help us with airline reservations. With their help, we'd go to reservation centers and give presentations to the agents. We'd do things like offer them commissions, because a lot of times you get a situation where travelers are just looking for a getaway, and if they aren't able to get an accommodation that they want, then it is up to the agent to sell them on some other destination. Reno (unfortunately, we're usually the ones that have availability) was easy to sell. These trips that RSCVA arranged to reservation centers were one of the more effective things that they've done. We had some success, and the industry really pushed RSCVA in that direction.

The other area where the RSCVA has been somewhat successful is with the charter airplane people and the airlines. They would organize what's called product-launch parties. We did a lot of this in Canada with Canadian Airlines in conjunction with RSCVA. The Canadian Airlines season would start in September. In August, they would pull together the travel agents that they worked with and the hotel-casinos that did business with them. We would go to Vancouver, Calgary, Edmonton, Regina, and Toronto. We'd have hors d'oeuvre parties with cocktails, and we'd talk about our properties, and Canadian Airlines would make their presentations about their new product. Other airlines do the same thing, and RSCVA has facilitated it.

26

Trying
to
Get
Out

IN 1995 WE WERE APPROACHED by a couple of men from Las Vegas, one of whom had been a banker for many years in Idaho and in southern Nevada. He had formed a little investment company composed of three or four different individuals, one of whom had hotel experience and one of whom was an attorney who'd had some gaming experience. Another individual was a wealthy man who had recently sold a chain of movie theaters in the Northwest, principally in Oregon and Washington. He had owned the real estate, as well as the businesses, and he'd sold them to some chain, so he'd gotten quite a sum of cash. It was in the neighborhood of a hundred and sixty million dollars, so they were looking for a place to invest this money.

These men were the sole owners of Tara Corporation, which had some real estate investments in southern Nevada and California. They became interested in hotel-casino acquisitions, and we were one of the properties that they thought about purchasing. We were a public company, and their thinking was that they could put all of Tara's holdings in the Sands Regent, the public company, and thereby they could become a public entity themselves.

We were not thinking about selling at the time. It probably was a good time to do it, but I had been involved so long in the business that I couldn't visualize not being involved on a twenty-four-hour-a-day, seven-day-a-week basis. It had never dawned on me that maybe it was time to sell. However, when we got the proposal, I got to thinking.

My sister had had cancer; my brother was very ill; and my daughter Toni was never interested in working in the business. She always wanted to do something on her own, so that people wouldn't say that she was successful just because she went into her father's business. She was very independent that way, and I encouraged that in her. My son was working in the business, and he was very diligent. He worked hard, and he would have gone on and stepped into my shoes, but I sensed that he wanted to do something else. At any rate, we talked to these Tara folks, and we came to an agreement with them.

Our stock price had deteriorated somewhat because of the problems in Mississippi, and the sale price that we arrived at was seven dollars a share. For stockholders like us, that had bought the stock before it split, that meant fourteen dollars a share for the old stock. We had gone public at twelve dollars, so it wasn't a big increase, but it was enough, as we weren't trying to squeeze the last dollar out of the company. We were more interested in an exit strategy that would leave the company in good hands—we had formed the company, and we didn't want to walk away from it and see it fail. We wanted it to grow and prosper, and we wanted to protect all outside shareholders, as well.

Along those lines, because Tara didn't really have the necessary expertise, they asked me to stay on and be the president and CEO for a period. After that I was going to stay on the board and still be involved, but not be the CEO, which appealed to me. It would give me something to do and allow me to do what I could to make it successful. It seemed like it was going to be a good fit. There was only one more thing, and that was the licensing issue; but we had done extensive preliminary work on the background of these folks, and we didn't find any reason to believe that they could not get licensed. So we made the deal, and they applied for their license in Nevada. They also had to apply in the state of Mississippi, because we were in business down there, as well.

Unbeknownst to us, after the deal was made, and after they'd made their applications in the state of Nevada, they had some internal discussions as to whether, in fact, they wanted to go through with the deal. They had put up half a million dollars that was non-refundable if they backed out, but for some reason they became reluctant to submit the applications for their Mississippi license. They kept telling us that they were having some trouble filling them out, and time went on. They had paid their fees to the state of Nevada, and Nevada had started their licensing procedures, but they never did turn in an application to the state of Mississippi.

Several months went by, and it was becoming more apparent to us all the time that there was a problem. We finally asked for a face-to-face meeting to try to determine exactly what the situation was. The best I could get out of it was that the man with the money, the man who had sold those theaters, either found a better place to invest his money or decided he didn't want to be in the gaming business or decided that he didn't want to go through the licensing procedure. That does happen. As much as you warn people about how stringent the procedures are for a gaming license, I don't think anybody is really ready for such an in-depth examination of one's background. There may have been something in one of their backgrounds, but I don't know, so I shouldn't speculate. I never did find out what the real situation was.

That half-million-dollar deposit stayed in escrow for awhile, and when they did not become licensed, we got the deposit, and that's pretty much the end of it. We didn't hear much more from Tara after that, and we didn't feel that bad

about it. We weren't actively out there trying to sell the company, anyway, and we got the half million. That was the end
of the Tara deal.

Our situation in Mississippi kept getting worse. The worth
of our company, because of the Mississippi situation, was declining, and our stock price had declined. We thought that if
we could straighten Mississippi out, then our company's stock
price would climb back up again, and we could sell our shares
in the company for a lot more money. However, before things
had improved any, we were contacted by a man named Shawn
Scott, whom I had met one of the times that I had gone to
Las Vegas to meet with the Tara group.

Shawn was an acquaintance of the Tara folks and had
done business with them. He was essentially a real estate investor who had started a couple of little casinos in Henderson,
Nevada. They were small operations, but he had been licensed by the state, so he had gotten over the licensing problem. Shawn was acting not only for himself, but as a broker
for a group of investment bankers in New York that had done
a couple of gaming deals. Shawn had also gotten them into a
deal with the Ormsby House in Carson City, trying to bring
it back from the dead. The SEC could give me no reason to
believe that they'd ever been anything other than above
board, so we talked among the family. Even though the stock
price had dropped dramatically, I was a couple of years older,
so we got to thinking more and more that maybe it was time
to sell.

We knew that if we sold, we were not going to make the
kind of money that we would have made with the Tara deal,
because the stock now was worth three dollars instead of
seven. However, all of my family have enough money to live
on and then some, and it was never our desire to be wealthy
just for the sake of being wealthy. We felt that our life and

our time here on earth were worth more than a few extra dollars, and that was the feeling of my children, as well.

My son's real desire was to go to law school, and he wanted the freedom that would come with selling. (Pete was always a great help to me, somebody that I could depend on and rely on. He was honest, and he'd been working in the business ever since he graduated from college.) Also, I had recently remarried and had a child, my third, born in 1991. At my age, I wasn't going to be around as long for her as I was for my older two children. I wanted to spend more time with her, and that was quite an incentive for me to go into the deal.

It looked like it was going to work. We again asked for a half-million-dollar, non-refundable deposit. The investment bankers began to buy our stock, as well, and that encouraged us, because we thought these folks not only like our company and are willing to finance this sale, but they see a future for the company. We thought this deal would certainly go through, and the outside shareholders would be protected, as well. I was to stay with the company, because Shawn wanted somebody to stay and help him run the company, and I was amenable to that. I had an open-ended deal, so that if I decided I wanted to stop working, I could. So we went down that road, and it looked very promising. Then the Ormsby House deal that Shawn was brokering for the investment bankers fell apart.

Shawn had also gotten the bankers involved in the financing of the Reno Ramada sale, and the Reno Ramada loan also went bad. Several deals that Shawn had put them into were turning sour, and they began rethinking the idea of whether they really wanted to finance him in the purchase of our stock. They sent a letter to Shawn and myself where they agreed the purchase price was six million dollars, and they agreed to put up five of the six million that was required, but either my family was going to have to take a million dollar discount, or Shawn or someone was going to have to come up with that other million. I disagreed with that and said we were not going to discount our stock. It was way too cheap as it was. We had the deposit, and we had done everything that we had committed to do, so if the deal didn't go through, Shawn would forfeit his deposit.

Well, essentially, the deal did not go through, but the investment bankers had bought 8 percent of the Sands stock. (I think they eventually got it under 5 percent so they wouldn't have to be licensed.) We made a settlement with Shawn Scott on the $500,000 deposit. We felt rightfully that it was ours, but because we didn't want to get involved in a lawsuit, we agreed to keep some of that money and let him have some back, so that we could settle the whole matter without having to go into court. It left a bad taste in our mouth. But in another sense, we thought we were just going to have to keep this company going on!

Well, along in March or April of 1999 I had a call from a man named Judah Hertz. Mr. Hertz had been referred to us by Wells Fargo Bank, because the mortgage that we had on our property was held by Wells Fargo. Because of our problems in Mississippi, Wells Fargo was becoming somewhat uneasy about the mortgage, and they were asking us for some advance principal payments to be made on that loan—we had some covenants with them that if our cash flow dropped below a certain level, we needed to reduce the loan by a certain amount of money. I was resisting, because I felt that it was unfair, even though it may have been written up like that. They also wanted to increase our interest rate, which they had the right to do, according to their loan agreement, but as a public-relations matter and as a matter of taking care of a good customer, I didn't think that it was proper.

Wells Fargo had done business with Judah in southern California. Judah lived, and still lives, in southern California, and he's a very wealthy man, worth in the hundreds of millions of dollars. He became attracted to us after the owner of the Colonial Motor Lodge, which is right across the street from us, put an ad in the *Wall Street Journal* to sell his place. Judah came to Reno to look at the property, and he almost made a deal with Bob Hallahan, the owner. Then, in the last minute, they had some kind of a falling out. During his trips to Reno to talk to Hallahan, Judah took the opportunity to walk around town and look over other properties. His method of purchasing properties down through the years was always to go to the lender when he was interested in a property. So he went to Wells Fargo, because Wells Fargo had most of the loans in downtown Reno. In his conversations with them, he found that they had had an ongoing disagreement with us about our loan. Also, a similar kind of situation was going on over at the Comstock.

The Comstock had approximately an $8 million mortgage with Wells Fargo, and Wells Fargo sold the mortgage to Judah Hertz for $5 million. (This is what Judah told me—I never discussed this directly with the bank or with the Douglass family that owns the Comstock.)He bought the place at a really reasonable price, because the Comstock has 300 rooms, and if you just rough that out at $5 million for a 300-room hotel, I think you come out at $17,000 a room, or something like that, which is extremely reasonable. If you were to build one like that today, it would cost you fifty, sixty thousand a room, at least. Judah also got all the casino equipment, and he made a deal with the Douglass family to lease it all back to them so they could run it, because, of course, he was not licensed.

Judah applied for a license to be a landlord, and then, just to show you the kind of operator he is, he turned around and got a mortgage from a bank back East for three million, so he was only in the place two million himself, and he was getting $40,000 a month rent from the Douglasses. So it was a great deal, and that's the kind of deal the guy has made in his business career—he described deals to me like that that he'd done in other cities, as well.

My family owns 46 percent of the Sands Regent's stock. In may of 1999, we agreed to sell Judah Hertz all the stock that we owned in the company if he could arrange refinancing of the $11.5 million balance on a loan we had with Wells Fargo that was coming due. If he wasn't able to accomplish that in a specified period, the sale wouldn't go through. The agreement further called for him to put up $1 million as a deposit, $300,000 of which was to be used to buy 100,000 shares of our stock, should he be denied a license. Because we had had difficulty with the previous buyer, we also had a clause in the contract that said, should Judah withdraw during the licensing procedure, or should he not diligently pursue licensing, then he would forfeit the entire million dollars. He agreed to that, and we signed that agreement.

Judah was a frequent visitor to Reno, and I introduced him to Ferenc and to Dave Wood, our chief financial officer. He would talk to us about other deals that he was looking at and about his ideas for the company, and he kept us updated on his efforts to refinance the company. His idea was to use our public company, once he became the major stockholder, to acquire other gaming properties and put them into our company and get stock in the company for these properties. He looked at the Flamingo Hilton, across the street from us, and made them an offer. It was exciting for our company, because even if we were going to sell all our stock, we still wanted the company to grow.

Judah asked me to stay on as a consultant if the deal went through, because I had a lot of experience in the business, and he felt I'd be helpful. He didn't know anything about the gaming business, and he had developed a great deal of confidence in Ferenc and Dave Wood, and he didn't want to change management, at all. As a matter of fact, he named Ferenc to be his key gaming employee for Sapphire Gaming, the entity that he was going to use to acquire all these other properties and merge them with Sands.

It was a real exciting thing for the company, so we cooperated with him, and we went to Las Vegas and looked at two or three different properties there that were for sale, to give him our ideas on them. We also went to Los Angeles and looked at a poker parlor he was thinking about buying, and we looked at two or three properties here in Reno. He had applied to the Gaming Commission for his license, and he hired one of the best gaming attorneys in the state of Nevada, Frank Schreck.

Eventually the investigators went to look through Judah's books. They spent several weeks in Los Angeles at his office, going through all his books and records. We had talked at length about the licensing procedure, and I had questioned him as to whether he knew that he had to show them all his personal checks and his bank accounts and the contents of any safety deposit boxes. I wanted to make sure he understood how difficult it was to get licensed, because I didn't want to go through what we'd gone through before. I didn't want to have happen what eventually did happen! [laughter] And I was sure, knowing Frank Schreck's reputation, that Frank had advised him of all these matters and told him exactly what he had to go through.

We proceeded in this manner for several months. We were looking at properties, and we did a lot of pro formas on the properties, and our company did a lot of studies on these properties, especially the Flamingo, to show the savings that we could make in operating them by using our department heads and by all the synergies that we could develop when we folded these properties into our company. I think the Douglasses had a short-term lease at the Comstock, and Judah talked at length about when the Douglasses' lease was up, that the Comstock would be folded into the Sands, and so it looked like a great future for our company.

In the meantime, we talked to several lenders that Judah had contacted on our behalf. He felt that there was a good opportunity for us to be refinanced by Lehman Brothers. They had a type of loan that's called a CMBS, Commercial Mortgage Backed Security. They bundle up a bunch of real estate loans, and then they sell them on the market. Lehman Brothers was working on a bundle of lodging loans, and our conversations with them were directed to a situation where they'd put us in one of these bundles of hotel loans and buy out our loan and pay off Wells Fargo and then loan us back the same amount of money. It would be a ten-year loan, and the interest rates were very reasonable. However, the gaming end of our business really caused a problem there, so we never were able to get into that package.

We talked to several other companies, and eventually Judah got a major amount of interest from a mortgage company called Foothill Capital. Ironically, Foothill Capital is a subsidiary of Wells Fargo Bank, but it seemed as if those people didn't really talk among each other. Foothill had done some other gaming loans, so they understood gaming. They eventually agreed to do the loan for us, but there were some contingencies. One was that Foothill only wanted to put up $8 million of the loan, so Judah agreed to personally put up the other $2 million. He gave Foothill $2 million of his money, so the loan was paid down to $10,800,000. Then, the Sands paid off $800,000, Foothill made the $10 million loan to the Sands, and we bought Wells Fargo out. That all happened right at the beginning of 2000.

So Judah had fulfilled his first contingency. We got refinanced for a five-year loan, and we had every reason to believe that he was sincere. In the meantime, he was going through the licensing procedure, and we thought that about

June 2000 he would be coming up for licensing. All through the spring, we felt fairly confident that Judah was going to get licensed. From time to time we'd ask how his licensing procedure was progressing, but his lawyer told us that it was just going to take some time.

In June of 2000, Judah's lawyer wrote a letter to Gaming asking to withdraw his application for a license. He didn't tell us until the latter part of July or early August. We said to Judah, "What's the meaning of all this?"

He told us at that Gaming wanted to go to Israel to talk to some of his business connections there, and that the people that Gaming wanted to talk to did not want to talk to Gaming, and that was the major reason that he wasn't going to get licensed. So it appeared as if, from what he was telling us, that it wasn't his fault. He said, "I'm sorry about all this, but this is the way it looks, and so I guess we're just going to have to withdraw."

Months passed with a lot of legal maneuvering over whether Judah had forfeited his deposit with us. In the midst of this, he resubmitted his application for a gaming license, then again he tried to withdraw. We pressed Gaming to proceed with a hearing anyway.

Eventually, Gaming set a hearing for December 2000. We did not attend that meeting, but we do have a copy of the transcript. The chairman, Mr. Ducharme, said that Mr. Judah Hertz had not met his burden. Then they went on to say that there was "a magnitude," and I'm quoting here, "of negative information in respect to this applicant, and we do not believe that he should be allowed to withdraw." That fact "prohibits him from contracting with other gaming licensees within the state." And there they were talking about the Comstock Hotel situation, where the Douglasses were leasing from him. So what they were saying to him was, "You're not even qualified to be a landlord. Therefore, you have to give up the lease that you have with the Douglasses at the Comstock." Even though the board had asked Judah to appear personally, he did not show up.

Judah appeared to have potential tax-fraud issues with the government. So the Gaming Commission's action in this matter was to deny Mr. Hertz's application for a license and deny it with prejudice. What that means is that he'll never be allowed to apply for a gaming license in the state of Nevada again.

We believe that the fact that Reno is growing at such a great rate will help the local business, and a great deal of our competition has gone away, closed its doors. You're getting fewer and fewer casinos in Reno, and you're getting more and more local business.

I have heard of no plans at all for any existing casinos to expand. Growth in the hotel-casino business seems to have come to a standstill in Reno, and for good reason—we don't know what's going to happen with Indian gaming. The weak guys have pretty much been weeded out, but there may be one or two more out there.

27

Stakeholders and Lobbyists

IN THE LATE 1990S, the Atlantis and the Peppermill, on South Virginia near the convention center, began booking more conventions into their hotels. (John Ascuaga's Nugget and the Hilton had long had conventions as an important part of their business strategy.) That business was growing, so these folks—principally Mr. Farahi, who owns the Atlantis right next to the convention center—felt that it would be very helpful to their business if the convention center were expanded. They got their lobbyists to work, and in 1999 Senate Bill 477 was introduced by the government affairs committee, supported by the city of Reno and the county of Washoe. As originally proposed, the idea was to raise the room tax enough to pay for bonds to expand the convention center, approximately doubling its size from what it was at that time.

In the beginning it appeared that the bill was going to pass without a problem, but strong opposition developed, especially from four major hotel-casinos in downtown Reno: the Circus, Silver Legacy, Eldorado, and Harrah's. These folks had powerful lobbyists in the legislature, and the bill reached an impasse. It looked as if it might not pass, so negotiations took place between the lobbyists and the lawyers that represented these different interests, and a compromise was reached. The downtown . . . the four hotel-casinos that I've just named, who later became known as Newco, agreed with the outside casinos that they would put in this bill a mechanism to also create funding for a Downtown Reno Project, as they called it, to promote tourism business in downtown Reno. It would have to be located in the narrow downtown police district that runs roughly from Arlington to Lake and from Sixth down to the river. When that sort of language was inserted into this bill, Newco agreed to support the bill.

From my point of view, what's insidious about the whole matter is that you're really just helping Newco and those four casinos. The rest of downtown Reno gets very little help, because when you put this project within a block or two of these four casinos, they're the ones that are going to be the major benefactors. And once people get into one of these casinos, the rest of the town never sees them. This was really a mechanism to help these four major downtown casinos, at least in my view, and wasn't something that all of downtown Reno would benefit from. But because of the powerful lobbying and the agreement with the outside property owners, there was very strong support for this bill to be passed.

The rest of us at that time really didn't understand the full import of this bill, because we did not know what kind of a project was planned for downtown Reno. And in effect, neither did anyone else, because all the bill says is that it's some kind of project that would help downtown Reno. So it was a wide-open thing at the time, and we were all hopeful that in the end it would be something that would help *everybody* in downtown Reno.

SB477 set up the Truckee Meadows Tourism Facility and Revitalization Steering Committee, to decide where and what the project was going to be in downtown Reno. It was funded by a portion of the 3 percent increase in the room tax that the bill set up. This committee later became known as the Stakeholders Group. It was set up by SB477, "to consist of three persons appointed by the board of directors of the RSCVA, one of whom must be a member of the Nevada

Resort Association." All four of the Newco properties were members of the Nevada Resort Association, as were the Hilton and the other out-of-town casinos: the Nugget and the Atlantis and the Peppermill.

Besides those three persons, you then had three members from the Reno Redevelopment Agency, which would be appointed by the chairman of the agency to be members of this board; and, as we know, Reno Redevelopment Agency is really the city council. So that means three members of the council and three persons appointed by the Nevada Resort Association from its members whose properties are in the designated district. Those were the Newco properties.

So, although it didn't name them by name, the way the bill was written, the Newco properties would be on this Stakeholders Group. All of them would be represented, but there couldn't be any other people from downtown casinos on the board, because you had to be a member of the Nevada Resort Association and you had to be in the police district. These four downtown hotel-casinos have seen fit to support the city council financially and also have their lobbyists very closely in touch with the members of the city council. And so, because they had good relations with the city council, and because of their financial support, once the committee was put together, they pretty much had control of it. Well, let's not say "pretty much"—they *definitely* had control. [laughter] They had their three votes, and they had the three council votes on a board that totaled nine members.

During the Stakeholder deliberations the Newco group said they were going to put $20 million of their own money into the project. They said that $5 million each from these four Newco properties would go into the project, but they didn't say whether it was an equity infusion or a loan . . . whether they were supposed to be repaid or what the terms really were. But they talked a great deal, and initially they may have even believed that it was going to be a public/

private project, and the private part was the $20 million they were going to put in.

They then began to talk about where the site would be, where this thing would be located. Quoting the steering committee, the Stakeholders Group were "mandated to develop a master plan which identifies proposed capital improvement projects that the committee determines to be advisable to promote tourism in Washoe County in methods pursuant to which proposed capital improvements will be financed and where it will be located." And "these capital improvements *must* be located" in this police district that was earlier described. That was a very small area of downtown Reno. It pretty much mandated that this thing was going to be built very close to these four properties.

Just outside that mandated strip, there is a large amount of property that's in the redevelopment district. Most of Sierra Street and most of the area along First Street and along the north bank of the Truckee River has been torn down or closed or abandoned, and Redevelopment owns it. There was a parking garage built down there, and a logical place to build this thing would have been somewhere along Sierra Street and First Street, somewhere in that area there. All those buildings down there are vacant and you already had a parking garage sitting there partially empty most of the time; but, of course, Newco didn't want it to go there. Newco wanted it to go where it would benefit them.

Another feature of the plan supported by Newco was to build a shopping center in the designated district, anchored by a tenant like Nordstrom's or someone of that stature. This project would be placed between Center Street and Virginia Street, and between Commercial Row and Sixth Street. And then, of course, across the street, you had three of the Newco properties, and just to the south you had the fourth property.

When you looked at that whole thing, what you really had was an area with a shopping facility, a convention center, and a bowling center that were all within walking distance of, and would almost specifically benefit, *these* four hotel-casinos. But the selling point used by Newco people on the city council (like Mayor Griffin, who was *fully* in favor of this) was that, "Oh, it's going to help *all* of downtown Reno."

The gaming industry in northern Nevada knows, because many surveys have been taken, that tourists, or even local people who come to downtown Reno, will visit normally a total of only three casinos. So if you get people in this, one way or the other, the probability is very high that they're only going to visit three hotel-casinos. Therefore, the *vast* majority of the business that this was going to create would accrue to these four hotel-casinos, and the rest of us simply would help pay for it.

In the end, very little came off as planned. Several hundred thousand dollars were spent by the Stakeholders Group for plans that David Cordish developed for a shopping area attached to a convention center, whatever it was going to be. Then, after a couple of years, Cordish left the scene without going forward with any of this stuff.

As designed, the facility was placed just north of the bowling center. It was a two-story structure, and it went from Fourth Street to Sixth Street and from Center to Lake. No parking was ever designed into the project, and I think Newco was part of this. They may have said, "We've got lots of parking in our structures, and eventually the City of Reno is going to build a parking structure somewhere over on Lake Street, so that'll take care of the future problem." There was a lot of talk about moving the RTC, the bus station, from where it is to some other location and then maybe putting a parking garage in there.

SB221 was introduced on February 21, 2001, by the committee on natural resources in the senate. That bill was to authorize the city council of the City of Reno to "increase tax on rental transient lodging and levy special assessments to pay costs of certain capital improvements." So the idea was to not only raise room taxes, but to levy a special assessment in order to help finance the bonds that would underwrite this project. Under the bill, the mandated district could be expanded by four blocks in any direction that the council approved, and those properties that were closer to the downtown convention center would pay a bigger assessment than those properties that were further away. There was an effort to create assessments based on this benefit ratio, and there was a lot of controversy about what the ratio should be and how far out you should go with it beyond the police district. There were people that argued that they had no benefit.

George Karadanis, from the Sundowner Hotel-Casino, and I started a group that we called the "No Taxation Without Benefits Committee." We sent out a mailer to all the downtown property owners, except the major hotel-casinos, and asked them if they cared to be assessed both room tax *and* a special assessment to pay for this convention center. Out of the 120 or so letters we sent out, we got back eighty that said they did not wish to be taxed for this project because they didn't feel it was going to be that beneficial for them. That was my feeling, as well, and George's feeling. We argued strenuously that this room tax and this assessment district ought to be confined maybe to a block or two either side of Virginia Street, from about Sixth Street down to Second Street, or maybe even to First, because that was definitely the only area that was going to benefit from this project.

Eventually, Newco agreed in writing with Mr. Karadanis that they would pay $700,000 of the $900,000 that was to be collected in the property-tax-assessment district. That tells you pretty much that the assessment district was extremely important to Newco. They needed it.

Once SB477 got passed, and the Stakeholders Group got set up, and Cordish was brought in, and the project was defined as to where it was going to be and what it was going to be, the four big hotel-casinos that were not downtown became very uneasy. They could see that what was going to happen was you were going to have a *competing* convention center – competing not only with the South Virginia convention facility, but also with their *own* convention facilities, the Nugget's and the Hilton's especially. When they could see the way things were going, they then banded together, hired a lobbying firm, and actively began to oppose these plans.

This committee that George and I formed, the committee for no taxation without benefits, could have been influential in the whole downtown convention project. Unfortunately, the committee agreed to the payment of $700,000 by Newco, on an annual basis, of the $900,000 in total property tax assessments that were going to be collected. With the payment, the committee agreed to support the project. Once that happened, these eighty property owners were on record as supporting the project as Newco espoused it. Therefore, our strength went right out the window.

I argued with George and two or three of the other members of the committee that we needed to hold out. We had a strong group, and we could have played a prominent part in the whole thing, and we could have done a job that would have been very helpful to the rest of downtown Reno property owners.

While I was away in Maui for a couple of months, the folks on that committee saw fit to sign this agreement with Mr. Francovich, who represents Eldorado. In that signed, written agreement, they agreed to support the project. It's unfortunate that that happened. Eventually the bill was passed by the legislature and signed into law.

If the Stakeholders Group proposal was approved by the city council, Washoe County, and RSCVA, Newco would operate the downtown convention facility. What they intended at the time—and they told everybody—was that they would actually turn the facility over to a professional operating group that operated other facilities like this around the country. But they wanted control of it, and their commitment of $20 million was tied up in that situation.

Newco said in the beginning, "Well, we're going to put in $20 million. We're going to operate it. We will get this professional group to operate it, but . . . ." They made no bones about it: Newco would control it, and they could put in whatever events they wanted, when they wanted them. They said, "Well, we will allow other people to bring events to us." For example, if the Sands or the Sundowner or somebody had an event, we could go to them and say, "You know, we have an event. We want to do it on x date. Is it open?" But that was a highly unlikely situation.

About that time the RSCVA hired a new director named Beckelman. He kind of got into the middle of it, and he came up with a proposal to help solve the matter, wherein RSCVA would operate and maintain this downtown convention center, as well as the one out on South Virginia. They would have control of it, rather than Newco. Newco eventually agreed to that proposal, but they said, "If that's the way it's going to be, then we hereby withdraw our offer of a $20 million loan." (It was to be repaid from the receipts of this center with 6 percent interest.)

When it came to light that all Newco had intended to do was loan the money, and expected to be paid back, even though it was *after* the bonds were paid for, there was a big uproar. Newco hadn't necessarily misrepresented what they were going to do initially, they simply were vague about it until they *had* to say how they were going to do it.

As it turned out, the City of Reno is going to float these bonds, and the City of Reno will *own* all of this stuff, and the City of Reno is going to be *behind* this $100 million bond issue. So if something happens and room tax doesn't get collected or whatever, taxpayers of the City of Reno are going to pick up the tab.

28

Marriages and Family

My second wife and I were married in the spring of 1981. This coincided with my father's stroke, which led to his death. He was in Honolulu. It was his ritual to go to Honolulu for the winter. Usually, he'd leave around Thanksgiving and come back in March. In 1981 he was there with his second wife—he'd gotten married three or four years after my mother passed away—and he had a stroke. His right side was paralyzed, and he lost his ability to speak. He was eighty-seven years old at the time.

Although Dad was in very good health for a man his age, he didn't last much longer. We didn't have any reason to believe that he was going to go then, and it was a tremendous shock to us . . . maybe even a bigger shock to me than my brother and sister. I had worked for so many years under his tutelage. He was my mentor, and we had done so many things together. Because we had come so far, and because we had fulfilled his dream, and because his dream had become my dream, I missed him terribly.

When the realization hit me that I would no longer have him to fall back on when I needed him, I was depressed. Many years before I had reached an adult understanding of things and an adult capacity to keep myself from getting in difficulties: I knew what the right path was; I knew right from wrong. I knew that I ought to do right, and, essentially, that's what I'd been doing for many years, but without my dad I was afraid that I could lose my way again.

I was around fifty years old at the time. The mid-life crisis is real, and I went through it. Maybe not everybody goes through it, but I know that I went through it, and it was complicated by my dad's death. I had been divorced from my first wife since 1977. We had separated in 1972, and I had attempted for three or four years to heal the marriage and put it back together, because I did have two young children that I was concerned about. I knew that divorce wouldn't be helpful as far as they were concerned, and usually it's the children that suffer in a marriage when there's a divorce. Well, my first wife took it upon herself to force the divorce, and I got the decree. We were divorced in 1977.

During the time that I was separated from my wife and living apart from her, I met Patty Sakelaris, a lady who was in the same situation as I. She was separated from her husband, and she had children, and we had similar problems. She was married to a Greek fellow whom I knew, and I had known her before they separated. We became attracted to each other for more reasons than just the fact that we were in similar situations. Both of us, because of our failed marriages, and because of the children involved, pretty much agreed that we did not want to be married. That was not an answer, especially in our situation. When we both got divorced, we liked each other enough that we decided to live together, rather than be married. Our children got along very well, and that helped us, because we had a family situation that we and the children were happy in.

Patty had graduated from college in California, and she wanted to become an audiologist; but she had three children, and it was difficult for her to do that. She had an aunt who was not working, who was real good with children, and we arranged for her aunt to watch the children, and she began to work on her speech therapy and audiology degree at the University of Nevada. Her children were four, five, and six, or somewhere in that area—maybe even a little younger than that. Her two daughters became close friends with my daughter, Toni, and they're still friends.

I agreed to help Patty go to college and on to graduate school. Then, when my father passed away, there was this huge void in my life, and I settled on the idea that the way to fill it was to get married. So I talked Patty into it, and we got married in 1981. Looking back on it, if we had not gotten married, we probably would have lived together for a long time without a great deal of difficulty, but we got married for the wrong reasons. If I had waited awhile, I would have realized that no one could fill the void caused by my father's death. It was going to have to heal itself. But we did get married, and it wasn't too long before we realized that we had done it for the wrong reasons.

My first wife and I had joint custody of our children, and they spent much of their time with us. The older they became, the easier it was for us to see that the children really weren't going to suffer as much as we thought they were. My second marriage lasted approximately three years, and we mutually agreed that it was probably better for everyone concerned that we get divorced. It was an amicable separation.

I am happy that I was instrumental in Patty getting her degree as a speech therapist and her certification as an audiologist. I was also helpful in getting her to understand that audiologists are professional people that do the testing, but the real money to be made in the hearing industry is in selling hearing aids. I'm proud that she went on and got into business with the financial help I gave her during the divorce, and she owns the Reno Hearing and Balance Center in Reno.

My son Pete was born in November 1958. My daughter from that marriage was named after my mother, Antonia, but we call her Toni. Neither gave me anywhere near the trouble that I gave my folks.

Pete III went to the University of Colorado, and he graduated with a degree in business. After graduation, Pete came to work for us at the Sands. Over the years, he was given many different responsibilities and did an outstanding job in each of them. Eventually he was made a vice president and a member of the board. Pete left the Sands in September of 1999 to enter McGeorge Law School.

In 1958, when my son was born, we built a home out on the end of Canyon Drive, and we lived in that home until 1971. Toni was born in 1964, so she attended Roy Gomm School, where her brother went, and then she went on to Swope, and then she also went on to Reno High, just like Pete III did. I had very little difficulty with Toni. The usual things—the drugs, the girlfriend and boyfriend problems— simply didn't happen to either one of my children. If they experimented with marijuana and other kinds of drugs, it wasn't very much, and Toni was very selective in her choice of boyfriends. I was spared all those problems, and I've been so thankful for that.

The Three Petes at Harrah's Steak House, 1975. Right to left, my dad, Pete Sr.; my son, Pete III; and me, Pete Jr.

Toni was a little bit more independent than my son. I wanted her to go to the University of Nevada, but she wanted to go to the University of Colorado. So I agreed to let her go, and she went for a year and a half, maybe two, and then her independence came out again.

Toni dropped out and lived in Boulder for awhile, working as a waitress. Then she went back to the University of Colorado and got a teaching degree. After graduation, Toni re-

Antonia "Toni" Cladianos. *"Toni was a little bit more independent than my son."*

turned to Reno and taught at the Sparks Middle School and the Mendive School. She later got a degree in counseling and is now working on a Ph.D. in educational psychology at the University of Nevada. Toni has one child, whose name is Hannah.

I've been married to my third wife since 1989. Her name is Althea. She was born in Reno, and her parents, Nick and Vaslie Pappas, are Greek. Althea was born in 1949. Her grandparents and her parents were friends of my parents, and I remember all of them from my youth. We were in the AHEPA together. We attended the Greek church together, and we used to celebrate the Greek holidays together, along with the rest of the small Greek community. Both her mother and father were leaders in the Greek community, and her mother was a charter member of the Daughters of Penelope, along with my mother. I knew her family very well.

When it came time for Althea to go to college, she decided to go to Chicago. She has relatives in Chicago, and it was a natural place for her to go. She attended Lake Forest College, graduated with a degree in American Studies, and was awarded a teaching certificate. She taught in the Chicago area for several years and then she got a job selling life and health insurance and worked at that for a few years.

In 1987 Althea had been home for Christmas to visit her family, and she was returning to Chicago. I was on my way to Chicago, as well, for a meeting with some travel agents. When I got on the airplane in Reno, she was sitting in a seat in one of the first seven or eight rows, and the seat next to her was empty, so I sat down next to her and talked with her all the way to Chicago. She told me about her life, what she'd been doing all those years, and asked me to meet some of her cousins, who I had never met. We got together, and we went to some great Greek restaurants, which I enjoyed immensely, because good Greek restaurants are difficult to find. And I met her two aunts, who I knew from our younger days in Reno, and I found them to be wonderful people.

I came back to Reno. At the time we were trying to develop a package business from the Midwest, because we had some pretty good airline connections in those days. (That was right after deregulation.) We were doing a lot of marketing in that area, and I was flying back there a lot. I'd make the initial contacts, help create the package with the wholesalers, and then I'd turn it over to other people. Chicago was a fairly new market for us, because after deregulation there were so many airlines flying back and forth. Althea had a wonderful knowledge of the Reno-Tahoe area, and she liked it a lot. She'd come back whenever she could to visit. It occurred to me that she would be a great sales lady for the Reno-

Tahoe area, because she was very knowledgeable and enthusiastic about it.

One of the problems that we faced when we went into a new market was that hardly anybody knew anything about Reno. When you'd mention Reno, a lot of people would say to you, "Well, where's that?" They had no idea, and most of them didn't know that Reno was so close to Lake Tahoe, or that we had the mountains and all the other wonderful things that we have to do here. You had to sell Reno. If you could sell Reno, then they'd come. Saying, "Well, you know, I have a hotel-casino; why don't you come visit me?" simply didn't work. It worked a lot better to sell Reno first and all the attractions that Reno had, and *then* you could say, "And by the way, we have gaming, and we have a hotel-casino, and we have these packages."

I broached the subject with Althea about being our representative in her area. We did shows in cities that were close to Chicago: Milwaukee, Cleveland, Toledo, Toronto, and Minneapolis. I thought if we had a representative, then that rep could go to these shows and sell Reno and at the same time pass out our brochures. It would be less expensive for us, and it would take a lot less of my time. Somebody enthusiastic like her, I felt, would really be good for our company.

Althea's job wasn't a nine-to-five kind of job. She was out on the road most of the time. She didn't have to be at work any particular time, and she worked on a commission. She was very interested in my idea, and her boss agreed, because a lot of this work took place on weekends. We worked out a deal with her to do these shows, and I went back there for the first few times and did the shows with her. I tried to train her in how I wanted her to do these shows, and because of the time that I spent with her, I got to know her very well. Then I became very fond of her . . . but I liked her ability, as well. She was doing a wonderful job for us, and I got her working with Canadian Airlines.

I got to where I found myself making excuses to spend time with Althea. She was very attractive, and I was happy that she was doing such a great job for our company and that I liked her so much. Eventually, I proposed marriage to her. We talked about it for quite awhile before she eventually agreed to marry me and return to Reno. Althea and I have a good marriage, and my in-laws are all wonderful, so I've added them to my family, and I feel good about it.

It was our plan right from the beginning to have at least one child, if not two, and I was excited about it, because I've always loved children. I knew that I was at an age that having children may not have been the wisest thing to do, especially for the child, because I might not be around for long, but Althea wanted it, and I agreed with it, and so we planned it. I was dubious from the beginning that it would happen, but I was hopeful that it would.

Lo and behold, in 1991 we had a baby girl that we began calling Kiki even before she was born. Her given name is

"I found myself making excuses to spend time with Althea. She eventually agreed to marry me . . . ."

Leslie, but I call her Kiki. My godfather's oldest daughter was nicknamed Kiki. I always liked the name.

My brother John was born in 1938. He was nine years younger than me. He was born a month later than he should have been, and the doctor had to deliver him by cesarean operation. When he was born, he had a broken collar bone and contracted pneumonia. He was very ill when he was a baby.

Kiki at age six.

In the 1930s childbirth was a lot more difficult than it is today. The doctors didn't know nearly as much as they do now, and my mother had a very difficult time for a year or two.

Because of the difference in our ages, John and I never got to go to the same school together. I never really got as close as I wanted to, and then I began my college career; and, looking back on it, I should have been a better brother to him. I think I was a little too self-centered. I don't think I gave it the kind of effort that I should have, and my brother had even more difficulty with my dad than I did in certain matters.

After high school, John went to UNR for a year, and then he went to Arizona State University at Tempe for a year or so. Then he just dropped out of school and wouldn't go back, and it caused a problem between him and my dad.

That all healed over eventually, and he came back and went to work in the business with us, and he was a wonderful help. He took to the business very well, and he liked the gaming end of the business. He learned it, and he worked hard at it, so I was able to pretty much relegate the slot machines and the pit to him.

Slot machines about that time were changing. The old mechanical machines were going out of existence. The new electromechanical machines were coming into play, and so the slot machine that I knew, that I had grown up with and knew how to operate, was disappearing. My brother came along just at the right time. He learned a great deal about the new machines, and I concentrated on trying to run the overall business. It was a wonderful situation for all of us, because he had a place that he liked and was good at, and I could depend on him.

At my brother's urging, we put in live games, because he could see that it would make us a real casino, rather than just a place with some slot machines. As we grew and prospered, my brother and I saw eye to eye, and we became great friends. We used to water-ski a lot together. We hunted together, and we became the companions that I had wanted earlier in my life.

Unfortunately for my brother, he inherited my mother's genes. My mother died when she was fifty-four years old, and she had a great deal of cardiovascular difficulty and diabetes, and my brother wound up with a blocked artery in his right leg. He had to have an operation in 1981, and the doctor told him he was afraid that at some point in the future he might lose that leg. Eventually, he did lose his leg. He must have had over forty operations over a period of twenty years.

When we went public in 1985, John sold some of his stock, so he was able to retire, and he moved to Hawaii. He bought a fishing boat, and he and a couple of partners were taking people out deep-sea fishing. But he did not take care of himself as he should have done. He needed to diet stringently and quit smoking and cut down on alcohol, but he just had this idea that what was going to be was going to be. We lost him in October of 2000, and he suffered mightily before he died. It was fortunate, I think, that he finally let go, because the pain that he went through was simply terrible.

Right to left: John, Katherene, and me, 1995.

When John passed away, he had been married over twenty years to his second wife, Sandy. He had previously been married to a lady named Linda, and they had two children, Adrienne, who died of cancer at the age of thirty-eight, and Jonathan, a doctor in New Orleans. Jonathan and his wife have two boys who are two and three years old. John was very proud of his family.

My sister, Katherene, is only two years younger than I am, so I was, in a sense, closer to her for a longer time than I was to my brother. We were a lot closer to the same age, and we had some of the same experiences, although she did have a much different experience than I did growing up. My father was an old-fashioned Greek, and amazing as it seems today, he wouldn't let her date when she was in high school. [laughter] When she entered the University of Nevada, my dad still had this same idea. She began to date, anyway, and didn't tell him about it. It was a very difficult position for her, and it was her feeling that eventually my dad was going to find a "nice Greek boy" to marry her, and she was afraid that he was going to try to force her into an arranged marriage. I understand exactly why she would feel that way, because of the way things had gone. It took a great deal of courage for her to do what she did.

The only way that Katherene could see out of that whole situation was to run off and get married. Now, there may have been another answer, but that was her answer. She was eighteen years old. It came as a great shock to all of us. My mother understood, but my father and I didn't. My dad refused to speak to her for two months, but my mother finally prevailed, and that situation changed. The marriage wasn't the best marriage in the world, and after a few years they divorced. She had one child whose name is Deborah, who lives here in Reno and has two children of her own, so my sister has two grandchildren.

During the years that we grew up as children, looking back on it now, I feel guilty that I didn't treat Katherene better than I did. She was my younger sister, and it's hard for me to put this in words, but I didn't want to be bothered with her. I guess that's the feeling I had. My mother would say to me, "You have to look out for your younger sister."

And I'd say, "Ah, gee, Mom. Do I have to do that? You know, I got my friends, and I have things I want to do, and I don't want to be concerned about her."

But my mother and father did instill strong family feelings in me, and even though I resented it, I tried to do the best I could. I'm sure I could have done a better job. I'm positive I could have done a better job.

Katherene is a very talented person. She always made very good grades in school. She's a person who has deep powers of concentration, and she's been a tremendous help to me and to our business. She began to work in the business, just like my brother and I did, after she'd gotten divorced. She did a variety of things, but she was particularly talented at furnishing and interior and exterior decoration.

Katherene is married to Mark Latham, who also has worked for us for many years. Mark was a construction engineer, and when he retired he wanted something to do, so we brought him into the business to work for my brother. Mark is a great host, and he knows many of our customers.

By 1997 it was apparent to me that the gaming business in northern Nevada was becoming increasingly dependent upon attracting locals to its casinos. I had no experience in local business—my success had come through appealing to tourists, charter groups, and others from out of town. Also, I was approaching 70, and I had a young daughter with whom

Right to left: My son, Mark Latham, me, and four Alaska Salmon.

I wanted to spend more time. It was time to step down and get someone else to run the company. As luck would have it, Ferenc Szony became available when the Hilton, which he was running, got sold.

Ferenc took over from me as president and CEO in January, 1998. He's done a great job. The year that ended June 30, 2000, was the first profitable year for the Sands since 1995. We added a new restaurant, Mel's Diner, so we were able to close our Palm Court Restaurant on the second floor. (Mel's Diner took its place.) Mel's is on the ground floor, which is always good in a casino, because restaurants on the second floor are difficult for people to get to; and, because it's situated on Fourth Street, it pulls a lot of people in off the street. Not only are they able to service our customers, but they actually pull people into our casino. We've noticed a decided increase in the slot play in the area adjacent to Mel's.

In the last several years, our company has had an amazing turn-around with Ferenc at the helm. Since 1995, we've gone from a company that was losing as much as $2 million or $3 million in a year to one that is showing a healthy profit. Our prospects for the future look good. We've changed the direction of the company. The company now has a large local business, and it's grow-

Ferenc Szony. *"We had an amazing turnaround with him at the helm."*

ing all the time. Ferenc has developed a team of people that are motivated and that are doing a great job.

My sister Katherene is still chairman of the board, and my son Pete III is treasurer and sits on the board. Together with Ferenc, they are providing the leadership and vision we need to prosper in a changing operating environment. A recent step toward further diversifying and building our business outside of downtown Reno was our June, 2002 purchase of the Gold Ranch Casino and California Lottery Station on the state line at Verdi.

My father was a penniless immigrant who couldn't speak the language when he got off the boat in Ellis Island in 1912. From that start, for our family to have gotten to where we are today is amazing. I consider myself extremely lucky, far luckier than I am smart. I am my father's son. He gave me opportunity, direction, and guidance; and he forced me, in some cases, to do things that I needed to do. I was very lucky to have my mother and dad there for me.

I'm proud that I had a hand in building what my family has now, and I hope in some way that both my mother and father can see where we are today. Even though we had some difficulties, we're on our way back up, and I have confidence that we will continue to achieve great success in our business and in our personal lives.

Glossary
of Terms

THE GAMING TERMS in this glossary were defined by Dwayne Kling. When using the glossary the reader should keep in mind that these terms have evolved informally from within the gambling subculture. Their meanings are often imprecise; they may have meanings not listed here; and their use may be idiosyncratic or specific to certain times and places in the history of gaming in America.

This glossary is meant for general use. In addition to defining terms that appear in *My Father's Son*, it includes many others widely used by people associated with the gaming industry.

agent, n. A cheater working with a dealer to cheat a casino.

bill acceptors, n. Devices built into slot and video poker machines that accept paper currency (e.g. $1, $5, $20, and $50 bills).

blanket roll, n. A controlled roll of the dice made on a blanket or a bed.

bottoms, n. Mis-spotted dice. Normal dice are spotted so that opposing sides add up to a total of ten, but this is not the case with mismarked dice. (See also "tops.")

box man, n. A person who supervises the craps game and is responsible to the pit boss.

breaking card, n. (Twenty-one) A card that will give a player or a dealer a total over twenty-one, thereby causing the player or dealer to lose.

brush games, *n.* (Keno) A game in which the keno writer marks the ticket with a brush in the traditional Chinese style (as opposed to the method currently used by most casinos in which the writer marks the ticket using a black crayon).

bust-out man, *n.* A cheater who specializes in switching crooked dice in and out of a game.

card counter, *n.* A twenty-one player who tracks, by suit and by number, the cards that have already been played in a game.

catwalk, *n.* In early casinos, an area in the ceiling above the casino floor, usually concealed by one-way mirrors through which one could observe the games. In most casinos this type of observation has been replaced by video surveillance. (Also called a "lookout.")

clean up, *v.* To take illegal dice out of a game.

coin bank, *n.* A cabinet with drawers in which a change person stores the portion of his/her bankroll that is not currently in use.

come bet, *n.* (Craps) A bet on the next roll of the dice after a point has been established.

conditioning, *n.* (Keno) The procedure of inscribing, on the right-hand side of the ticket, the total price of the ticket, the number of ways, and the price of the ways (i.e., it describes the player's wager).

crimp, *v.* To mark cards by bending them slightly to allow identification of a card.

crossroader, *n.* A person who cheats casino games.

daub, *v.* To mark cards with coloring to allow identification of a card.

daybook, *n.* A daily report in which supervisors enter anything of importance that happens in a twenty-four-hour period.

dead game, *n.* A game that is open but has no players.

deuce dealing, *n.* A form of cheating in which the top card of the deck is not dealt, but rather the second card, or deuce, is dealt.

do side (to bet on the), *v.* (Craps) To bet the dice will pass (or win).

doing something, *v.* Cheating a game.

don't side (to bet on the), *v.* (Craps) To bet the dice will not pass (or win).

double odds, *n.* An "odds bet" taken by a player at twice the original bet.

draw, *n.* 1) A keno ticket with the winning numbers punched out for a given game, used as an overlay by keno checkers to determine winners and payoffs; 2) A specific keno race, game, or drawing.

drink stamp, *n.* An instrument used by a pit boss to authorize free drinks at the bar.

drop, *n.* 1) The total amount of cash handled plus the markers drawn at a game during a given time frame; 2) The amount of money emptied from a slot machine.

drop box, *n.* A receptacle under a gaming table in which currency used to buy chips or tokens is deposited (or "dropped") by the dealer.

eighty-six, *v.* To ban from a casino.

end play, n. A wager made with very few cards left in the deck, when a card counter could have an advantage.

eye in the sky, n. An observation post (or person in that post) used for purposes of monitoring casino activity.

field bet, n. (Craps) A bet that covers the numbers 2, 3, 4, 9, 10, 11, and 12 and pays double on 2 and triple on 12.

flat, *adj.* Illegal or crooked (relative to casinos or particular games).

flat bets, n. A bet that pays even money.

flat dice, n. Dice which are not true cubes (i.e., crooked dice).

floor man, n. A person who supervises a specific area of gaming (e.g., slots, pit games).

from the shoulder (to bet), *adv.* To make a high first bet.

full comp, n. A situation in which every item is complimentary (i.e., there is no charge to the customer).

going for the money, *v.* To cheat someone out of his/her money.

hard eight, n. A roll of the dice consisting of two fours, one set of fours on each die. (A hard six would be a roll involving two threes, a hard ten would have two fives.)

heat, n. Pressure from authorities or customers.

heavy, n. A person who engages in an illegal action during a game.

high roller, n. A bettor of high and consistent action.

hit a keno ticket, *v.* To win on a keno ticket.

hitting into stiffs, *v.* (Twenty-one) Taking a card when one's current total is 12 or over.

hold, *n.* The amount of money won by a slot machine or a table game.

horn bet, *n.* A one-row bet on the craps table covering the numbers 2, 3, 11, and 12.

juice, *n.* Connections with important people.

key man, *n.* A person working on the casino floor who performs minor repairs on slot machines and in some cases pays jackpots.

lammer, *n.* 1) A small disc used to indicate the amount of credit extended to a player; 2) A disc used to designate the value of a chip or a check, usually on a roulette wheel.

layout, *n.* The cloth covering on a gambling table.

lookout, *n.* (See "catwalk.")

marker, *n.* An instrument used to extend a certain amount of credit to a player.

mechanic, *n.* A dealer who manipulates the tools of the trade (e.g., dice, cards) in an illegal manner for the express purpose of altering the outcome of a game.

Megabucks, *n.* A dollar-operated, progressive slot-machine game, linked via network to casinos throughout Nevada.

microfilm, *v.* (Keno) To make a film record of tickets as they are written to discourage cheating.

muck, *v.* To illegally enter extra cards into a deck.

number one, n. (Keno and pit games) Person who is in charge of a department for an eight-hour period (comparable to a shift supervisor).

on and off bets (to pay), v. (Craps) To use a dealer's shortcut method of paying a player's come bet that is coming off a number at the same time that the same player's new wager is going on that number.

one dice, two dice, etc., n. Table numbers for the various crap games in a pit set up.

peek, v. To sneak a look at the top card of the deck.

point, n. (Craps) A number established by the shooter on the first roll of the dice.

progressives, n. A group of two or more slot machines electronically linked to share a single, common jackpot payoff amount. The payoff "progresses" as coins are inserted into any of the linked machines.

proposition bets, n. (Craps) One-roll bets or bets on the "hard ways" (i.e., on numbers 4, 6, 8, and 10).

Quartermania, n. A quarter-operated, progressive slot machine, linked via network to casinos throughout Nevada.

read the table, v. To count the bankroll, or the total amount of chips, on a table.

reel strips, n. Strips, usually made of plastic, which are attached to the reels on slot machines. The arrangement of various symbols on the reel strips (e.g., cherries, bells, and bars) determines the payoffs on the machine and therefore affects the percentage of the slot machine.

repayment, *n.* The paying back of a credit marker.

sand, *v.* To mark the edges of playing cards with sandpaper. The location of the sanded area allows the cheater to know the denomination of a card.

score, *v.* To win a lot of money.

shift manager, *n.* The individual in charge of an entire casino for an eight-hour shift.

shift supervisor, *n.* The individual in charge of a particular department for an eight-hour shift.

spotting, *v.* Marking the numbers on a keno ticket.

squares, *n.* Legal dice.

station-operated game, *n.* A keno game for which bets can be taken at an annex or "outstation".

stick man, *n.* The dealer who calls a craps game and moves the dice to the shooter.

stiff, *n.* (Twenty-one) A hand that could go over twenty-one if a player or dealer takes a hit.

store, *n.* A club or casino.

take and pay, *v.* (Twenty-one, craps, and roulette) A procedure in which a dealer collects the losing bets before paying the winning bets.

third base, *n.* The last position on a twenty-one game.

tokes, *n.* Tokens, monies, or chips given to dealers by players as gratuities or tips.

tops, *n.* Mis-spotted dice. Normal dice are spotted so that oppos-ing sides add up to a total of ten, but this is not the case with mismarked dice. (See also "bottoms.")

totaling of payoffs, *n.* (Twenty-one, craps, and roulette) The procedure in which a dealer, when paying a player who has won more than one wager on a single decision, pays one total amount rather than paying each wager individually.

track, *v.* To keep records on the amount of gambling action re-ceived from particular customers.

unit, *n.* (As in "unit bet" or "unit deal") A fixed amount through which bets are made (e.g., "He bets in five-dollar units.").

way tickets, *n.* Keno tickets with the spots grouped so that two or more arrangements are bet on by the player.

whip the dice, *v.* (Craps) To send the dice back quickly.

Index

C